Praise for SHORT NIGHTS OF THE SHADOW CATCHER

"[Egan] artfully frames a stunning portrait of Edward Curtis that captures every patina of his glory, brilliance, and pathos. [Egan] writes with passion and grace." — *Christian Science Monitor*

"The author gracefully transforms the past into vivid scenes that employ all five senses . . . an honest portrayal of a man obsessed with capturing the final days of this nation's first people."
— *Minneapolis Star Tribune*

"Powerful . . . Egan's biography is indeed the life story of Curtis, but he also seeks to tell a larger arc about the changes of the American West, and the decimation of Native American culture." — *Seattle Times*

"[A] captivating tribute to a treasured American and the treasures he created." — *Dallas Morning News*

"Egan's superb biography is actually a double portrait — of Curtis and also the Native American struggle to resist assimilation." — *Newsweek*

"A remarkable story." — *Oregonian*

"*Short Nights* is not only the marvelous and rollicking account of the life of one of America's extraordinary photographers. It is also a book about the extreme personal cost of outsize ambition. Edward Curtis undertook one of the most epic cultural projects in American history — photographing and documenting the vanishing ways of life of some eighty American Indian tribes. It cost him almost everything he once was. And still he persisted, turning out some of the greatest photographic and ethnological work ever done. Egan has found yet another great subject, and has crafted yet another great narrative around it."
— S. C. Gwynne, author of *Empire of the Summer Moon*

"Egan's keen sense of place, people and history makes *Short Nights of the Shadow Catcher* an exceptional marriage of author and subject."
—Bloomberg

"Lucent prose illuminates a man obscured for years in history's shadows." —*Kirkus Reviews*, starred review

"With a reporter's eye for detail, Egan delivers a gracefully written biography and adventure story." —*Publishers Weekly*, starred review

"Ace popular historian Egan makes Curtis' story frequently suspenseful, always gripping, and monumentally heroic."
—*Booklist*, starred review

"This fascinating biography is recommended to readers interested in the American West from the late 19th through early 20th century."
—*Library Journal*

"[Short Nights] mesmerizes—it's instructive, entertaining and a joy to read . . . When it comes to superlative historical writing, this is as good as it gets . . . Dazzling." —*Shelf Awareness*

Also by Timothy Egan

Short Nights *of the* Shadow Catcher

THE EPIC LIFE *and* IMMORTAL PHOTOGRAPHS *of* EDWARD CURTIS

TIMOTHY EGAN

MARINER BOOKS

HOUGHTON MIFFLIN HARCOURT

BOSTON   NEW YORK

First Mariner Books edition 2013

Copyright © 2012 by Timothy Egan

For information about permission to reproduce selections from this book, write to trade.permissions@hmhco.com or to Permissions,Houghton Mifflin Harcourt Publishing Company, 3 Park Avenue, 19th Floor, New York, New York 10016.

www.hmhco.com

Library of Congress Cataloging-in-Publication Data
Egan, Timothy.
 Short nights of the Shadow Catcher : the epic life and immortal
      photographs of Edward Curtis / Timothy Egan.
     p. cm.
  ISBN 978-0-618-96902-9 (hardback) ISBN 978-0-544-10276-7 (pbk.)
  1. Curtis, Edward S., 1868–1952. 2. Photographers — United States —
      Biography. 3. Indians of North America — Pictorial works. I. Title.
 TR140.C82E43 2012
 770.92—dc23   2012022390

Book design by Melissa Lotfy

Printed in the United States of America
DOC 10 9
4500649920

Frontispiece: Edward S. Curtis, self-portrait, 1899

We are vanishing from the earth, yet I cannot think we are useless or else Usen would not have created us. He created all tribes of men and certainly had a righteous purpose in creating each.

— GERONIMO APACHE

What is life? It is the flash of a firefly in the night. It is the breath of a buffalo in the wintertime. It is in the little shadow which runs across the grass and loses itself at sunset.

— CROWFOOT BLACKFEET

In memory of Joan Patricia Lynch Egan,
mother of seven, who filled us with
the Irish love of the underdog and of the written word.
She was sustained by books until the very end.

CONTENTS

1

FIRST PICTURE
1896

THE LAST INDIAN OF Seattle lived in a shack down among the greased piers and coal bunkers of the new city, on what was then called West Street, her hovel in the grip of Puget Sound, off plumb in a rise above the tidal flats. The cabin was two rooms, cloaked in a chipped jacket of clapboards, damp inside. Shantytown was the unofficial name for this part of the city, and if you wanted to dump a bucket of cooking oil or a rusted stove or a body, this was the place to do it. It smelled of viscera, sewage and raw industry, and only when a strong breeze huffed in from the Pacific did people onshore get a brief, briny reprieve from the residual odors of their labor.

The city was named for the old woman's father, though the founders had trouble pronouncing *See-ahlsh*, a kind of guttural grunt to the ears of the midwesterners freshly settled at the far edge of the continent. Nor could they fathom how to properly say *Kick-is-om-lo*, his daughter. So the seaport became Seattle, much more melodic, and the eccentric Indian woman was renamed Princess Angeline, the oldest and last surviving child of the chief of the Duwamish and Suquamish. Seattle died in 1866; had the residents of the village on Elliott Bay followed the custom of his people, they would have been forbidden to speak his name for at least a year after his death. As it was, his spirit was insulted hourly, at the least, on every day of that first year. "Princess" was used in condescension, mostly. How could this dirty, toothless wretch living amid the garbage be royalty? How could this tiny beggar in calico, bent by time, this clam digger who sold bivalves door to door, this laundress who scrubbed clothes on the rocks, be a princess?

"The old crone" was a common term for Angeline.

"Ragged remnant of royalty" was a more fanciful description. She was famous for her ugliness. Nearly blind, her eyes a quarter-rise slit without noticeable lashes. Said to have a single tooth, which she used to clamp a pipe. A face often compared to a washrag. The living mummy of Princess Angeline was a tourist draw, lured out for the amusement of visiting dignitaries. When she met Benjamin Harrison, the shaggy-bearded twenty-third president of the United States, during his 1891 trip to Puget Sound, the native extended a withered hand and shouted "*Kla-how-ya*," a traditional greeting. Though she clearly knew many English phrases, she refused to speak the language of the new residents.

"*Nika halo cumtuv*," her contemporaries quoted her as saying. "I cannot understand."

Angeline was nearly alone in using words that had clung like angel hair to the forested hills above the bay for centuries. Lushootseed, the Coast Salish dialect, was her native tongue, once spoken by about eight thousand people who lived all around the inland sea, their hamlets holding to the higher ground near streams that delivered the *tyee*, also called the Chinook or king salmon, to the doorsteps of their big-boned timber lodges. "Angeline came to our house shortly before her death," a granddaughter of one of the city's founders remembered. "She sat on a stool and spoke in native tongue. We forgot her ugliness and her grumpiness and realized as never before the tragedy of her life and that of all Indians."

They could appreciate the tragedy, of course, in an abstract, vaguely sympathetic way, because they had no doubt that Indians would soon disappear from what would become the largest city on the continent named for a Native American. Well before the twentieth century dawned, there was a rush to the past tense in a country with plenty of real, live indigenous people in its midst. Angeline, by the terms of the

Point Elliott Treaty of 1855, was not even allowed to reside in town; the pact said the Duwamish and Suquamish had to leave, get out of sight, move across the bay to a sliver of rocky ground set aside for the aborigines. The bands who had lived by the rivers that drained the Cascade Mountains gave up two million acres for a small cash settlement, one blanket and four and a half yards of cloth per person. Eleven years later, Seattle passed a law making it a crime for anyone to harbor an Indian within the city limits.

Angeline ignored the treaty and the ordinance. She refused to move; she had no desire to live among the family clans and their feuds on the speck of reservation land that looked back at the rising sun. The Boston Men, as older Indians called the wave of Anglos from that distant port, allowed tiny Angeline to stay put — a free-to-roam sovereign outcast in the land of her ancestors. She was harmless, after all: a quaint, colorful connection to a vanquished past. *Poor broken Angeline. Is she still here, in that dreadful shack? God, what a piteous sight.* She was even celebrated in verse by the early mythologists of Seattle:

> Her wardrobe was a varied one
> Donated by most everyone.
> But Angeline deemed it not worthwhile
> To put on others' cast-off style!
> And much preferred a plain bandanna
> To 'kerchief silk from far Havana.

The children of the new city, the American boys in short pants, had no verse or kind words for her. Angeline was prey. Great fun. They taunted the gnarled Indian, threw rocks at her. These urchins would lurk around the waterfront after school, looking to catch Angeline by surprise, then they would fire their stones at her and watch her squawk in befuddlement.

"You old hag!" the boys shouted.

But she gave as good as she got. Under those layers of filthy skirts, Angeline carried rocks for self-defense. She didn't leave the shack without ammunition. She didn't hide or retreat, but instead would sink an arthritic hand into one of her many pockets, find a stone and let it rip back at the boys. *Take that, you bastards!* Once, she hit Rollie Denny, he of the founding family whose name was all over the plats of the fast-expanding city. Hit him square with a rock for all to see, at the corner of Front Street and Madison. This also became part of the verse, the poetic myth: the crippled, sickly, elfin descendant of Chief Seattle nailed the snot-nosed kid, heir to much of the land taken from the native people.

> For once he hit her with a stone
> And she hit him back and made him moan!

No one was certain of Angeline's age. Some accounts said she was near one hundred, though that surely was an exaggeration. Most placed her at about eighty. The year 1896 was particularly hard on the princess. For days at a time she kept to her cabin, which she shared off and on with a roustabout grandchild. The boy was born to Angeline's daughter, who had been living with a white drunk, Joe Foster, who beat her on a regular basis. After putting up with the abuse for years, the woman strung a rope from the rafters of her home and hanged herself. From then on, Joe Foster Jr. was in Angeline's care. When the Indian was sick, people left baskets of food on her doorstep, though feral dogs would sometimes get to the food before the princess could. Whenever a church lady stopped by, Angeline would wave her off. A glimpse inside her cabin found dirty dishes stacked high, a cold bunk, cobwebs in the corners, Joe Foster Jr. nowhere in sight.

She had a deep cough, from tobacco smoke and the ambient chill. They cared about Angeline, these fine women of new Seattle, because for all her surface squalor she was believed to be saintly. "She is the only Indian woman I know whose morals are above reproach," said one of the church ladies. A backhanded compliment, to be sure, but a contrast to the characterization of another member of a Seattle pioneer family. "The Indians at best are but a poor, degraded race," wrote Catherine Blaine, wife of the Reverend Blaine, in a letter home to the Midwest, "far inferior to even the lowliest among you." The reverend had a harsher view. "The coarse, filthy, debased natives," he called the inhabitants of this beautiful region. "Pitiable objects of neglect and degradation," he wrote. "They lie, gamble, steal, get drunk and all other bad things almost as a matter of duty."

The good ladies insisted that Angeline seek medical attention. She must not spend another day in the sloping shack by the shore or she would soon die. Against her will, the Indian was taken to the hospital up the hill. There she sat, sphinxlike, not saying a word. A doctor got her to put down her cane, take the pipe out of her mouth, remove the scarf and bandanna, and strip away a few layers of skirt. She had been diagnosed with pneumonia once before, and this current bronchial congestion and deep wheezing indicated another round of a feared and possibly fatal sickness. She needed care, the doctors told the church ladies, a warm, clean bed, some ointments and hot soup at the least. But Angeline was done with this place. When the doctor left the room, she quickly put the layers back on, wrapped her scarf around her head, reached for her pipe and cane, and fled, rocks clanking in her pockets. Out the door she went, mumbling, mumbling. What was that she said? Something about the hospital being a *skookum* house — a white man's jail. Away she went to the shore, to her shack, to the reliable music of water slapping sea rocks. Enough of the church ladies and their nickels and baked goods and castoffs, enough of the doctors and their probing instruments.

And that is where twenty-eight-year-old Edward Sherriff Curtis found Princess Angeline. He knew *of* her, of course. Everyone did. Despite her ugliness — or, more likely, because of it — she was the most famous person in Seattle, her image on china plates and other knickknacks sold to visitors who flooded into Puget Sound as the weather warmed. A sketch of her face once adorned the pages of the *New York Sun*, which hailed her as "the pet of the city." If she was not the actual last Indian of Seattle, people in town certainly treated her that way: her very existence served as a living expression of how one way of life was far inferior to the other, and that it was the natural order of things for these native people to pass on. Just look at her.

"Your God is not our God! Your God loves your people and hates mine!"

So said Chief Seattle himself in his famous treaty speech. Well, maybe not. His translator, Dr. Henry A. Smith, was an eloquent fabulist, and only relayed these words many years after the Duwamish tribal head had passed away, in 1866. But for the inheritors of a moisture-kissed land so stunning it was hailed by the British explorer George Vancouver in 1792 as "exhibiting everything that bounteous nature could be expected to draw into one point of view," they expressed the prevailing sentiment. And so these haunted words went into the chief's mouth, the speech refined along the way as it was chiseled into American history and twined to the city's creation myth.

"Our people are ebbing away like a rapidly receding tide that will never return."

And:

"A few more moons, a few more winters and not one of the descendants of the mighty hosts that once moved over this broad land or lived in happy homes protected by the Great Spirit will remain to mourn over the graves of a people once more powerful and hopeful than yours."

And:

"These shores will swarm with the invisible dead of my tribe."

When Curtis saw Angeline moving along the shore, the visible nearly dead, using that cane of hers more like a blind woman trying to find her way than an old lady struggling for balance, she looked at once like the perfect subject. There against the deep waters of Puget Sound, there with the snow-mantled Olympic Mountains framed behind her, there with the growl of earth-digging machines and the snorts of steamships and loading crews and the clatter of streetcars and trolleys — with all of that, Curtis saw a moment from a time before any white man had looked upon these shores. He saw a person and nature, one and the same in his mind, as they belonged. A frozen image of a lost time: he must take that picture before she passed.

Curtis had come bounding down the steep hill from the big house into which he had just moved his ever-expanding family, at 413 Eighth Avenue. And what a vision of style, manliness and ambition he presented. He was positively glowing as he moved, already a master of the fastest-growing city in the American West. With his six-foot-two-inch frame, he towered over Angeline. His Vandyke beard, his polished boots, his hat tipped rakishly to one side, barely above the heavy-lidded eyes, made him look like a bit of a dandy. There was style to his swagger. He had the kind of charisma that came from a combination of looks, confidence and good luck. "He has a dreamy, sort of drawly voice," one male admirer wrote. "His blue eyes are sleepy ones with a half-subdued air of humor lurking in their depths."

But what the merchants who waved to him and bid him "Good morning, Mr. Curtis" and the strangers who smiled warmly at the sleepy-eyed man in full did not know was how much of his persona was forced, a creation young Curtis had forged in a remarkably short period of time.

Yes, he owned the fancy studio downtown, six blocks from home, with a portrait-filled parlor that alone was worth a visit. Yes, he was married to a gorgeous woman, dark-haired and intelligent, with one child and a second on the way, and they shared that house up the hill with his mother and other family members. And yes, the discerning *Argus,* well read in the region by the well fed, had pronounced Curtis and his partner the leading photographers of Puget Sound a mere five years after Curtis mortgaged the family homestead to buy into a picture shop. "One of the greatest examples of business energy and perseverance to be found in Seattle today," the paper said. If you had any money and beauty, or desired both, it was de rigueur to pose for the master who worked behind the standing lens at Curtis and Guptill, Photographers and Photoengravers. The things they could do: the shadows, the painterly effects, the daring nudes (not advertised)! It was portrait photography—art—a bit risky for its intimacy and far ahead of the routine pictures that every family of means displayed in its drawing room. The finished picture could be printed on a gold or silver plaque, a method that was "original to Curtis and Guptill," the *Argus* noted, "brilliant and beautiful beyond description."

Curtis had developed a reputation for finding the true character of his subjects. He did the civic leaders—Judge Thomas Burke, the progressive hero who had stood up to a mob trying to force the Chinese out of Seattle by rifle and pitchfork. And the Gilded Age rich—Samuel

Hill, public gadfly and railroad man, who dreamed of building a European castle on a bluff above the Columbia River. But he also captured the face of the trolley car driver who had saved a month's pay to sit before Curtis in his spiffy uniform, of the sailor who planned his shore leave around a session in front of the camera. He brought out the radiance of the young strivers, women of seventeen convinced that a Curtis portrait was a passport to a better life. Visiting celebrities were guided to the studio, there to be charmed by the tall, dashing young man with the silk ribbon around his hat, smoking cigarettes between takes, constantly in motion, in and out of the dark veil that cloaked his camera. In the manner of the instant cities that looked out to the Pacific, Curtis had risen so quickly, had come from so little to be so much. If only they knew. But this was the Far West, where a man's past, once it was discarded, buried or lost in a distant land, stayed that way.

What Angeline did to stay alive, the grubbing and foraging and digging and cutting, was what Ed Curtis had done in his early years. Curtis had been the clam digger, up to his knees in Puget Sound muck. Curtis had been the berry picker, his arms sliced with surface cuts from rummaging through thorny thickets above the shore. Curtis had scraped away at whatever he could find in the tidal flats, whatever could be felled or milled or monetized to keep a family fed. He'd lived a subsistence life, his hands a pair of blistered claws, his joints raw from the rock-moving and log-rolling, just like the crone in the red scarf. His father was called, in the term of the day, dirt poor. A Civil War private and army chaplain, Johnson A. Curtis was sickly and in foul temper for much of the great conflict; after being discharged, he never found his way or recovered his health. One thing he brought home from the dreary War Between the States was a camera lens. Not a camera, just the lens. It sat for a dozen years, untouched. Johnson Curtis married Ellen Sherriff, stern-faced and bushy-browed, started a family—Edward was the second child of four, born near Whitewater, Wisconsin, on February 16, 1868—and bounced around the rural hamlets of Le Sueur County, Minnesota, trying to turn the ground for food or a soul for Jesus. He was miserable, a complete failure. Ed Curtis supplemented the meager offerings at the family table with snapping turtles and muskrats he caught in the creek; one made a soup, the other could be smoked and eaten as a snack. It was never enough.

Education, sporadic at best, was in a one-room schoolhouse. The sickly father, when he felt up to it, hit the road spreading Bible verses. The preacher took his boy along on many of his ministry forays. They went by canoe, just as the Indians had done, plying the waterways of still wild Minnesota. Ed learned to make a fire and cook a meal out of whatever fish or salamander he could find or warm-blooded critter he could shoot. The gothic Christianity of the United Brethren Church was not for him; it was so joyless, so life-smothering with its rules and prohibitions. But the outdoors, the open country—there was a church Ed Curtis could feel at home in. His formal schooling ended in sixth grade. About the same time, at the age of twelve, he discovered his father's Civil War lens. Following instructions in *Wilson's Photographics*, he built a camera consisting of two boxes, one inside the other. It was a primitive device, but transformative and thrilling, for it could capture life in the marshes of Minnesota and in the faces of family and friends. It made young Curtis feel like something other than a mule.

When his oldest brother, Raphael, left the house, Curtis had to put the camera aside. The preacher grew more sickly and useless. The fatal taint of the war had never left him. At fourteen, Ed Curtis inherited a heavy burden: he would have to support the whole family, including both parents. He got a job working for the railroad, rising to become a supervisor. Because of his height, he looked much older than his actual age. He killed muskrat and turtle still, brought more fish to the family table, tilled a large garden, used his earnings for cloth and sugar and tobacco. The winter of 1886–87 nearly finished off the Curtis family. The preacher was bedridden during the cold months, wailing and complaining. In the spring, the fledgling crops of the new season died in a seizure of frost. The money from the rail job dried up after one of the periodic panics that shut down the unregulated American economy. Broke, facing real hunger and no future, the Curtis family was left with no option but to look west.

In the fall of 1887, Ed Curtis and his father arrived in the Puget Sound area, which was opening up to land opportunists after treaties had removed most of the Indian, and all of the British, claims to the region. Danes, Swedes and other Nordics were flooding into Washington Territory, marveling at how the fjords and forests reminded them of northern Europe. Irish and Germans came because of good word of mouth from family members. But mostly, the fresh-starters were other midwesterners, leaving the flatlands after the economic busts of the 1880s for another chance at a tabula rasa. Here was Eden in the mist. "Bays within bays, inlets on inlets, seas linking seas—over 12,000 square miles of surface, the waters come and go, rise and fall, past a splendid succession of islands, promontories, walls of forest and towering mountains," a reporter for the *Atlantic Monthly* wrote, describing perhaps the most primeval patch of temperate zone then under the American flag. "The old Indian names which still haunt the shores heighten the illusion. The wilderness is dominant still."

That first winter for the Curtis homesteaders was wet but mild—the lows seldom falling below freezing, snowfall a rarity even though the region is farther north in latitude than Maine. The Curtis men claimed a piece of land across the water from Seattle, near a town called Sydney. Their acreage was crowded with evergreens, alders and maples, and sloped down to the sound. In the clearing, Ed Curtis could look out at tall ships on the way to Seattle, Tacoma and Port Townsend, and could see what would become a magnificent obsession—the 14,411-foot cone of Mount Rainier. From sea level to the glacial top, Rainier was the highest freestanding mountain in the United States. Everywhere Curtis turned, he took in a view dramatically unlike the Midwest. On one side were the Olympics, which held their snow until midsummer, and on the other side were the Cascades, the spine that ran down the entire midsection of the territory, dividing it between a wet half and a dry. Water was the dominant element and master architect. The green was all-encompassing.

Edward cut down spruce trees—light, straight, easily split softwood —on the family claim and built a cabin with the timber. The centerpiece was a stone fireplace, which heated the home fine. Fruit trees were planted. A big garden was established. The rest of the family—a teenage girl Eva, the youngest boy Asahel and the preacher's wife Ellen—

bundled up their belongings in the spring of 1888 and took the train out west to join the men. But just as the light of May was bringing the land to life, the old man took a turn for the worse. He had pneumonia when his family arrived, with no appetite and no energy. The Reverend Johnson Curtis died three days after the reunion.

At age twenty, Ed Curtis took up where he had left off before the move, trying to support the clan. He fished. The salmon were huge—big Chinooks weighed thirty pounds or more—and millions of them flooded the waterways that emptied into Puget Sound; all a man had to do was be minimally alert and modestly competent with net or pole. He fixed things for hire, helping widows and disabled men with bent axles and faulty stoves and broken plows. He picked berries. The orange ones, salmonberries, were the most exotic; the purple ones, huckleberries, the tastiest, though he had to hike into the foothills to get at them. He plucked oysters from the mud, dug clams, chipped mussels from half-submerged logs. He cut wood, splitting firs and spruce for house-framing purposes, and alder and maple for stove fuel. He aspired to fulfill his father's dream to open a brickyard. In a formal photograph taken not long after Reverend Curtis died, Edward is the image of earnest ambition: clean-shaven, strong-jawed, a white tie against a white shirt, looking resolute. But then his life came to a halt after he took a terrible fall from a log, mangling his spine. At twenty-two he could barely walk, let alone lift a beam or heft a bundle of bricks. Just like his father, Curtis was confined to bed for almost a year, "limp, thin and bleached," a neighbor boy recalled.

It was awful not being able to get around, watching his mother put together a meal of boiled potatoes and bacon grease. Out the window, though, was a world that gave flight to his spirit. He became a close observer: how the color of the land would change subtly in shifting light, the moments in midmorning when the fog lifted, or breaks in the afternoon between rain showers, when he could see the spectrum of the rainbow in a single drop held by a rhododendron leaf.

A sixteen-year-old girl, Clara Phillips, started visiting the bedridden man in the homestead cabin. She had a mane of thick dark hair, worn well past her shoulders, and exhibited a feisty independence. Clara's family had moved around: from Canada to rural Pennsylvania, where she was born, and then to Puget Sound. The Phillips girls, Clara and her sister Nellie, were different from the other homesteader children; they used fancy words from books and were curious about things beyond the little community that would become Port Orchard. When she met Curtis, Clara had not yet finished with her schooling, and she fascinated him with all the things she knew that he did not. When Curtis talked of what he wanted to do when he regained his mobility, she alone seemed to believe him. There would be no more berry-picking or clam-digging, no more wood-cutting or fence-fixing, no more brickyard. He would no longer put his back into his living.

Clara visited one day and found Edward sitting up, enraptured by a contraption on the kitchen table: a 14-by-17-inch view camera, capable of holding a slice of life on a large-format glass-plate negative with such clarity it made people gasp. The camera was not cheap, the price much derided by Edward's mother. He had bought it from a traveler looking to raise a stake on the way to goldfields. Ellen Curtis thought it was a waste: what was he going to do with that costly and fragile thing? Even *Wilson's Photographics,* which Curtis had used to help build the camera back in Minnesota, had warned that photography was "a circus kind of business, and unfit for a gentleman to engage in."

The healing invalid's plan was bold: he would borrow $150 against the property and use the cash for a move to Seattle. He had heard about a picture studio in town, and it needed a new partner. The big, bustling place across the water was a short boat ride from home, but a world away from the sodden ground of the homestead. "They call it the Queen City and talk about its great future although it wasn't very long ago there were Indian attacks on the town," the preacher Johnson Curtis had written his family after he and his son put their first stakes in the ground. "It's over 10,000 people and there's a university in the middle of town and hills all around it. Edward says they have telephones, 120 of them!" With the 14-by-17 view camera, Curtis vowed to leave the subsistence life forever.

Newly mobile in 1891, Curtis went off to Seattle to make a go of it. What he knew about studio photography was laughable. And who would support the family? But in a new town, in a new land, he could fail almost without consequence. What he brought to the city, his sister Eva recalled, was unbridled curiosity—"always nosing into something interesting." In Seattle the $150 stake was enough to buy Edward a name on a storefront, "Rothi and Curtis, Photographers," and an apprenticeship to a dominating partner. Clara joined Curtis in the city, scandalizing her family. She lived in a boarding house—the same one as Curtis. Her mind was set, as was his. They married in 1892. She was eighteen, he was twenty-four.

Success came quickly. Curtis left Rothi and joined Thomas Guptill in a much bigger enterprise, a studio on Second Avenue with photoengraving facilities. The Curtis couple lived above the shop until a baby, Harold, born in 1893, prompted a move up the hill. By 1895, just four years after his prolonged convalescence, Curtis was a Seattle celebrity, his name known around the Pacific Northwest. He had money to stuff the house on Eighth Avenue with fine furniture. More importantly, it was big enough to bring the rest of the family over. His mother, his sister Eva, his brother Asahel, Clara's sister Nellie and two of her relatives —they all moved in.

Curtis himself was seldom home. He not only mastered the artistry of working with a box to capture light and shadow and the way a personality could change with a gaze one way or a tilt of the head the other, but was equally skilled at technical details. "Finest photographic work in the city" was the claim of the studio in the Seattle directory of 1895. The next year, a Seattle paper backed that boast, predicting that "in a very few years these young men will have the largest engraving plant west of Chicago." Curtis grew the beard that became his trademark, wore stylish clothes, learned fast how to charm the leading citizens of the city. Photoengraving was laborious; each picture was finished by hand, with a honeyed sepia tone. More than a decade earlier, George Eastman, of Rochester, New York, had developed a much easier way to process a photograph: dry gel on paper, replacing heavy plates wiped with chemicals. "You press the button, we do the rest" was the marketing slogan, put to use when the Kodak Brownie was sold starting in 1901. But Curtis wanted nothing of the shortcuts. He preferred the

quality and detailing he could get with glass-plate negatives, no matter how heavy, dangerous and expensive. There was more than enough
work at the studio that Curtis could hire his brother Asahel, six years
younger, as an apprentice in 1895.

That Edward Curtis, at the age of twenty-seven, had made the journey from ragged forager with a dented spine to the talk of a robust
town full of similar self-confident swells of the Gay Nineties would be
enough for some men. But Curtis was hungry for the bigger dare. The
house, the business, the family, the gadgets, the praise from the press
and the nods of approval from moneyed gentlemen—it was a start.
Curtis also did those nudes: bohemian, exotic women showing their
nipples just above the lace, angelic faces looking bored in a gilded parlor. Curtis had left the grim-faced Christian sensibility of his father behind, like so many in the West.

His adopted city spread north, south and east, limited only by the
inky depths of Puget Sound to the west. The 10,000 people Reverend
Curtis had spoken of had become, in barely a decade's time, a city of
nearly 100,000, and that amount would double, and then some, in the
next ten years. The climate was said to be "salubrious," a wonderful
euphemism for a place that got thirty-six inches of rain a year, most of
it falling between November and March. The new inhabitants, having pushed away the Indians for a pittance, and with only a few minor
skirmishes, could not believe their good fortune. Here were seven hills,
the highest rising to just over five hundred feet, with the cornucopia of
Puget Sound lapping at one shore and the long, clear magnificence of
Lake Washington on the other, a mountain lake at sea level. You could
see ten feet down in the fresh, clear waters, all that glacial-rock-filtered
runoff clean enough to drink.

Between the two big bodies of water were other lakes, streams and
waterfalls, even a clearing of level ground where the tribes used to
gather to give away things and eat until they fell over, stuffed and happy.
A garden setting it was, just as the British explorer had said, requiring
virtually nothing from man to improve on it. Near Pioneer Square was
a low-lying island where the natives from the reservation used to park
their dugout canoes, there to sell shellfish to the three-masted schooners

anchored nearby; the island lost its natural moat when it was filled with debris. Cable cars moved smartly up and down First Avenue, and buildings with Romanesque and Palladian features sprouted overnight, rivaling in height the five-century-old trees that had been in their paths.

Curtis himself was put to work on behalf of the city's hagiography. He shot dreamy landscapes at the edge of the city, which filled a full page of a respected Seattle broadsheet, hailing "A New Garden of Eden." A story in that annual progress edition told of a visiting Oxford don who asked about Seattle's history. He was taken to see one of the pioneers who had been around when the city was started.

"Started!" the visitor said. "Do you realize how peculiar it is to an Englishman to hear of men who were present when a city was started?" Life in the new Northwest, the story concluded, was "wholly beyond the comprehension of the Europeans."

There remained in the tree-shaven, steam-shoveled, hydraulic-sluiced urban makeover the stubborn figure of Chief Seattle's last surviving child. Curtis approached Angeline now with a proposition. He tried a simple negotiation, laying out his idea. Angeline backed away, her hands deep in the pockets where she kept her rocks. Curtis used Chinook jargon, a few hundred words that had been a primitive trading language dating to the Hudson's Bay Company days. Angeline shook her head.

"Nika halo cumtuv."

Curtis opened his leather case and displayed a few portraits—beautiful, full-faced, radiant subjects. And such detail, like real life. He gestured to her and then to the pictures.

"Nika halo cumtuv."

At last he reached into his pocket and produced some coins. More hand gestures followed. A simple exchange did the trick: money for picture. Up the hill they walked, Angeline pausing to rest every few steps, to the studio at 614 Second Avenue. Inside, it took some time for Curtis to persuade Angeline to get comfortable. Plenty of people had taken her picture before. It was usually quick, followed by a growl from the native woman. Curtis had her sit and look around the room, daydream if she liked, gave her some tobacco for her pipe, maybe one of his cigarettes. Of course! After some time she loosened the bandanna and the scarf.

"No, no! Just as you are."

And the cane: he wanted the Indian's stick of worn hardwood to be in the portrait too. It was as much a part of Angeline as the faded calico skirts. She did not smile, not even an attempt, and he did not want her to smile. He was looking for the lethal glare she saved for the boys who threw rocks at her. He hoped to convey a face that had seen worlds change, forests leveled, tidelands filled, people crushed. As a girl, she never dug a clam or washed a bit of clothing. Her father had slaves from other tribes do the menial work. Her current status, the scrubwoman in the shack, was anything but quaint. Already, official histories had established a consistent narrative of natives welcoming the passage of one era to the next. "The advent of the white man was a pleasant episode in the lives of these savage people," one of the first chroniclers of Seattle said. "Their arms opened to receive them as superior beings, and the lands they possessed were freely offered for their acceptance." The face of Edward Curtis's last Indian of Seattle would say something else.

What Curtis knew of Indians was informed, in large part, by depictions of dead natives he had seen in a book as a child. More than a thousand Eastern Sioux had been rounded up following an 1862 raid on settlers in Minnesota. The carnage was widespread in villages and farms in the southwest part of the state; by one estimate, eight hundred whites were killed in what became known as the Sioux Uprising. The Sioux had been roused to violence by repeated violations of their treaty, and by the mendacity of corrupt government agents who refused to make the required payments from that pact. In defeat, after the uprising, the Indians were sentenced to death. At the same time, many in Congress demanded that all Indians be wiped from the map, echoing the view of their constituents after the Sioux had caused so many casualties. President Lincoln commuted the sentences of most of the insurgents. But the death penalty remained for more than three dozen of them. On December 26, 1862, they were all hanged, the largest mass execution in American history. Curtis had studied an engraving of the lifeless Sioux in Mankato, Minnesota. Necks snapped, faces cold—it haunted him. "All through life I have carried a vivid picture of that great scaffold with thirty-nine Indians hanging at the end of a rope," he wrote.

But the Curtis of 1896 was no crusader. Not for him was the growing movement of missionaries and government policymakers to bring Indians into society, to get them into tight-fitting shoes, suit jackets with watch fobs, with proper haircuts, to Christianize them and force them to tend a farm, just like any yeoman American. Indians and their treaty rights, political autonomy and property disputes—all of that was somebody else's fight. Politics. Injustice. Blah, blah, blah. Who cares? Curtis wanted pictures. The exchange between photographer and subject was purely a business proposition.

He gave Angeline a dollar for her time, equal to a week's worth of drudge work. What emerged from the many takes and the alchemy of developing chemicals was a face that could knock a door down with its slit-eyed stare. A tuft of silver hair peeks out from under Angeline's scarf. The lines of her face are so deep, so prominent, they look like scars from a knife fight, as if someone had carved her visage from a pumpkin. Her mouth is downturned. Curtis allowed light to fall on her cheekbones and nose, enough to contrast with the sad, dark eyes, looking away at another time. Beneath her chin, where the scarf is tied in a knot, is another bit of hair. The shawl is wrapped completely around her shoulders, held together by a safety pin. That simple pin stands out as a diamond brooch might on a society matron. In the bottom corner of the photo is the knob end of Angeline's cane. To look at the face and not see humanity is to lack humanity.

The portrait of the princess was magnificent, and Curtis knew it, for everyone who saw it was impressed. But the picture was not what he'd had in mind when he first spied Angeline against Puget Sound. Over the following weeks Curtis returned to Shantytown. He saw Angeline in the mudflat, stooped and dark-cloaked, shovel in hand—the clam digger in her element. This was more like what he had seen in a flash that day on the shore. The sitting portrait was fine, but he was drawn to something more natural. Angeline had to fit her background, and that could never be the studio on Second Avenue. Nor was he interested in the image of the shrew, the hag, the crone. He gave her money to continue her grubbing and prying, as she had for decades. From these everyday scenes came the inspiration for two pictures. One he called *The Clam Digger*, the other was *The Mussel Gatherer*. No frowning, vanquished Indians here. No starving, bedraggled aborigines. No warriors. They were neither threats nor objects of pity. The subsistence life was front and center, an ageless figure digging for food in front of a tranquil bay, with a distant island and benign clouds in the background, no sign of a city at all. No face was visible either — just the hunched-over silhouette. Through his camera, Curtis gave the backbreaking work, which he never considered anything but lowly, a noble patina.

From Angeline, Curtis learned about other Duwamish and Suquamish people who lived at the edges of the city, upriver, hidden from view. They saw the Point Elliott Treaty as a betrayal and had never signed on to it. Curtis waited along the riverbanks for them to return from picking hops in the fields, their dugouts loaded down, baskets on the shore. When they saw his camera the Indians would shy away, or force an expression.

"No, no. Please. Just as you were."

From other Indians he learned about the reservation to the north, the Tulalip, where he was told he could see native people living the old way. He went to that little patch of the Indian realm, became acquainted with the tribal policeman and his wife, and spent hours watching the unremarkable rituals of daily life. At home in Seattle, the paying work was backing up: so many engagement pictures to be taken, ingénues to immortalize, businessmen to satisfy. He would get to all of it, but what stirred him most was the Big Outside — mountains, brooding forests, a saltwater inlet untouched by machines, and these nearly spectral people who seemed to belong to the land.

Curtis paid the Indians on the Tulalip reservation, just as he had paid Angeline, buying access. But again, he stressed to his subjects that all he wanted was to observe them going about their day, gathering shellfish, weaving baskets from reeds. He wasn't there to tell them how to do anything. Just the opposite.

"I will work with you," he said. "Not at you."

These pictures had elements of a seventeenth-century Dutch master framing the common class—Vermeer's *The Milkmaid*, or even his *Girl with the Pearl Earring*. Curtis did not consider himself to be doing a historian's work or that of a journalist or ethnologist. Still, it was important to get it down, and get it right. "The people in the main were sedentary, inhabiting well-made wooden houses," he wrote of his new acquaintances, trying to correct a false impression of Indian mobility in every part of the West. And if people in Seattle thought native home-building was nothing more than a variant of the primitive shack of Princess Angeline, Curtis knew better; he had seen the glories. They didn't live in leaky animal-skin tipis or under a roof of bug-ridden brush. "The triumph of their architecture," he wrote, included a communal lodge that was "520 feet long, 60 feet wide, 15 feet high, supported by 74 split timbers" and built by Angeline's people just a half century earlier without modern tools. "Agriculture was unknown" to the Coast Salish, he explained, not because Indians were too stupid to till the ground, but because "the ease with which food could be had from the sea left no incentive for development of agricultural life." As a witness, young Curtis sensed the value of a diminishing world; it occurred to him in a stark epiphany that if he could capture these closing hours, he would have something of lasting value.

Princes Angeline died in her cabin on May 31, 1896.

ANGELINE IS NO MORE
AGED INDIAN PRINCESS
PASSES INTO SPIRIT LAND

So blared the page-one headline of the leading morning paper, the *Post-Intelligencer*, accompanied by a sketch drawn from the Curtis studio portrait. City dignitaries hailed Chief Seattle's daughter without reserve. "Princess Angeline was the best known and most picturesque Indian character of the Pacific Coast, or possibly in the United States," said one prominent Seattleite. She was easily the most beloved of "the dusky daughters of the soil," said another. For her funeral, the church ladies solicited money to build a casket in the form of a dugout canoe, which was prominently displayed at a mass in Our Lady of Good Help

Church. She was buried under a big slab of rough-hewn granite at Lake View Cemetery. On the stone was chiseled: "Angeline, Daughter of Sealth, May 31, 1896." Her cane was passed on to a civic grandee. In death, she gave the mythic poem of her life its last lines:

> There she lies, the Indian Queen
> Wrinkled, wise old Angeline.

At the far southern edge of the city, near Lake Washington, a street was named for the princess. Her passing was news across the United States, detailed in a lengthy wire-service article. "She is almost certainly the last of the Duwamish Tribe," the story concluded. And with that, the new inhabitants of this part of the Far West closed the book on a people whose presence had gone back to at least the time of the Roman Empire—most everyone, that is, but young Edward Curtis. For him, Angeline was the start of the largest, most comprehensive and ambitious photographic odyssey in American history. The second step would be upward, into the clouds.

Princess Angeline, the last surviving child of Chief Seattle. Curtis took this photo in his studio in 1896, shortly before Angeline's death, at a time when it was illegal for Indians to live in the city named for her father. He paid her a dollar for the sitting.

2

ENCOUNTER ON A VOLCANO
1898

TEN THOUSAND VERTICAL feet above the confines of his studio in Seattle, Curtis positioned himself now on Mount Rainier at the magic hour of a midsummer day — a time when glaciers that had been blue would blush for a few minutes. He set up his camera on a platform overlooking two downward-thrusting fjords of ice, wrinkled with crevasses eighty feet deep or more. He was shooting in black and white with his 14-by-17, but even glass plates without the ability to hold color could mirror something that few eyes had seen, there in the alpenglow of the volcano.

For two years, Curtis had stalked Rainier in all its moods, catching the savagery of its storms, the exuberance of its wildflower burst, the listlessness of dead-zone fog that wrapped the mountain in spooky silence. In order to get close enough to understand Rainier, Curtis had to become a mountaineer. And in those two years of exploration, the sickly cripple of seven years earlier had become an accomplished climber. Curtis would find his way over ice and above the clouds, would crawl over crumbling lava rock and slow-tread along shaky snow bridges, making his own path. Intimacy — as with Princess Angeline — was what he sought with this subject.

The natives in canoes and the big mountain sixty miles southeast of Seattle struck him as the most authentic parts of a region rapidly remaking itself. In the city, forests and hills were leveled, rivers were pinched, and boulders that had been left from the last glacial epoch were dynamited. Ports were dredged ever deeper and fields gouged open for canals—all in a great hurry to form a new metropolis. In defiance of the setting, the people of Seattle intended to bring the city's bedrock hills down to something closer to the streets of their hometowns of Cleveland and Chicago. Giant hoses sluiced away the tops of Denny and Jackson hills, the mud running downslope to fill in the tideland near Angeline's old shack.

The younger Curtis, Asahel, was drawn to the urban creation, and spent his free time shooting industrial pictures, buildings rising, scrub brush turned to broad avenues. He was trying to establish a name outside the studio where he had worked for his brother since 1895. The boys shared a belief that their entrée into the larger world would be through a camera. While Asahel shot the mess of a city's dawning, Ed Curtis was pulled to the bigger palette that started at Seattle's edge. And if getting close to Rainier meant he had to warm himself in steam vents at the summit to keep from freezing, or duck into a snow cave that might smother him in a seismic shrug, he was game for it. The studio restrained him, even more so after he shed his partner in 1897 and went out on his own as "Edward S. Curtis, Photographer and Photoengraver." In the city, he was the maestro with a trademark fishhook signature and a calendar full of appointments. In the high country, he was Curtis the climber, going places no photographer had gone.

In the fading light now he looked down across the Nisqually Glacier and saw what appeared to be a small party on this summer's eve. The clouds swooshed in on an ocean-borne current. Camp Muir was often a reliable bench above the evening fog. But with a strong westerly wind, the clouds could be pushed upward, obscuring the white wilderness. A few minutes was all it took for what had been an uninterrupted view in all directions to disappear, visibility reduced to nothing. Curtis lost sight of the climbers below, though their voices remained.

"Helloooooooo," came a cry through a purgatory of gray. Curtis bellowed back. He sealed his camera and tucked it in his knapsack. Using his six-foot-long alpenstock, with a metallic pick at one end, he stabilized himself as he took small, quick steps downward toward the human sound.

"Over here!"

After some back and forth, silhouettes appeared in the soup, accompanied by much chattering and staccato grumbling. They were a half-dozen men, adrift and confounded on one of Rainier's most treacherous glaciers, the Nisqually, an ice field nearly five miles long.

"We're lost." The climbers were middle-aged and well outfitted, and looked to be fit and robust for their age. They were shivering, mist collected on their mustaches, clothes soaked. Curtis knew that dusk could be disorienting and deadly at this altitude. Down below, the flower meadows were known as Wonderland, and a campsite was called Paradise. Up high, names were as hard as the eternal snow: Cadaver Gap and Disappointment Cleaver. Rainier was the most heavily glaciated peak in the then United States—thirty-five square miles of permanent snowfields and ice. One step was all it took for someone to fall into a slit of the Nisqually, the body never to be retrieved, part of the mountain's buried memories.

In Curtis, the lost men had stumbled upon a climber known as much for his ascents on the high, unknown terra of the Pacific Northwest as for his leadership. They could not have been luckier.

"Follow me."

He guided them slowly upward, making sure they stayed close together and took small steps, to his refuge at Camp Muir. He had hauled firewood over the previous days, and built a rock shelter where he could stoke a blaze and get out of the wind. He got the campfire going, and while sipping hot drinks the climbers revealed something about themselves. They were from the East, from New York and Washington, D.C. Men on a mission: studying the mountain for science, part of a campaign to give Rainier formal protection, which would happen the following year when it became the nation's fifth national park. Yes, of course Curtis recognized their names, at least some of them. He had rescued two of the most famous people in America.

The year before, Curtis had made national news—but not with his camera. The Mazamas, one of the best organized of the climbing clubs sprouting in postfrontier America, had ventured north from their home in Portland, Oregon, in the third week of July to attempt a record: most people to summit Mount Rainier. The traveling group of two hundred included women, in keeping with the progressive bent of the club, and several scientists. Though the mountain had first been scaled twenty-eight years earlier, it remained somewhat of a mystery. How active was the volcano? How thick were the glaciers? What forms of life thrived in the year-round snow? Even the exact height was in dispute, a question the Mazamas hoped to resolve. Among their members was Professor Edgar McClure, a University of Oregon chemist who brought along a mercurial barometer he planned to deploy on the summit as a way to settle the question of Rainier's precise elevation. "Never before has there been such an excursion," the Portland *Oregonian* reported, and quoted a leader thusly as he informed those they met along the way: "We were the pick and flower of Portland; our boys were all fleet of foot and strong of limb and our girls were all young and handsome."

The climbers arrived at Longmire, a base in the old-growth forest with hot springs for bathing. Then it was upward and onward, by foot to a meadow at Paradise camp. There, the climbers met a self-confident woman and her husband, an engaging, hyperkinetic man loaded down with camera equipment: "A certain Mr. E. S. Curtis of Seattle," the Mazama journal noted. Clara, the mother of two young children, had no plans to aim for the summit, but she loved tramping around the high country with her husband. Curtis knew the mountain like his living room. He warned the climbers just before nightfall: should they awaken to a sound—"a deep, hoarse roar"—it would be an avalanche, off in the distance. Enjoy it, he said.

The expedition was a massive undertaking, involving four tons of gear, two beef steers, seven milk cows, assorted beasts of burden and a brass band. That first night in Paradise, Curtis was summoned to help with an emergency: a man from California, "not accustomed to the dangerous vagaries of mountain storms in the Northwest," in the Mazamas' official account, had gone missing. Curtis set off in the darkness without hesitation, his wife unfazed. "Never shall I forget the heroic example that Mrs. Curtis gave us of womanly courage when she bade her hushed goodbye as he started out into the fog, the gale, and the dangerous darkness of the mountain the first night in camp," wrote Dr. Weldon Young, the team's doctor. They found the frightened, shivering Californian on snow two miles from camp. This rescue, and Curtis's expertise on the mountain, so impressed the Mazamas that they asked him to lead their expedition. Curtis agreed. He also welcomed all female climbers who wanted to make a go for the top, and named one young woman from Portland, Ella McBride, as a coleader. McBride was a schoolteacher, with great stamina and athleticism that Curtis admired. Per a Mazama request, Curtis gave in to one custom of the club: the ladies were required to wear bloomers.

After a prayer, up into the clouds they went in single file, accompanied by a slow-trudging, often slipping group of musicians carrying heavy instruments. Just before dusk, when they reached the snow camp named for the naturalist John Muir, the party was ordered by Curtis to cook up soup and stew, then bed down before nightfall. The brass band played "The Star-Spangled Banner" and all went to sleep. They rose a few hours later, just after midnight, stomping their calked boots on compressed ice, a fat moon overhead, blankets wrapped around their upper bodies. Frozen lips pressed against frigid mouthpieces as the band tried to give their Mazama partners a tuneful sendoff. The first hour was all doubts and cold hands, Curtis encouraging the climbers to stay positive: it would get better after sunrise. They had so many questions: *What should they eat?* Very little. Their stomachs would be turbulent from the altitude. *How slippery would the ice be?* Hard, until midday. *Are there many crevasses?* Numerous ones, some hidden by snow bridges, deep and dangerous. Prod first with the alpenstock before taking a step.

The push to the summit was a steady march past monoliths of rotten rock and aged ice. Sunrise came with a burst of rose-colored light and a view of the long blue wall of the Cascade range just to the east. As the day went on, the sun softened the snow, making it difficult to walk. The altitude made several climbers sick; they dug into the snow to wait out the climb. By 3:30 in the afternoon, what was left of the main party crested the crater and walked past steam vents to the summit. The volcano was alive, they realized, by the strong smell of sulfur and the hissing from the openings at the highest point of the Pacific Northwest. The Mazamas obtained their record, putting fifty-nine people on the summit. At 4:30, Professor McClure set up his mercurial barometer and took several measurements. Later, his figures were computed to an altitude of 14,528 feet, which would make Rainier the tallest peak in the contiguous United States. The altitude was off, as it turned out—too high by 117 feet.

Curtis did not allow the party to stay long on top. He knew the snow that had been mush on the way up would quickly harden when the sun left it, and also that the way down was the most dangerous part of any climb. The exhausted party followed Curtis. Just after dusk, two climbers lost their footing and slid, falling quickly toward a ledge. They caught themselves before tumbling over a cliff. Curtis went after the frightened, scuffed men and led them back to the main group. Just before 10 p.m., all of the climbers collapsed at Camp Muir.

In the confident afterglow of their success, several Mazamas, including McClure, decided to go all the way to Paradise, a drop of five thousand feet, instead of spending the night at Camp Muir. Midway through that final descent, McClure hopped up on a rock to take in a moonlit view; he knew instantly he had made a mistake. "Don't come down here," he shouted. It was too late for him. He slipped, and was gone in a whoosh. The other climbers said they barely heard a thing. McClure fell hundreds of feet, bouncing over sharp rocks. Much later, when the Mazamas found his body, it was bloody, broken and perforated with deep wounds from sharp stones.

The Oregon professor's demise was the first recorded death on Mount Rainier, and it was news across the country. The mountain had become a gentleman's Everest for a certain kind of American adventurer. In the consensus view of the fatality, as later detailed in *Harper's Weekly*, Curtis was not held accountable. He was praised as a brave soul who had not only led a historic climb of men and women to the top, but rescued two people on the way down. "Mr. Curtis proved the right man in the right place," one account noted. "A better selection could not have been made." After the climb, the Mazamas made Curtis an honorary member, joining John Muir and a few other notables. And they became appreciative fans of his outdoor photography, which Curtis advertised in a small brochure, "Scenic Washington." (Sample offering: "A panoramic view of Rainier, framed, ready for hanging—$25.") Within a year, the club boasted, "We now have the finest collection of Rainier views in existence."

Back at Camp Muir, Curtis tried to explain the quirks of the volcano to the men from the East he had rescued. The mountain has its own weather system, he said. In the summer, the radiant glow of the sun off the snow is so intense it burns the skin even inside the nostrils. In the winter, up to ninety feet of snow can fall in a single season. At dusk, the pyramidal shadow of the peak stretches to the crest of the Cascades. At the top of Rainier, well below the surface, is a lake—melted water from the heat that pushes up the nearly three-mile-long throat of the mountain. And the Indians, who had called the peak *Takhoma*, never climbed it beyond the snowfields above the timberline. Only a fool or a Boston Man would try such a thing.

The climber most fascinated by Indians was a man who introduced himself as Bird Grinnell. *That Grinnell?* Yes, George Bird Grinnell, founder of the Audubon Society, editor of *Forest and Stream* and considered the world's foremost expert on Plains Indians. He traced his ancestry to the *Mayflower*. He knew George Armstrong Custer long before the yellow-haired officer became an impetuous Indian fighter. He had grown up with people like Cornelius Vanderbilt—at one time the richest man in America—as a guest at the family house in Manhattan. He counted among his best friends an ambitious young politician, Theodore Roosevelt, just gearing up that summer to run for governor of New York. Ten years earlier, Grinnell and Roosevelt had founded the Boone and Crocket Club, devoted to preserving wildlife in order to have the opportunity to shoot it later. Oh, and it was *Doctor* George Bird Grinnell, a Ph.D. from Yale, though Curtis could call him Bird. Please.

Another mustachioed man warming his hands at Camp Muir was Clint Merriam. *That Merriam?* Yes. C. Hart Merriam, cofounder of the National Geographic Society, a zoologist and ornithologist by trade. He was the chief of the U.S. Biological Survey. In that duty he had conducted an inventory of the natural world in the United States, a sort of Noah's ark accounting of native plant and animal life before much of it disappeared. Though he knew more about birds than perhaps anyone else in the country, Merriam's lasting contribution to the study of the land was his theory of "life zones," used to classify the bioregions of the United States. Merriam's wild turkey, among other species, was named for him. He was a doctor of medicine as well, though Curtis could call him Clint.

As for Mr. Curtis? He had dropped out of school before his twelfth birthday and later operated a picture studio in Seattle. His wife, now pregnant with their third child, helped to run the shop, along with other family members. Curtis wasn't going to fake it. He could not fathom their academic argot. The names being tossed around — Roosevelt, Pinchot, Vanderbilt — he recognized from the papers. He was nobody compared to them, an itinerate preacher's kid trying to make a name for himself in the city on the shores of Puget Sound.

Much of that reputation-building was linked to gold from Alaska. The rush to the Last Frontier had started a year earlier, bringing a stampede through Seattle and making a fortune for merchants — from the outfitting, financing and fleecing of hapless sourdoughs. Ever the opportunist, Curtis himself had taken advantage of the last great American gold rush, dispatching his brother Asahel to the frozen fields of the Klondike. Curtis followed him shortly thereafter. Back in Seattle, he dashed off a letter to *Century Magazine*, a leading popular journal. "I have just returned from a trip over different trails to the Alaskan gold fields, and have secured the most complete and the latest series of photos," he wrote. He had witnessed the raw side of the scramble—dead horses in piles, flimsy tent villages, ramshackle towns. "In fact, these views depict every phase of the mad rush to the gold fields and portray the situation and the difficulties to be encountered more clearly and truthfully than can any mere pen picture." It was quite a claim: a young man with no experience in journalism boasting that he had captured something that everyone else had missed in a big national story. But the gamble paid off. The March 1898 issue of *Century* carried a gripping narrative and pictures—"The Rush to the Klondike."

The article made a splash for Curtis, but the professional triumph was a personal disaster on one level. His brother Asahel, who'd established the contacts in Alaska, taken some of the pictures and hauled thousands of glass-plate negatives and developing chemicals all through the Klondike in service of Curtis Inc., received no credit. He was furious. He said Edward had no right taking his photographs—the product of many frozen days in the wretched gold camps—and claiming them as his own. On the contrary, Edward said, those pictures belonged to the Curtis studio; his brother was an employee. After an explosive spat, Asahel quit. He took all his belongings from Edward's home and promised to go out on his own and compete with the other Curtis. From then on, the brothers would not speak to each other. At chance encounters around town, they turned away, as to a stranger.

After detailing his somewhat exaggerated Alaskan experience to Merriam and Grinnell, Curtis told them he also knew a thing or two about Indians, though again, not from books. He had learned by observation. His pictures of Indians around Puget Sound had just been chosen for an exhibition sponsored by the National Photographic Society —the most prestigious showing in the country. And a few weeks earlier, while leading another Mazama expedition, to the top of Mount St. Helens, Curtis had come upon two Indians drying bark in the woods. He stayed behind to chat with the men and photograph them. This early Indian picture, owned by the Mazamas and almost never seen, is a startling piece of photojournalism, showing natives deep in a forest at the base of a restless mountain; they are wearing long pants and white men's shirts, grimacing at the camera.

Grinnell and Merriam were intrigued by this lanky man who'd appeared out of the fog on a glacier, all blue eyes and bounce in his step. Just before Curtis "thawed them out and bedded them down," as Curtis later conveyed to a friend, he mentioned a few more details about the tribes of the maritime West. This business of the potlatch, the Indian ritual of giving away worldly goods, was an extraordinary event. There was nothing more honorable. And yet government agents were trying to ban the potlatch—they considered it barbaric, unfit for a race that needs to join the lot of civilization. Canada had made it a crime for Coast Salish people to participate in their most esteemed ceremony. The two men leaned into their rescuer: *Tell us more.*

A few days later, Curtis hosted the distinguished gentlemen at his studio, a showroom of the finest faces in Seattle and the most gloried scenery in the region. But the easterners were fascinated by his Indian pictures. A big part of his business now came from selling "Curtis Indians," as they were advertised in a brochure, and his search for native people had taken him well beyond the city, east of the Cascades, where he found a band of the Nez Perce living at the edge of the Columbia River on wind-raked scablands. And farther east, into Montana, he'd gone for glimpses of buffalo-dependent tribes. His Indians were a startling departure from the usual depictions of these people. There were, in the faces, distinct human beings, not character types. How did he do it?

Good pictures, Curtis explained, are not products of chance, but come from long hours of study. Though he'd gone many times to Rainier, much of the mountain had eluded him as a subject. He said it could take years to get it right, years when he might return from the glaciers empty-handed. You had to understand the essence of a thing before you could ever hope to capture its true self. And yes, he was trying to bring a painterly eye to the process, a subjective artistry. No reason to apologize. He believed that no two people could point a camera at something and come away with the same image. But, of course, photography involved a mechanical side as well, and there too, you could shape the final product to match a vision—to bring the right image to light from a stew of chemicals, to touch it up in a print shop, to finish with an engraving pen. Curtis never turned it off, never took time to play or let his mind roam, even at home. At night in the big Seattle house, "he studied pictures," Clara's cousin William Phillips recalled, "the whys and wherefores; the ifs and the ands: landscapes, portraits, marine views and studies from old masters. He reveled in such, in his musings, in his thoughts and conceptions."

Curtis often slept in his studio, working until first light. In the early morning, when his wife arrived to open the shop for business, she would find him slumped against a wall, fresh-printed pictures spread all over the floor, his clothes wrinkled, cigarette stubs in a pile. And then he would snap to, rub his face and resume his work as if he'd never taken a break. He boasted that he needed very little sleep to function well; he had a prodigious amount of energy. His tank was always full.

"Wait till you see the next picture I make," he would exclaim. "It's going to be a crackerjack!"

His labors would be rewarded with one of the biggest prizes in American photography. The pictures prompted by Princess Angeline's routine and repeat visits to the Tulalip reservation—*The Clam Digger* and *The Mussel Gatherer*, along with *Homeward*—had made the finals. And *Homeward*, which showed Puget Sound Indians in a high-bowed canoe backlit by the sun-infused clouds of early evening, won the grand prize: a gold medal from the National Photographic Society. Soon, those pictures would tour the world.

As impressed as the visitors were by Curtis the photographer and Curtis the mountaineer, they were equally interested in Curtis the amateur anthropologist. He had collected bits of mythology and tribal narratives along his picture-taking path, and wrote up summaries of these scraps of the Indians' inner world. For decades Grinnell had fought to save the American bison, using his influential mouthpiece, *Forest and Stream*, to shame speculators of buffalo hides and skulls, the mindless poachers with rapid-fire rifles who had reduced a bounty of perhaps sixty million to a few hundred stragglers. Grinnell's passion for lost causes was now focused on Plains Indians. The Pawnee, the Blackfeet, the Cheyenne—they'd been pushed to the brink, and their culture was being erased from the land of their grandparents. In Grinnell's view, the way to understand Indians was to become more like them, rather than insist that the tribes become more like us. He had lived with Plains Indians for twenty seasons, could speak the language and many dialects, and had published *Pawnee Hero Stories and Folk-Tales.* The Blackfeet had made him an honorary member of the tribe. Grinnell feared that in just a few years' time, these natives might end up like the buffalo.

To Grinnell and Merriam, departing from the Pacific Northwest after a fortuitous encounter on the region's highest peak, this Curtis man seemed like quite the resourceful fellow. He knew Alaska, mountains and Indians. He was fast on his feet, quick with a joke, full of practical knowledge, physically heroic.

Over the winter, they stayed in touch. And in the spring of 1899 Merriam made a proposal to Curtis: how would he like to join the largest scientific exploration of Alaska ever undertaken? The idea came from the Gilded Age titan Edward Henry Harriman, who had just gained full control of the Union Pacific Railroad as part of a bigger scheme to monopolize rail traffic—much to the annoyance of his chief rival, J. P. Morgan. The deal-making had left Harriman, at the age of fifty-one, exhausted; his doctor recommended a long cruise. Harriman turned his hiatus into something much bigger. He strode into the Washington, D.C., office of C. Hart Merriam with a plan to stock a large ship with the finest zoologists, geologists, botanists and ethnologists and go forth in search of the unknown. Merriam would organize the scientific party. Harriman would pay for it all. It was to be the last great exploratory expedition of its kind in North America, dating to the Lewis and Clark journey a hundred years earlier. Curtis would be the official photographer.

The steamship *George W. Elder* left Seattle on the final day of May 1899, loaded down with milk cows and chickens, a well-stuffed library and a well-stocked bar, and 126 people, including two medical doctors, a chef and sous-chef, a chaplain, taxidermists, guides and the Harriman family. Curtis was the youngest and least credentialed member of the expedition, and he brought along an assistant, Duncan Inverarity, a friend from Seattle. Among those sailing north were the two best-known naturalists in America, John Muir and John Burroughs, both long-bearded and long-winded, called "the Two Johnnies." Also on board was a lanky gentleman with faraway eyes whose name was constantly in the papers: Gifford Pinchot, a man of the woods, from a wealthy family. At night, the ship's salon hosted arcane discussions by the scientists, speaking mostly in Latin, "fearfully and wonderfully learned," as Burroughs put it. The German-born forester Bernhard Fernow played Beethoven on the grand piano. Pinchot went on at length about how the outdoors made him feel most alive. The Two Johnnies argued, a flutter of white beards and spokes of fingers poking each other's chests. By day, the scientists would disembark in a particular bay, and then bring back all sorts of plants, fish and wildlife to the ship, where they were picked apart. The *Elder* steamed past the rainforest shores of southeast Alaska, up into Glacier Bay, through the inlets of Prince William Sound, out along the far edge of the Aleutian Islands, touching the Siberian shore — where Mrs. Harriman wanted to leave a footprint in Russia — and then back, a nine-thousand-mile round-trip. No junket, the expedition claimed to have discovered six hundred species new to science, putting some of the best minds of new-century America to good use.

For Curtis, the *Elder* was a floating university — an Ivy League one at that. From E. H. Harriman he learned how to operate an audio recording device, a wax cylinder that could pick up and preserve sound. It was an expensive, newfangled toy for the railroad tycoon and his seven-year-old son, Averell. Curtis realized the recorder could be used to preserve the songs and words of the people they observed along the way. Outside Sitka, the machine recorded a Tlingit chant. Curtis was closest to Grinnell, an easterner who acted more like a westerner and who conveyed a sense of urgency about the passing of so much that was original to the continent. Grinnell was a member of the expedition because of his knowledge of birds, but he seemed more interested in the native people they met. These villagers in animal skins and furs were ogled at by most of the scientists, treated like exotic species or fossilized relics. When the ship sailed into a bay where women were skinning seals, most of the Harriman elites were repulsed by the smell and carnage. Curtis waded ashore and spent a day talking to the natives and taking pictures. The photographs show people who seem annoyed, at best, by the intrusion of well-outfitted Anglos. There are no moonlit silhouettes, no soft-focus portraits. The photos have a hard, documentary edge.

The Curtis method was simple: get as close as he could. He worked the same way with the landscapes. In shooting nearly five thousand photographs for the expedition, he sometimes leapt from iceberg to iceberg, slipped on polished stones in freezing streams and hiked to the edge of crevasses. Once, in his canoe in Glacier Bay, he tried to get close to a heaving ice field that was calving big chunks. Crewmen on board the *Elder* watched in amusement as Curtis paddled toward an enormous, berg-shedding glacier. He took several glass-plate impressions, then moved in closer. And then—horror. A calf of ice nearly ten times the size of the steamship broke away with a thunderous crack and splash, sending a wall of waves toward Curtis's tiny canoe. "About half a mile of the front fell at once," Burroughs wrote. The photographer paddled directly into a wave, a suicide impulse, it seemed. But instead of being crushed and drowned, Curtis rode the high waters to their crests—to the amazement of those watching from the deck of the ship. He lost some plates and equipment, but returned alive, his sense of invincibility hardened.

The famous men assembled by the railroad tycoon liked the photographer. He was self-deprecating, brash, tireless, able to handle the repartee of big egos in tight quarters—and certainly obsequious without being annoying. He was also sincerely interested in learning from them. "His earnestness, industry, simplicity and innocence are positively contagious," wrote William Phillips, in explaining the most attractive qualities of young Curtis.

Near the end of the Alaskan summer, the ship steered into what appeared to be an abandoned Tlingit village on Cape Fox—a ghostly place to the Harriman experts. But the empty village was alive in a way the experts could never know. The artwork, the totem poles and posts, the masks, the carved raven heads and salmon designs were animate objects to the Tlingit, each with a power of its own. The scientists took hundreds of artifacts from the village, to the disgust of John Muir, who felt his shipmates were no better than common looters. These distinguished scholars would never haul away paintings and statues from an empty church in Europe. The men were preserving culture, they insisted, not robbing a village. Plundering a native community was justified as a rescue for the sake of science; the artifacts were bound for museums in the United States.

To Grinnell, who'd been brooding for much of the trip, the majestic but strangely empty site on Cape Fox only confirmed what he'd been saying about the inhabitants of the big land: their way of life was passing. Every collision between the native world and modernity was a hopeless mismatch. The Indians were doomed. And here was all the evidence he needed: a dead village, like a body still warm to the touch. He confided these concerns to Curtis, who said he also was appalled that educated and celebrated men would steal so many priceless objects. Next year, Grinnell said, he planned to return to a place that curious outsiders had yet to pick apart, to take in a native ceremony on the high plains of Montana, and to do so in a respectful manner. For centuries, the people who lived where mountain and prairie came together had gathered during the longest days of the year to praise the sun. Missionaries and the government's Indian agents were closing in. The Indians' central ritual would soon be gone, outlawed like the potlatch. Grinnell was privileged to witness the ceremony because of his standing among the Blackfeet. He planted an idea with Curtis: why not see for yourself and get it down for posterity? On the deck of the ship as it steamed back to Seattle, Grinnell made an offer that would set the course for the rest of Curtis's life. "Come with me next year," he said. "You'll have a chance to know Indians."

The climber: Curtis on Mount Rainier in 1897, from a booklet he published of mountaineering photos and adventures. (The picture is cropped.)

Two Indians drying bark in the woods of Mount St. Helens. Curtis took this rarely seen picture in 1898, while on a climbing expedition with the Mazamas.

3

THE BIG IDEA
1900

I N THE SUMMER OF 1900, Curtis boarded the Great Northern Railroad for a trip east to an Indian land that existed only in the imagination of most Americans. His train chugged through a long tunnel inside the Cascade Mountains, out past the glacier-scarred indents of coulee country in central Washington, straight to the rail center of Spokane. From there the tracks headed north, nearly to the Canadian border, and then east again. The train huffed across the Rockies of western Montana, up, up, up, straining to straddle the Continental Divide at Marias Pass, 5,215 feet above sea level, the highest point of the most northerly of the nation's transcontinental railroads. Through the mountains that would be enshrined by decade's end as Glacier National Park the train went, and then down, down, down, a dramatic transition from forest green to prairie brown and high flat ground to a knot of small buildings, a dwelling house, two hotels, a store. His destination, Browning, Montana, was a whistle stop on the Great Northern line, but also the heart of the Blackfeet Nation.

The emptiness startled him. The wind nearly knocked him down. A one-man expedition, Curtis gathered his cameras and notebooks, his sketchbooks and tent, his sleeping roll and extra clothes and a wax cylinder recorder. As the dust flew in early evening, he was met by Bird

Grinnell, a warm reunion. It was the Pawnee from the Great Plains who had first given the doctor from Yale the name of Bird, because he appeared every year in the spring and then would migrate somewhere when the cold weather came. And it had been with the Pawnee, in 1872, that Grinnell had witnessed their last great buffalo hunt, an adrenaline-surged spectacle of half-ton prey chased by nimble athletes on horse-back.

The wind from the prairie, gathering momentum as it swept down from the province of Alberta, made it difficult to hold a conversation outside the leaky frame walls of the Browning general store. Curtis could see why a tree was unable to cling to the hard earth at four thousand feet on the Montana high ground. The men outfitted their horses, then took off at a trot back toward the mountains, where the plains buckled up and rose. They were crossing twenty miles or so of buffalo country, amber fields of grass pocked by hollows where the bigheaded beasts took dust baths to keep mosquitoes away. But there was not a bi-son in sight; few had been seen for two decades, Grinnell told his aco-lyte. Bird turned fifty that summer, almost twenty years older than Curtis, with half a lifetime's knowledge from living with Plains Indians to impart to the younger man. Their purpose was one part adventure, one part anthropology and one part mercenary, for both men knew their access to this lost world could fill a lecture hall later.

This trip to the Blackfeet Nation was also the test of an idea starting to take shape—that those "Curtis Indian" fragments sold by his studio could form part of a much bigger picture story. Grinnell encouraged Curtis, urged him to be expansive, but he also stripped him of his more romantic notions. He was both mentor and tormentor. *What are you really looking for?* Grinnell asked Curtis. *Why are you shooting all these pictures of Indians in the first place?* Curtis explained that he was doing it "for his own amusement," as Grinnell wrote later. Also, Indian pictures were a lucrative part of his business. He could charge a premium for a typical studio portrait, but those branded Curtis Indians—the pictures he'd taken around Puget Sound and on the Columbia Plateau—were selling for much higher prices. It was telling that Curtis put every surplus dollar back into the "amusement" work; that was what made his heart race now, even more than climbing mountains.

Grinnell pressed him further. He wondered if Curtis had ever thought about putting together a book, or an exhibition at the Smithsonian, where Americans could see what was slipping away. Curtis could rouse the nation to action, as Grinnell had done on behalf of keeping a small bison herd intact in Yellowstone. Grinnell's crusade had won over many influential people, including Teddy Roosevelt, who'd just made the step from governor of New York to vice president of the United States. Indeed, Curtis replied, he had thought about doing something grand and consequential. "The idea dawned on him that here was a wide field as yet unworked," Grinnell wrote. "Here was a great country in which still live hundreds of tribes and remnants of tribes, some of which still retain many of their primitive customs and their ancient beliefs. Would it not be a worthy work, from the points of view of art and science and history, to represent them all by photography?"

Curtis had tried to take pictures of these plains natives two years earlier, in 1898, but came home with little to show for it. Now, with Grinnell, Curtis had a flesh-and-blood passport to something an outsider could not see on his own. With Bird at his side, he was a tourist no more —he was in training.

As for the late-afternoon thunderheads, twirls of dust devils and biting flies drawn to horse flesh and the softer human kind—who could complain? Push on, Curtis urged, push on. He'd been promised much more than a peek: a chance to witness the Sun Dance, the oldest and most important religious ceremony to the Piegan, Bloods and related tribes, resettled on the Blackfeet reservation because of common bonds. Any inconvenience was a trifle compared to what lay ahead.

They crossed a plateau, the wind tossing thistle over the prairie, and galloped ever higher, to the near exhaustion of their mounts. Grinnell signaled a slowing as they seemed to run out of ground. Dismount, he ordered. The two men took the reins of their horses and walked toward a cliff's edge, Curtis curious and willful, Grinnell's eyes trained ahead. They stepped up to the rim of a high precipice. Below was an encampment, a circle of large tipis, more than two hundred of them by Curtis's count, forming an enclosure a mile or so in diameter. The Indians had brought horses, wagons, carts, food and the painted buffalo skins that stretched around pine poles to form their lodges.

Ever since the daughter of Chief Seattle had caught his eye in the tidal flats, Curtis had been looking for a community of Indians to cast in lasting light on his camera glass. Mostly he'd found only snippets of life here and there, broken from the whole. There was nothing of a people living in continuity with the past. Nothing intact. But here — look at it! — just below the cliff were generations, as many children as grandchildren. By historical standards, the Piegan encampment was small, but Curtis had never witnessed so many Indian people together in one place. The only thing to compare to this group, for sheer numbers, was the engraving he had seen as a child of Indians hanged in that mass execution in Minnesota.

Take it all in, Grinnell told him. *Take a long, long look*. To Bird Grinnell, the scene below the cliff already belonged to yesterday. For one thing, the Holy Family Mission, aided by government Indian agents, was doing all it could to put an end to this ceremony. The Sun Dance was considered savagery, matching the law's description of an "immoral dance." Under the Indian Religious Crimes Code, anything deemed unwholesomely pagan could be banned — dances, feasts, chants led by medicine men. The regulations were specific: "Any Indian who shall engage in the sun dance, scalp dance, or war dance, or any other similar feast, so called, shall be deemed guilty of an offense." As punishment, the agents could withhold food rations and imprison participants of traditional religious ceremonies for up to ninety days.

The churches had been given broad discretion from the government to spread doctrine and charity among the Indians, a clear violation of the First Amendment's religious establishment clause. Few politicians seemed to mind. "The Indians," said Thomas J. Morgan, the man appointed by President Benjamin Harrison in 1889 to oversee their affairs, "must conform to the white man's ways, peaceably if they will, forcibly if they must." The churches would give them spiritual sustenance; the government agents would dole out food and goods. The system was fraught with corruption, and enforced by patronage hacks and militant missionaries. "This civilization may not be the best possible, but it is the best the Indians can get," said Morgan. "They cannot escape it, and must either conform to it or be crushed by it." Forced assimilation never had a more clearly stated goal.

After the mission was established on the Montana prairie in 1890, young Blackfeet were taken from the tribe and sent to a three-story brick boarding school, fifteen miles from Browning. The idea was to rinse the native out of them and cleanse them with western Christianity. A big part of that effort was to get the boys to reject the illegal Sun Dance. A year's worth of missionary reeducation could be undone by just a few days in summer at the traditional ceremony. If the Piegan were to avoid the fate of Angeline's people, they would have to start the new century by joining the modern world, the clerics insisted. Give up the chanting and dancing, the prayers to the sun and the earth, the mumbo jumbo. An ancient festival paying homage to a blinding star was barbaric.

In 1900, census takers were in the field, making a concerted effort, at long last, to count every Indian—this at a time when all violent hostilities between the original inhabitants of the continent and the new residents had finally come to an end. The frontier was closed, the U.S. Census Bureau had announced a few years earlier—there was no longer a line to push west nor a big empty space on the map to be filled in with immigrants. This caused a great fuss among the pulse takers of American life. The early reports of the count were not good: the number of Indians was down, dramatically so. And the population figures conformed with other indicators of decline: by 1900, the tribes owned less than 2 percent of the land they once possessed. Entire languages had already disappeared—more than a loss of words, a loss of a way to look at the world. All of this had been predicted for some time, and was taken as accepted wisdom. As far back as 1831, the prescient observer Alexis de Tocqueville had said this of American Indians: "They were isolated in their own country, and their race constituted only a little colony of troublesome strangers in the midst of numerous dominant people."

Throughout the afternoon and into the early evening Curtis took pictures of these "troublesome strangers" from above: the encampment; the practical lodges, big enough to provide shelter for an extended family; the stretched animal skins outside, painted with symbols that told a story in a compact wraparound. Curtis worked without pause, moving across the cliff's edge, reacting to the changing light, slipping the heavy plates from his camera into a sealed container, then reloading.

Grinnell was impressed by his passion. Two years after meeting Curtis on the volcano, he saw in him a rare combination. Here was "a professional photographer, equipped with all the skill required in the technical part of that business," Grinnell wrote, "but he is also an artist, seeing and loving the beautiful and longing to reproduce it." And everything below, the sweep of tradition and majesty on one of the longest days of the year—it was fantastic, yes, Grinnell said. But the view was superficial as well, offering only a glancing impression.

"Their humanity has been forgotten," Grinnell said of the predominant way most outsiders looked at Indians—as either savages or victims. The Piegan had gathered to pay homage to the Great Mystery, Bird explained. And if Curtis expected to understand that mystery, in order to take pictures that were true, he would need to go down below and get to know the people. The glory was in the eyes, in the faces, in understanding how they thought and what they did in the margins of a day.

Bird took him to the encampment. It was important, he cautioned, not to come on too strong, too eager. Relax. Soak it all in. Smile. These people are not specimens, not fauna to be categorized and put under microscopes as on the Harriman expedition. They are just human beings, no more complicated or simplistic than others, no more heroic for their survival or tragic for their loss. Laugh at yourself. Don't be afraid to appear stupid: imagine an Indian walking into an Elks Lodge in downtown Seattle, uninvited. Curtis said he had established a rule, born in part by his revulsion at the Harriman party's looting: he would not take a picture without offering to pay, or without the subject's permission. A fine guiding principle to Grinnell, but he urged the young man not to start in right away with cash and exchanges. Take time to get acquainted. Here is White Calf, chief of the Blackfeet—a friend, nearly sixty years old. Over there is Tearing Lodge, another revered elder, seventy years old. And that hard-eyed man on horseback, scowling as he circles the edge of the encampment, that is Small Leggins. *He doesn't like you.*

The whites had said many things about these plains dwellers, commenting on their rituals of self-mutilation and fasting, their soaks in sweat lodges and their naked dashes into the snow, the way they dispatched enemies, torturing and gutting them and taking the women as slaves. Little of what had been written was accurate, Grinnell said. George Catlin, the most famous American graphic documentarian of Indians in the nineteenth century, had come home with many fanciful drawings and even more fanciful conjectures. Catlin had called the Blackfeet "perhaps the most powerful tribe of Indians on the continent." They certainly had a reputation for toughness, for feuding fiercely with other tribes, for violence that didn't follow the norms of Anglo-European warfare. But "most powerful"? No, not by any stretch. They were too small in number for that. The Comanche, the hard-riding, merciless Lords of the Plains, who dominated much of Texas and the Southwest, could rout the Blackfeet in an afternoon, had they come into a fight.

If the stories are contradictory, Grinnell continued, put two or more sources together and try to settle on the truth. Ask the same question repeatedly—but ask it of the people themselves. Don't bother with those who profess to know Indians because they live nearby, the merchants who scorn them or the ranchers who run cattle over the old buffalo grass. Nor should he waste his time with the anthropologists of eastern colleges or European universities, who divided themselves between the Noble Savage school and the racial determinists who saw Darwinian roadkill in the collapse of the tribes. And he certainty should avoid the do-gooders in black robes who were oh so sorry for the poor, pathetic Indians as they worked to tally converts. Finally, Grinnell reserved special scorn for government agents, the frontline enforcers of assimilation, the faces of a conqueror who made sure no sensible policy would ever be practiced.

Taking Grinnell's advice, Curtis established another plank for the cathedral of a plan he was building in his mind: "Information at all times must be drawn from the Indians." Over the days, Curtis listened. The Indians were skeptical, of course, of this stranger that Bird had brought into their midst. Small Leggins followed Curtis with his eyes, an orbit of staring. The man with the camera and wax recorder heard stories of their origins, their hopes, the great losses they had suffered from disease and a deathly hunger that followed the collapse of the buffalo herds. In one winter, 1883–84, the Piegan lost a fourth of their population to starvation—a "winter of misery and death," Curtis wrote. He wondered about a few of the more dark-skinned natives, and was told they were descendants of a black slave called York, who had passed among these people nearly a hundred years earlier with Lewis and Clark. Curtis smoked a ceremonial pipe. He learned that a person should never look his mother-in-law in the face or talk to her directly. He was invited into a sweat lodge. He stripped naked and sat as the water poured out of him, until he nearly passed out, delirious and hallucinating, "until I heard far-away music where there could be no music," as he wrote to a friend back home. But he remained Edward S. Curtis of Seattle, the portrait photographer. He would not try to fake or play at being an Indian.

Curtis found these people very "likeable," and among the most courteous he had met, of any race. At the same time, Chief White Calf warmed to him. A trust was developing, but it took a great deal of time, much of it spent in silence. His questions often went unanswered. "To ask the Piegan . . . any direct question bearing on the subject of religion yields scant light," said Curtis. "It is necessary to learn rather from the everyday life of the people." When the stories came, even in dribs and drabs, the breakthrough was thrilling to Curtis—like learning to swim after hours of flailing in water. See how easy: just let yourself float.

After several days, the chief informed Curtis that he would be allowed to do portraits of those tribal members who agreed, for a negotiated price. Curtis could shoot the encampment, the lodges, the gathering of wood for fires, the horses taking a long drink in the afternoon, everything but the Sun Dance itself. He was allowed to witness it, but this ritual could never be stolen by an outsider's camera. It is the highest of religious ceremonies, the annual fulfillment of a pledge to the sun. People would sweat in the lodge, burn sweet grass incense, offer dried buffalo tongues to the sun, sing and dance. He was allowed, somewhat to his surprise, to record the songs, using the "magic machine," as the Indians called his wax cylinder.

The formal Sun Dance lasted five days. "Wild, terrifying, elaborately mystifying," Curtis said. "I was intensely affected." He coaxed a handsome young man to pose inside a tent, with a full peacock sprout of erect hair, bedecked in necklaces and shells, cloaked in a light rawhide coat of symmetrical designs. *A Piegan Dandy,* Curtis labeled the picture. One dandy taking a picture of another dandy — there was a projection of an artist feeling the full surge of his growing talent. The portrait was eventually processed as an albumen print, in which paper was coated in an emulsion of whipped egg white and salt, then dipped in silver nitrate before a negative was exposed onto it — the rarest kind of finish for Curtis. He set up his 14-by-17 on a tripod close to the village for ground-level pictures of natives collecting logs for the ceremony. As he worked, Curtis spotted Small Leggins in one part of the circle, riding his horse at a quick clip, coming right at him. The closer he got, the faster he rode, charging directly at Curtis. He intended to trample Curtis and smash his camera. At the last second, White Calf appeared, steering Small Leggins away. The chief "saved my life," Curtis said.

The photographer got his picture as well: a wide view in early evening, the tipis in the circle echoing the triangular tops of the summits in the background. This he called *Piegan Encampment.* The finished product was a photogravure, from a process in which the image was chemically etched onto the surface of a copper printing plate — a laborious method used by Curtis for most of his Indian pictures. (For his best work, he rarely printed an actual photograph in the traditional way.) And eventually, he even got Small Leggins to hold still long enough on his horse for Curtis to immortalize him. Another picture from that July was taken at the water's edge, where the Two Medicine River, shrunk by the summer sun, snaked through the grass of the plains. This was a trio of men on horseback, one riding an Appaloosa, looking away to the distance, the shadows of their figures reflected in the water. The resulting photograph was called *The Three Chiefs*.

Curtis talked White Calf into posing. He was drawn to the chief's head, which stood out because he was bald. At the appointed hour, the chief showed up—but he had donned a blond wig and was dressed in a faded blue army uniform, with a soldier's hat on top. Curtis got a laugh out of that, but nothing that was worth bringing to light later in the studio. This episode with White Calf showed the kind of conflict Curtis would face time and again, the clash of the old with the new. Curtis would always side with the old, no matter how much it had been supplanted, because the fast-disappearing past, he felt, was the authentic. The twentieth century had no place in the nascent Curtis Indian project.

Near the end of the Blackfeet summer, Curtis told Grinnell his mind was set. He would embark on a massive undertaking, even bigger than Bird had suggested: a plan to photograph all intact Indian communities left in North America, to capture the essence of their lives before that essence disappeared. "The record, to be of value to future generations, must be ethnologically accurate," he said. As sketched by Curtis, it was an impossibly grandiose idea, and he was vague on the specifics of how to pay for it, how inclusive it would be, how long it would take and how he would present the finished product. What's more, after recording the songs of the Sun Dance, Curtis further expanded his scope and ambition: he would try to be a keeper of secrets—not just a photographer, but a stenographer of the Great Mystery. And did Edward Curtis, with his sixth-grade education, really expect to perform the multiple roles of ethnographer, anthropologist and historian? He did. What Curtis lacked in credentials, he made up for in confidence—the personality trait that had led him to Angeline's shack and Rainier's summit. Bird loved the Big Idea.

When he boarded the train back to Seattle, on the same Great Northern line that had opened up Blackfeet land and doomed it as bison hunting ground, Curtis knew he was taking home photographic gold. The long hours, the respectful silences and the fair exchange of cash for posing had paid off. He could not wait to show the images to the rest of the world. A few months later, when his pictures went on display at the San Francisco art store of William Morris, they immediately "attracted a great deal of comment," a newspaper in the city reported. In an interview, Curtis was effusive. He gushed about how much the Sun Dance had affected him. But the paper made light of what Curtis considered serious work. "There is just one feat more difficult than introducing an Indian to the bathtub, and that is to make him face a camera," the story began. Dime-store Indians again, plenty of hokum; it was enough to make Curtis wonder if the public would ever care for his planned epic. Though Curtis had gone into considerable detail with the reporter about the glory, power and intricacy of the Sun Dance, the paper described the experience as "five days crammed with weird customs."

Back in Seattle, Curtis had to take domestic considerations into account. The project would involve so much time away from home, from the studio, from his growing family. Where would Clara fit in? What was her role? She had encouraged Edward to move across Puget Sound, to mortgage his homestead, to reach for Rainier's summit, and at every step she had followed—and occasionally led. But with three children, she knew the family had to balance the pragmatic with the idealistic. Who would tend to the debs, the prosperous and pink-faced merchants, those willing to make a special trip from out of town, waiting months to have Curtis take their picture? Beyond the paying work, Curtis was already famous among those who thought a camera could produce original art—what more did he need? This *dream* . . . How would the family live? Time in the field, deep in Indian country, would cost thousands of dollars, with the payoff well down the road, if at all. Curtis insisted that he could do both: oversee the studio business and grow the Big Idea. On some trips, he suggested, Clara and the children could come with him. Her cousin William Phillips, who lived with them, would be Curtis's first assistant for the Indian project. For the studio, he would hire a few more people and expand the reach of his name. As Clara noted, plenty of the city's newly rich would pay handsomely to have the name Curtis etched below their hagiographic mugs. And those people would indirectly finance the Indian work. Not to worry, the money will come.

"He had a living to earn, a family to support," Grinnell wrote later in a long article unveiling the Curtis plan, carried in *Scribner's Magazine*. "To do what he thought of meant much travel, great expense, and unending toil. But the idea refused to be rejected. It overpowered him."

He was home for only a few days that summer of 1900. His family and friends were perplexed: why the hurry? Because, Curtis explained, the subject was dying. His project would be a marathon at a sprinter's pace. Grinnell's description was apt — the idea had indeed overpowered him. Off he went by himself, in a dash of camera equipment and notebooks, clothes and cash and books and tents and plates, to the outer reaches of the American Southwest, by train deep into the wild, as far as the tracks would take him, to Winslow, Arizona Territory. Then, by horse-drawn wagon, bouncing and jostling sixty miles over rough terrain, to a bony, roadless expanse in the middle of the map — Hopi Indian land. The sky was big, the natives unknowable, the photographer not sure exactly what he was looking for. He chose the Hopi, and other tribes in the area, because their ancestral home in the arid Southwest had not been overrun by farmers and town-platters. From the Rio Grande to the Grand Canyon, there was a high concentration of tribes with sophisticated views of both the natural and the supernatural world — dozens of nations that had yet to give in to a larger nation. It was bristly ground, passed around by Spain, Mexico, the Republic of Texas and the United States, foreign to foreigners who were always looking for something like what they'd left behind in old Europe.

And for Curtis, too, the Southwest was far removed from anything he had seen — and he loved it. He rejoiced in the "harmonious, pastel shades of sand" and the "distant ranges of lavender mountains slowly transformed into turquoise as the lowering sun sinks behind them." He was captivated by the way unmarried women wore their hair in squash-blossom coils, and by the "remarkable stories of Hopi distance running" — tales of men who ran twenty miles a day to work their fields.

He found a native translator, put him on the payroll and started in with the questions-and-listening tour, mindful of Grinnell's advice, going from village to village trying to make himself known, but also to blend in. It was not an easy introduction, as Curtis quickly picked up on the Hopis' low regard for white people. They resented missionaries, who constantly told the Indians that everything they believed was sanctified garbage, and they despised government authorities two thousand miles away in Washington, who ordered the men to cut their hair or else face fines and imprisonment. "Here they live with the unavoidable minimum contact with the white race, whom they unostentatiously but cordially hate," said Curtis. As he found, it was a recurrent attitude in Arizona Territory.

Hopi communities were built atop high mesas, the homes constructed of clay, rock and sandy mortar, ceilings eight feet high, walls eighteen inches thick, sleeping quarters reached by ladders. The heat in the Arizona desert was intense, and few things stirred at the height of day. The land was the opposite of the green Pacific Northwest; it was the earth turned inside out, all exposed rock in shades of copper, yellow and rust. The Hopi lived southeast of the Grand Canyon, near the Painted Desert—an oasis of earthen villages surrounded by a sea of the much more populous Navajo, their longtime rivals.

And unlike the Plains or Puget Sound Indians, the Hopi were farmers, sedentary and dependent on the water that came coursing through arroyos during summer monsoons to irrigate corn, bean and squash fields. If the water didn't arrive, the people would starve. So, to ensure the annual rain, the Hopi prayed intensely during their biggest religious occasion, the Snake Dance. As with the Sun Dance, this was the most important ritual of the year for the Hopi. The ceremony could only be performed by members of the Snake Society, those who gathered rattlesnakes, hundreds of them. Though Curtis was allowed to watch the dance, as were others who put up with Hopi scorn for outsiders (including, on his first visit, members of the Harvard Glee Club), Curtis wanted much more.

"After witnessing the Snake Dance ceremony," Curtis wrote, "I was profoundly moved, and realized if I was to fully understand its significance, I must participate, if permission could be obtained." He asked the chief of the Hopi Snake Society, a man named Sikyaletstiwa, if he might learn the ways of the fraternity and participate—with the goal of shooting pictures. Curtis stressed that he was not trying to become an Indian. He just wanted inside, to try on the metaphorical clothes of the natives. The answer—forget it. Impossible, the chief said; no one outside the society could participate. Sikyaletstiwa told him that if he really wished to learn about the Hopi, he should come back next year, and the year after, and the year after that. Curtis promised he would do just that. Before he left, he made a portrait of a snake dancer, a man of about thirty, a jaunty figure not unlike the Piegan dandy he had shot the same summer in Montana. This picture, called *Snake Dancer in Costume*, stood out not just for the detail—a full-length, shirtless man, nearly naked but clothed in mystery, his body painted, shells and jewels hanging from his hair, ears and neck—but for the look on the man's face, at once defiant and self-confident, reflecting the mood of Curtis himself.

"These photographs are not like those which anyone has seen," Grinnell wrote in a glowing account of the Blackfeet and Hopi work. "The results which Curtis gets with his camera stir one as one is stirred by a great painting." But, he added, "while Curtis is first of all an artist, he does not think solely of his art."

Over the next three summers, Curtis returned to the Southwest, just as he promised he would, introducing himself to other tribes and trying to gain insight into their lives. The distances were vast. The land was a deeply eroded and vertiginous plateau, with few roads, spires appearing on the horizon like giant rock stalks—not easy to travel. It became clear that if Curtis was to follow through on his stated intention to Grinnell to photograph and document the ways of "people who still retained to a considerable degree their primitive customs and traditions," he would have to go to the cellars, attics and aeries of the continent. The Indians of the East, save for a few pockets, had been pushed out long ago, starting—systematically—with the Indian Removal Act of 1830. Yes, a few Cherokee still lived in Appalachian hollows, and a handful of Seminoles hunkered down in the Everglades of Florida. You could find a Choctaw or Chickasaw who had refused the forced march to Oklahoma, and in New England, a Pequot or Penobscot still pulled fish from the sea while living at the edge of a Yankee village.

America was stitching itself ever tighter, through rail lines and roads for automobiles; by decade's end, airplanes would fly with the birds in every part of the country. At the same time, the Indians who wished to continue living the old ways had to take refuge — to hide, essentially — from the dominant culture. The populous Navajo were spread throughout the north of Arizona Territory, over the border into the sandstone wilderness of Utah, down along parts of New Mexico. The Havasupai, a tiny band, lived literally out of sight: in a deep hole at the western edge of the Grand Canyon, thousands of feet into a slit carved by runoff into the Colorado River. The Mojave were farther south, their lives blended with some of the harshest desert of the world. To find the longtime nomadic Apache, Curtis would have to go high into the mountains and deep into pine forests. He would have to follow the Rio Grande above Santa Fe to encounter Pueblo people who had been conquered by the Spanish three hundred years earlier. All of this was just in the Southwest. If Curtis was going to do something definitive, exhaustive and encyclopedic, he would also have to spend much time on the plains, in the Rockies, in the fjords of British Columbia and Washington State, in the northern California mountains and the southern California desert, in the Arctic.

Curtis was confident he could do it all. He may not have had money or education, but he had robust health, he boasted — he felt strong, always full of zip, plowing through sixteen-hour days, seven days a week. Only on rare occasions in the first years did he express any doubt, and then as a way to solicit further encouragement. How many tribes would he have to visit to cover the full scope of native peoples living as they had before Anglo dominance? Twenty? Forty? Sixty?

"I want to make them live forever," he told Grinnell. "It's such a big dream I can't see it all."

The tribes may have been numerous, but the overall population was plummeting. When the results of the 1900 census were published, the government counted only 237,000 Indians in a country of 76 million people. This was the lowest number ever, scholars and Indian authorities said, down from perhaps as many as 10 million at the time of white contact in 1492. Typhus, measles, bubonic plague, influenza, alcohol poisoning, cholera, tuberculosis — the diseases introduced to the New World from the Old rolled across the big land and through the centuries, wiping out nations along the way. If these trends continued, in the consensus view of government policymakers, American Indians could vanish within Curtis's lifetime. Perhaps he was already too late.

A Piegan Dandy, 1900. The closeness of Edward Curtis to his subjects
made for a productive season at the Blackfeet reservation in Montana.
That summer changed Curtis's life, launching his photographic epic.

Piegan Camp, 1900. This was the first time Curtis had seen an entire Indian community, intact and vibrant. He was enthralled.

Snake Priest, 1900. After his first visit with the Hopi in Arizona, Curtis vowed to become a part of the Snake Priest society.

4

___

INDIAN NAPOLEON
1903

A FEW MINUTES BEFORE kickoff at the biggest football game of the year in Seattle, the crowd in the splintered wooden stands craned to get a look at an entourage leading a tall, full-haired dignitary to the sidelines. Chief Joseph of the Nez Perce was with his nephew Red Thunder, trailed by a knot of newsmen. He was known worldwide as the Indian Napoleon, a field genius who had outwitted the American cavalry and some of its best generals in a 1,700-mile retreat from his homeland in northeast Oregon to the Canadian border. The Nez Perce War of 1877 had made Joseph—a striking-looking man whose native name, *Hin-mah-too-yah-la-kekt*, or Thunder Rolling Down the Mountains, carried power and music in six syllables—a household figure in Europe and the United States. As the last of the great chiefs died, and the Indian world seemed an ever more distant era, Joseph's fame grew. Only Geronimo, the aging Apache warrior, was as well known.

"Rah, rah, rah!" The spectators at Athletic Field took up a chant, and one of Joseph's escorts said they were cheering in his honor. Turn and wave, he was told—they want to see you! The new boots on his feet were muddied by the stone-and-clay gumbo of the field, and the wind bit at his face. A thick woolen blanket was wrapped around his shoulders. It was late November, the darkest, wettest, bleakest time of the year, days when the sun might not be seen for weeks and the light would flee in midafternoon. "The most noted Indian now living," as the papers put it, was in Seattle at the invitation of the Washington Historical Society. What better exhibition could they put on? A famous Indian! An exotic from the past! See him and hear him and touch him while he's still alive! He was allowed to leave the virtual prison of his plot of reservation ground on the Columbia River Plateau, to cross the mountains and come to speak as the society's guest. Joseph had accepted the offer, not because he liked being on display, but because he hoped to persuade influential people to take up his cause.

Not since Teddy Roosevelt came to town a few months earlier had Seattle been so stirred by a visitor. The president gave a speech before fifty thousand people, urging citizens of the Northwest to conserve their salmon and forests. A big news story on the Sunday before Joseph's arrival included pictures of the chief on his latest trip to Washington, D.C., there to "plead with the Great Father for the return of the Wallowa Valley, the home of his fathers." He had met with Roosevelt on the visit, to little avail; the Nez Perce leader was poor, aging and without any leverage but his renown. That celebrity had given him access, if not influence, during his extensive travels over the past five years. In the spring of 1900, he'd met President William McKinley. While on the East Coast that year, he was very much in demand. Would he come to New York for the dedication of General Grant's tomb? No, the chief said, he couldn't afford it. Well then, Buffalo Bill Cody offered to pay his way and put Joseph up at the Astor House with him, which did more for the consummate showman than it did for the single-minded cause of the Nez Perce chief. In Manhattan, Joseph walked around town one day in a full war bonnet, at the prompting of Cody; the rest of the time he wore a suit jacket.

"Did you ever scalp anyone?" a woman asked him in New York. Joseph didn't speak English. But using a translator, he tried to convey a single message: the once mighty Nez Perce, beloved and celebrated by Lewis and Clark and expeditions that followed, known for their horsemanship, their good looks and manners, their prosperous villages spreading over three states, were in crisis. The Joseph band, which had never converted to Christianity and refused to acknowledge a clearly fraudulent rewrite of a treaty, had dwindled to 127 people. The war of 1877 had ended badly for the bedraggled tribe, an assemblage of elders, women, children, babies and very few warriors. They had eluded about two thousand American soldiers in a chase that took them to the depths of Hells Canyon, over the most rugged mountains of Idaho and into Yellowstone National Park, north through Montana to the Canadian border, where they would have been safe had they been able to cross over. Along the way, small groups of Nez Perce had twice surprised and attacked much larger battalions of American troops. Their luck ran out at Bear Paw, on the last day of September. The Indians were hungry, some of them frostbitten, when the soldiers surrounded them. Joseph surrendered with the memorable words, "My heart is sick and sad. From where the sun now stands, I will fight no more forever."

The survivors, and Nez Perce sympathetic to Joseph who were not part of the war, were manacled, shipped to a prison in Kansas and then to a six-hundred-acre compound that was little more than a POW camp in the designated Indian Territory of Oklahoma. During the first four years in Oklahoma, 103 of the 431 Nez Perce died. By 1885, Joseph and his followers were allowed to move to the Colville reservation of central Washington, home to more than half a dozen different tribal bands, none of them particularly friendly to the Nez Perce. Colville was still a long way from the green meadows of northeastern Oregon, which Joseph's people had been promised by earlier treaty. The struggle to see the sun rise again in the Wallowas consumed the last quarter century of Joseph's life.

The press in New York wasn't interested in any of that. Broken treaties were old news. The Wallowa Valley? Couldn't find it on a map. A wild Indian on Broadway, especially one so photogenic, in full-feathered head bonnet — that was a story. "The Red Napoleon," reported the *New York Sun*, was "tall, straight as an arrow, and wonderfully handsome."

It was on his second trip to the East, months before the football game, that he met Teddy Roosevelt. At the same time, his former enemy, General Oliver Howard, whose six hundred men had been surprised by one of the attacks from a small force of fleeing Nez Perce, invited the chief to speak at the Carlisle Indian Industrial School in Pennsylvania. This institution was a high-minded boarding school for Indians from all over the country. The students came in as savages, educators proclaimed, and came out as model citizens. Joseph spoke to the children in his native tongue, as always, which only a few of them could understand. What exactly did he say? The teachers and important guests gasped when they heard the translation: "For a long time I wanted to kill General Howard."

In Seattle, Joseph's escort was a red-bearded, buoyant young professor of history at the University of Washington, Edmond S. Meany. Like Curtis, Meany was a Northwest Renaissance man, drawn to the wonders of the fledgling city by the sea. And like Curtis, he had come from the Midwest and a family that had lost its father at a young age, forcing Meany to be the breadwinner while still a teenager. Meany did not look down on Curtis for his lack of education, and Curtis did not begrudge Meany his advanced degrees. They became fast friends. Meany was tall, persuasive, an intellectual omnivore. Before his thirtieth birthday, he had started a news agency, been elected to the state legislature —where he was instrumental in passing a bill that made tuition free at the two state colleges—and climbed the highest peaks in the region. He also founded his own alpine club, the Mountaineers. He was fascinated by native people, especially those east of the Cascades, and took up their cause while still a student, earning his master's degree in 1901 with a thesis on Chief Joseph. The professor and the tribal leader were so close that Joseph gave Meany an Indian name, Three Knives. It was Meany who publicized the notion that this most famous of living Indians was "practically a prisoner of war, receiving rations and requiring permission to leave the reservation." Though he taught forestry, American history and the occasional literature class, Meany was at his professorial best when expounding on Indian life. He wanted his students to see Indians not as an academic subject, not as trees to be closely examined or distant historical figures to be deconstructed, but as living people who understood the Northwest better than any who came after them.

On the day Joseph arrived in Seattle, Meany put him up at the Lincoln Hotel and said he would try to find a car to drive him to the game. The press would surely want a picture of that. Seven years after Angeline's death, just having an Indian in the city—any Indian—was a curiosity. Seattle had bulged to 150,000 people and was growing like blackberry bramble in midsummer; the roads were lined with horse-drawn carriages, streetcars, bicycles and sputtering automobiles. Mechanical sluicing machines and hoses hissed around the clock, leveling the hills. And down in Pioneer Square, a large cedar totem pole, carved by Tlingit Indians, was erected as the centerpiece for the historic heart of the city.

Meany introduced Joseph to the only other man in Seattle who knew as much about native people as he did—the portrait photographer with the studio downtown. And in Curtis the old chief found a motivated listener. They were the same height, well over six feet, though separated by thirty years. Curtis asked Joseph about his distinctive hairstyle, a combed-back upsweep rising several inches above his forehead, with long braids on his chest. In Nez Perce culture, Joseph explained, a man who had fought the enemy many times, or had scalped a living man, was entitled to this kind of proud, showy display. He talked about how much he and his fellow native northwesterners hated their exile in Oklahoma, where it was hot, dry, flat and windswept when it wasn't cold, tornado-lashed, hail-pelted or barren. His people had starved there, and longed to see green forests and blue mountains. But the most revealing thing the chief told Curtis was about the Nez Perce War of 1877. Contrary to what had been accepted by most historians, Joseph was not the Indian Napoleon. He was not a crafty general, or even a particularly good warrior. There were other Nez Perce who planned the attacks. Joseph simply tried to hold his people together, to speak for them and argue for a resolution that would prevent total annihilation. The fact that they had eluded the cavalry for so long was due to luck and guile, not good generalship.

Curtis was astonished: the official story was wrong. Here was another chance to correct the record. And he was moved by the saga. Who could hear of the last hundred years of the Nez Perce—from rescuing

Lewis and Clark at a time when they were starving, to being chased down as outlaws through the first national park—and not feel that a tremendous injustice had been done? But Curtis had vowed to Grinnell and in print at the start of his pictorial odyssey not to revisit Indian political fights or to get into contemporary clashes over treaty rights. The stories of mistreatment, lies and betrayal were not worth rehashing. He wanted more than anything to take Joseph's picture.

Would the Nez Perce leader sit for him? Joseph demurred. He would think about it. Curtis pleaded. Take a look, he suggested, at the work he had already done on the Nez Perce, some of it on the walls of his studio. One picture was a full-body portrait of a child no more than a few months old, tightly wrapped in painted buckskin against a wood backboard with a flower drawing on it, entitled *Nez Perce Babe*, from 1900. In that face was the future of Joseph's people. Another picture showed an adult man in all his glory. He had the good looks that the Nez Perce were known for, with a fine, prominent nose, a strong jaw and full-flowing hair, swept back from his brow in the way Joseph wore his, braids exposed down to the middle of his chest. His was not the face of a dying race or a conquered people, and it epitomized the positive feelings that Curtis had of this tribe. He labeled it *Typical Nez Perce*, from 1899.

OLD CHIEF LIKES CITY,
MEETS A FAMOUS INDIAN ARTIST
THEN TAKES A BATH

His every move was front-page news, even if the tone was patronizing and superficial in the extreme. Curtis was referred to in the *Post-Intelligencer* as a "professional Indian tamer," akin to a man who could calm lions in a circus tent. The centerpiece of Joseph's visit to Seattle was speech, sold out for weeks in advance, that the Nez Perce leader was to deliver at the city's largest auditorium on Saturday night. But there was something else on the calendar that November weekend that had people in a frenzy: the football showdown. "The championship of a stretch of country from the Rockies to the sea lay in the balance," the *Seattle Times* noted. "It was an important contest, beside which the corruption of the steel trust, the robbery of a canal or the polypus in an emperor's larynx sinks into insignificance." The 1903 Sun Dodgers of the University of Washington were in the midst of an unbeaten season. November 20 was the big match with Nevada. Joseph's hosts had concocted an idea that would bring the two worlds together: perhaps the Indian chief would like to watch the region's biggest football game? But how would this help him return to the Wallowas? And why would a contest with an odd-shaped pigskin be more significant than all the major news of the day? What could it possibly mean for the Nez Perce, or even for the polyp in the emperor's throat?

On Friday afternoon, game day, Joseph boarded a streetcar to make his way up the steep hill from downtown to the field on Capitol Hill. The chief, accompanied by Meany, was led to the Washington sideline, where he was handed three cigars. The game was a ferocious defensive battle: players without face protection slammed into cold mud, bones crunching on many of the tackles, blood splattering. The crowd did an Indian chant—common at Sun Dodger games—"Skookum, Skookum! Washington!" Newspaper stories said the chief watched the game in stony silence: "his face never changed expression except when the ball was kicked, and then he appeared to laugh." Late in the fourth quarter, Washington got a safety. The 2–0 score held, and the Sun Dodgers— later known as the Huskies—emerged triumphant, kings of the Pacific Coast.

NEZ PERCE CHIEF SEES FIRST FOOTBALL
SMILES THREE TIMES

After the game, Joseph was asked his impressions of this wildly popular American sport, a game that was coming under fire for its excessive violence and serious injuries. Joseph spoke for nearly a minute to Meany, who translated.

"I saw a lot of white men almost fight today," Joseph said. "I do not think this is good."

The address, the following day, was a disappointment. Joseph appeared tired, his posture showing his weariness. He did not engage the audience. He did not tell war stories, or give accounts of derring-do, or offer details about fighting white soldiers in Yellowstone National

Park, or explain how his people survived for so long on so little food, or drop the names of presidents and other important people he had met over the years. He spoke entirely in his own language, and what he had to say was the narrative of people who were always good to the Americans and had been betrayed for their friendliness. His life was full of broken promises. He wanted his homeland back. He wanted to return to ground rightfully belonging to the Nez Perce. "A lot of grunts" was how one of the papers summarized his talk.

On his last day in Seattle, Joseph went with Meany to visit Curtis again at his studio on Second Avenue. Three Knives had talked him into it: the chief would sit for a Curtis portrait. Curtis had watched Joseph's speech on Saturday, the audience growing restless when the chief failed to show up at the scheduled time, and then sitting on their hands while he explained the plight of the Nez Perce in words none of them could understand. Curtis had been moved by the chief's quiet charisma, on his insistence on returning to the Wallowas, and he was convinced that the tribe had been robbed. He made plans to visit Joseph at the Colville reservation, to study Nez Perce ways, record their language on his wax cylinder and shoot pictures of the tribe.

In a studio stuffed with Navajo rugs and Hopi baskets, Curtis had the chief sit with Meany and Red Thunder. They were entertained by ten-year-old Harold Curtis, called Hal, getting a glimpse of how his father worked with native subjects. Curtis tried to find the man in the face, experimenting with the light, studying the angles. The chief looked worn, older than his years, gloomy, and it seemed to Curtis that much of the life was drained from him. Curtis took a few shots of Joseph and his nephew sitting down, shrunken in their seats, Meany standing over them in the middle. All three men are glowering. Then Curtis had the chief sit by himself, and he tried a number of poses. One was with feathered headdress, looking directly into the camera, a shot later finished as a photogravure titled *Joseph — Nez Perce*. This portrait shows him with a dozen rows of shell necklaces, the traditional bonnet tied beneath his chin, no hair visible. The chief is frowning. His gaze is distant. Then a second portrait, this one with the full upsweep of Joseph's hair, no headdress. The light is less gauzy, more harsh, the stare intense, the frown still there but somewhat empathetic. The picture shows even more of the topography of Joseph's extraordinary face: scars and nicks, prominent lines formed from habitual sorrow. He's wearing two large shell earrings, each bigger than a silver dollar. This photogravure was also titled *Joseph — Nez Perce*. It has multiple dimensions and conveys multiple emotions: that stare, those eyes, that hair, that mouth. It is unforgiving, without a hint of artifice, full of life even as Joseph neared his death.

When Joseph returned to the reservation, the long winter siege had already taken hold of the little village of Nespelem, Washington. He told his family that his bones ached, his rheumatism was acting up, and he had trouble sleeping. He said, "I shall live to see one more snow." He died the following year, on September 21, 1904, never having returned to the Wallowas. In keeping with Nez Perce custom, Joseph's widow cut her hair short; she would not be allowed to remarry until it once again touched her shoulders. He was buried under a mound of stones not far from the geologic scar of the Grand Coulee, with a simple rock cairn atop it. It was widely reported that Joseph, in the estimation of the reservation doctor, had died of a broken heart.

"Well, our old friend Chief Joseph has passed on," Curtis wrote to Meany a few weeks later. "At last his long, endless fight for his return to the old home is at end. For some strange reason, the thought of the old fellow's life and death gives me rather a feeling of sadness." He had interviewed more than a dozen Nez Perce after first meeting Joseph, and felt that he understood his place and their place in history. Bill Cody had called him "the greatest Indian American ever," but Curtis was more specific in his assessment: "Perhaps he was not quite what we in our minds had pictured him, but I still think he was one of the greatest men that has ever lived." It was significant that Curtis did not qualify his last statement with "Indian" — Joseph was a great man, regardless of his race.

The restraints on the Nez Perce, members of a conquered nation living by the fiat of a faraway government, were felt even among the smallest of other tribes at the time of Joseph's death. When Curtis went to see the Havasupai on his summer trip in 1903, he heard the same kinds of complaints he had heard on the Colville reservation. For that trip, he traveled again by train to the heart of Arizona Territory, and then by coach and horseback to the high plateau in the north, to where it dropped into the Grand Canyon. From the great chasm's edge, he hired a mule, which was loaded with his gear, and hiked with a translator down the narrow trail, dropping more than three thousand vertical feet over nine miles, stepping gently over crushed pebbles and knuckle-sized stones through tiers of time wearing the colors of different ages, at last reaching the village of Supai, home of the People of the Blue-Green Water. "The strangest dwelling place of any tribe in America," Curtis called it. They had lived in the most remote area of the United States for about seven hundred years, the natives told Curtis, and been relatively undisturbed. Yes, they had trouble with the Navajo—who didn't? When Kit Carson burned the Navajo peach orchards to the ground and marched those Diné, as the tribe called itself, off to exile in New Mexico, the Havasupai were left untouched. They were too small a tribe to bother with, hidden in a deep pocket of the Colorado Plateau. Over the years, few whites had visited: a Spanish missionary, Father Garces, dropped into the canyon in 1776, and an American explorer, Frank Cushing, came along more than a hundred years later. They found well-watered little gardens of squash, beans and corn, and a tribe that wanted to be left alone. By the start of the twentieth century, the Havasupai were penciled into a tiny reservation just off the floor of the Grand Canyon, less than a single square mile. The Indians were tired of being told how to live and what to do by government agents—a familiar complaint in the Southwest. But they were powerless to do anything because of their peculiar limbo status: neither citizens nor foreign nationals. "We are no longer men," a Havasupai leader told Curtis. "We are like little children. We must always ask Washington."

What Curtis saw of the Havasupai was not a healthy people. Measles had started to ravage the tribe, killing the young, especially. They feared going hungry after their hunting range had been severely restricted. Curtis counted 250 tribal members. He recorded their language, wrote down their songs on staff paper, took pictures of families living in an extraordinary setting. The way the Blue-Green Water People had fashioned homes into the cliffs of the slot canyon in particular drew his photographic eye.

During the same trip to Arizona, Curtis went to see the Hopi and the Navajo. He tried again to get permission to participate in the Snake Dance. And again the head of the Snake Society, Sikyaletstiwa, turned him down. But the priest was friendly enough with Curtis that he let him take his picture. By this time, Curtis was referred to by one of his many nicknames, The Man Who Sleeps on His Breath, because of the air mattress he inflated at camp.

After a year's absence, Curtis noticed that natives of the Southwest had changed. Government agents had banned even more ceremonies. As in Montana, children were hauled off to boarding schools run by the missions, where their spiritual lives were handed over to another God. The boys were supposed to learn how to farm and read, the girls how to be homemakers and serve tea. Those who resisted were threatened with a loss of provisions and derided as "blanket Indians." The Hopi were torn between incentives for giving up the traditional ways and the uncertainty of staying the course. The tribe broke down into factions, and in those villages that had given over entirely to missionaries, it was forbidden to speak the native language. Would the Snake Dance, which was as important to the Hopi as Easter Sunday mass is to Roman Catholics, soon be outlawed? Feeling the sand slipping through the hourglass of his project, Curtis picked up the pace.

He hurried off to Walpi, one of his favorite places in the Hopi Nation. This village was perched atop bare stone on a high mesa, with views of open country below that stretched to the horizon. The sandpaper-colored walls of the houses looked as if they sprouted from the tabletop of rock. Walpi could have been a Tuscan hill town lost to time but for the absence of a church on the village skyline. The location and building style of Walpi gave it two strategic advantages for protection from enemies: it was camouflaged, appearing from a distance to be just another stone mesa, and it was an impossibly steep ascent, making it difficult to attack. In Walpi, Curtis found a Hopi man with feminine good looks, wearing hoop earrings, hair cut just at the shoulders, deep-set black eyes. Curtis had him sit with a simple army blanket around his shoulders; the austerity of the cloth brought out the attractive features of the face. The resulting picture, titled *A Walpi Man*, was developed as a platinum print, a rare and costly process with superb resolution.

As satisfied as he was with this and other Southwest portraits, Curtis slipped into periods of insecurity, at times panic, pressed by the urgency of time and the drain on his bank account. Perhaps he *had* taken on too much. He was shooting contemporary photographs, but the pictures looked like historical documents even before he developed them; the present seemed to morph into the past inside his lens. Next year, he wondered, how difficult would it be to find a young Hopi who could speak the language? "There won't be anything left of them in a few generations and it's a tragedy," he wrote Bird Grinnell. "A national tragedy."

Curtis picked up his gear and raced east, to the White Mountains of Arizona, where he hired an interpreter and went in search of Apache life. These Athapaskan-speaking people were epic wanderers over a broad swath of the arid West. Their name bespoke their reputation: Apache meant "fighting men," but was also translated as "enemy." After the Comanche had pushed them out of the high plains of Texas in the early 1700s, the Apache's mobile societies were sustained by thievery, trading, raiding and hunting. They never farmed. They preyed on sedentary Indians, feckless whites and unwary Mexicans in an area almost as large as Great Britain, from the Sonoran Desert to northern New Mexico. The White Mountain Apache were now confined to a reservation in the juniper- and pine-forested land of a sparsely settled American territory, far removed from any sizable Anglo town. It took days for Curtis, traveling first by horse-drawn carriage and then on his own mount, to find the Indian communities. When he met a stagecoach exiting the reservation, he was encouraged to find a dispirited missionary on his way out — the preacher's despair was a promising sign. He also ran into a government farm instructor, who complained that "teaching the dirty Indians" to till the ground was a hopeless task. Once among the Apache, Curtis found that Indian lips were sealed. Those well-meaning men of the cloth and the plow had certainly done him no favors—poisoning the well, as it were. Curtis devised a strategy: he would feign indifference.

"I asked no questions and indicated no special interest in more than casual externals," said Curtis. Every day in the field he watched—from first light until late at night. "They were up at dawn, and bathed in pools and streams that their bodies might be acceptable to the gods," he wrote. "Each man, in isolation, greeted the rising sun in fervent prayers." After several weeks, he was allowed to follow Apache women as they harvested mescal, roasted it in a pit and mixed it with other juices for a drink. Still, he was only scratching the surface—an embedded tourist. He wanted detail, detail and more detail. He heard whispered talk about a painted animal skin, a chart of some kind that was the key to understanding Apache spiritual practices. Curtis offered a medicine man $100—a fortune, more than anyone on the reservation could earn in a year—if he would show him the skin and explain what the symbols meant. His bribe was rejected.

"If I showed it to you," the Apache priest told Curtis, "I would be killed by the other medicine men."

"If I would give you $500, what would you say?"

"I would still say no. For if I was dead, the money would do me no good."

Tribal distrust of Curtis was widespread. Apache threw dirt at his camera, charged him on horseback, misled him, threatened him, cursed him, ignored him and laughed at him. They complained to government agents about this intruder in their midst, trying to record the sacred ways. When he left the Apache homeland in August, the rituals were unknown to Curtis, the Great Mystery just that, his money useless, his project among these people a bust. The larger narratives of how the Apache came to be were protected by the medicine men. Yes, he had written down names and terms that he'd heard repeated in ceremonies, but had no clue to their context. The few pictures from that 1903 trip to the White Mountains were taken by a photographer who was never permitted inside. One shot in particular, *Story Telling—Apache*, shows a half-dozen men at a hillside resting spot, two of them still on horseback. The picture is notable for the detail of the land—hard ground and scrawny trees, thin grass and stone trails—but reveals nothing of the people or their inner lives. He would return.

At home, money was tight. Curtis was bleeding funds, trying to finance an undertaking of vast anthropological and photographic scope with earnings from his portrait business. He had a family of five to support and a staff of a half dozen at the studio. He joined the Rainier Club, the most prestigious in Seattle, in part because it gave him a place to sleep on nights when Clara was mad at him, and in part because of the access it gave him to gentlemen who would pay a premium for Curtis to take their picture. The other way to expand his business was to sell more Curtis Indian prints, at higher prices. He started a line of Indian postcards for the mass market. When he held the first major exhibition in Seattle of his native subjects, in late summer of 1903, people flocked to buy framed photogravures, just as he'd hoped. On display, and for sale, were images from seven years of work among the Indians of Puget Sound, the Great Plains and the Southwest.

Another influential man in town, the newspaper publisher Alden J. Blethen, was backing Curtis with barrels of printer's ink. A native of Maine, Blethen had come to the Northwest on a visit, liked what he saw and purchased a small-circulation newspaper, the *Seattle Times,* in 1896. Both men had found their life work in the same year. Using splashy graphics, color, big headline type, broad photographic display and partisan Democratic Party editorials in a city dominated by the progressive strain of Roosevelt Republicanism, Blethen made the paper into a major voice of the Northwest. Curtis gave him perfect pictures, which set his paper apart in a highly competitive market. Full-page Curtis Sunday features, with the Indian photos taking up the majority of space in artful layouts, were a hallmark. In the paper, the Seattle photographer was written up as a dauntless adventurer, going where no white man had gone, living on his wits and his guile, charming exotic natives, proving all the experts wrong. Curtis was physically strong, movie-star handsome and, at a time when the first nickelodeons were being cranked on city corners, artistically brilliant. "He lived Indian," the *Times* said in one piece, though in fact Curtis did no such thing. "He was heap white brother." Curtis exuded an otherness, a dash of the bohemian "He's an artist," the paper said, but "he doesn't impress one as being part of the Latin Quarter, really. There isn't any long hair about him, nor the stale smell of beer . . . his light yellow beard is a bit of the Du Maurier order."

Curtis promised he would include the family in future travels in the field; they would all go together, the clan in Indian country. "Joy of joys," Hal, the oldest son, recalled upon hearing the news. "What a summer that promised." He was eleven at the time. As it was, the family saw very little of Curtis from then on. In a letter to the Smithsonian in which he tried to impress its officials with the size of his ambition, Curtis said he planned to be back in Indian country in January of the new year, and then spend almost all of his time until the fall on work among the tribes. When his family did see Curtis, his mind was elsewhere. He seldom socialized, despite a surfeit of invitations to the best parties. He was still not on speaking terms with his younger brother Asahel, a photographer with his own growing reputation. And the feud drew in their mother; she moved out of Edward's house and into Asahel's.

It hardly seemed to matter; the Indian project had taken over Curtis. He talked of nothing else. "One of us would ask what he was doing or thinking about, or where he had been when he was away from home all day taking pictures of Indians," recalled his sister Eva. "Most often, he didn't seem to hear the question, so preoccupied he was." The majority of his time at the studio, working well after everyone else had left, was spent not on businessmen from the Rainier Club or on the bright young things in silk dresses, but on bringing more detail and light to half-naked figures from the desert. How could a middle-aged banker with a bulbous nose compare to a Walpi native in his prime?

Clara found something in the *Ladies' Home Journal:* a contest to discover the Prettiest Children in America. The artist Walter Russell would select from thousands of entries a handful of pictures, which he would then paint in oil portraiture. The contest was a perfect opportunity to expand the Curtis name to the broadest possible audience— something more in keeping with the paying work of the premier portrait photographer in the West. From the studio archives, a picture of a Seattle girl named Marie Fischer was selected as the Curtis entry in the contest.

During the summer following the death of Chief Joseph, Meany asked Curtis to go with him to the grave of the Nez Perce leader for a reburial. It troubled Meany that the chief had not been given a proper memorial. Working with the state historical society, the professor arranged for a white marble shaft to be shipped east, to the Okanogan Hills on the Colville reservation. Joseph, of course, had wanted to be buried in the Wallowa Valley, but was denied in death what he'd been denied in life. Meany, Curtis, Joseph's widow, about forty members of the Nez Perce community and a crowd of cowboys and their wives in Sunday clothes gathered on June 21, 1905 — the longest day of the year, and one of the hottest in the arid midsection of Washington State. A large American flag was strung to four skinny pine poles and stretched about fifteen feet above ground, over the grave, providing shade for the gravediggers. The ritual would involve uprooting the chief's remains and placing them in a new spot. The digging of the tough lava till was difficult, and done with little fanfare. It struck Curtis how awful the soil was in the sun-blanched reservation and how it was impossible to expect anyone to farm this ground. The cemetery was on a slope above the village of Nespelem, treeless, the grass brown and matted, with a view toward the scablands. This Indian dumping ground was not far from the big gash in the earth that would, within a few decades, hold the fresh-leashed flow of the Columbia River in the largest dam yet built — the Grand Coulee.

Curtis was surprised that no prayers or songs were offered at this occasion.

"Last year we buried him," explained a Nez Perce in a war bonnet that fell all the way to his ankles. "This time, just move him."

Suddenly the Indians stopped working and dropped their shovels. They retreated to the shade under the sagging American flag and sat, saying nothing. The temperature climbed. Meany asked about the delay: they couldn't just squat in the heat of the midday sun of central

Washington, a desert that sometimes got less rain than Arizona, with two half-completed holes in the ground. The Indians shrugged but kept silent. Again Curtis wondered about the lack of a formal ceremony. The natives shook their heads. For Joseph, they said, there would be "no Boston Man's talk."

After a long pause, one native pointed back at the grave and gestured at the professor and the photographer.

"Let the white men do the digging," he said. "They know how."

Curtis rolled up his sleeves and went to work. He chipped away at the gravel and dun-colored dirt, putting up piles all around the grave. "It was no small task," Curtis wrote. "I dug, pried, tugged . . ." With Meany's help he lifted the simple coffin from the ground and dragged it to the new hole. It was not yet deep enough, so Curtis went back at it, shoveling into the afternoon. At last, Chief Joseph of the Nez Perce was slid into a divot in the earth, and Curtis buried him under several feet of Columbia Plateau soil. The white marble shaft, seven feet high, was planted atop the grave and cemented to rock. On one side was a carved image of the chief. On the other was his real name: *Hin-mah-too-yah-la-kekt.*

The next day, Joseph's widow held a potlatch, giving away her late husband's possessions. Over two days, she handed out blankets and baskets, carvings and bedding, beadwork and utensils, fishing gear and hunting rifles—all his earthly goods. She cried loudly when she came upon an item that was dear to their marriage or prompted a particular memory. But nothing must be kept back—all was gifted. At the end of the potlatch, the Indians tore down Joseph's tipi, so that nothing remained to remind the living of the dead man. Curtis left the reservation feeling drained, but also relieved.

"No more will he beg of the Great White Father and say: 'All I ask is to go back to the old home in the Wallowa Valley; my father's home, and the home of my father's father,'" he wrote in an account for *Scribner's.* "His troubled life has run its course."

In the two years that had passed since Joseph visited Seattle on a rain-swept autumn weekend, no one could remember what he said in a speech intended to sway prominent leaders. And the football game, all those white men "almost fighting," which had been given so much significance, was forgotten as well. What lasted for another century, growing in stature with every decade, was the picture Curtis took of the chief of the Nez Perce during the final November of his life—"his most famous portrait," the art scholar and collector Christopher Cardozo later called it. Curtis made Chief Joseph live forever, and Joseph did the same thing for Curtis. But at the time, Curtis did not think his project could last into another year without help from the most powerful man in the United States.

Chief Joseph of the Nez Perce, 1903. Curtis took this
picture in his Seattle studio in the last year of Joseph's life.
Joseph died, his doctor said, of a broken heart.

5

WITH THE PRESIDENT
1904

THE VIEW FROM the study of the Roosevelt home at Sagamore Hill looked out on a sheltered slice of Long Island Sound, and it was quieter there on the second floor, though stuffy when the wind was down and the air heavy with summer heat. Edward Curtis and Teddy Roosevelt were talking about the West, a favorite subject of this polymath president. It was not easy to carry on a prolonged conversation without some interruption from the younger residents. This was as the family wanted it—the house had few boundaries for age or class. Children were to be seen *and* to be heard. Adults were to play, when they weren't giving the president some insight into a pressing global issue. Pets had free range of most rooms, and for a visitor a door could open to the surprise of something four-legged or feathered. At the dinner table each child was required to ask at least one question of a guest. In Curtis, the westerner who had spent the past seven years in places that Roosevelt considered as iconic to the young nation as cathedrals were to old Europe, the children had a source of stories about faraway people who could not seem more exotic to students of a New England private school. What were the Apache like? Why does a Sioux warrior eat the heart of a grizzly bear? How does a Hopi priest handle all those rattlesnakes? Are most Indians polygamous? What were Chief Joseph's last words?

Curtis had many questions of his own. He had learned why a Piegan man would spend three days fasting before praying to the sun, but he knew very little about which fork a gentleman was supposed to use for salad at a formal dinner. The East Coast took some getting used to. Not just the humidity, which made a resident of the Pacific Northwest sweat through a shirt before breakfast, but the customs and cultures. He would have to find his way without a translator — more difficult, in some respects, than trying to crack the puzzle of the Apaches' eternal secrets. How did one dress for lunch? Was it proper to swim with a woman, alone? Could he feign interest in the Harvard debating club? He was lucky to have the Roosevelt family of eight — Edith, Teddy and their six children — as his guides to the affairs of Long Island. For the only rule of the summer White House that Roosevelt cared for was that guests not be slothful or boring. The youngest president in the nation's history and the thirty-six-year-old photographer had much in common. Curtis was one of the few guests who knew, firsthand, all about those wondrous scraps of original America beyond the 100th meridian that Roosevelt was so passionate about, places he felt were in peril at this moment in the country's aggressive adolescence. They took to each other in no time.

"I had found a listener who not only gave his undivided attention to my expression of thoughts and desire," said Curtis, "but he concurred as well in my beliefs." Curtis lit up as Roosevelt told of his ranching days in the Dakotas, a refuge for a grief-stricken young man who had lost his wife and mother on the same day. He beamed when Roosevelt talked about riding an Appaloosa at dusk in Montana, or his more recent journey to the Grand Canyon. Roosevelt guided him through the rooms of the three-story, seven-bedroom Queen Anne–style house just outside Oyster Bay. The library was decorated with bearskin rugs on the floor and trophy antelope on the walls. "I soon learned of his special gift," Curtis said. Roosevelt "could read a page of a book at a glance, not a line at a time like most of us mortals."

The dining room was informal for such a big house, seating twelve at best; heads of bighorn sheep and Rocky Mountain elk stared glassy-eyed under a beamed ceiling. The table, Roosevelt explained, had come from Florence, bought while Edith and Teddy were honeymooning in Italy. Had Curtis ever been abroad? No, sir. Curtis discussed Indians, and on this subject he could always hold a room. But did he know that the Roosevelt compound was on land named for Sagamore Mohannis, the Indian chief who had used it as a meeting ground in the 1660s? That would not surprise Curtis: every corner of the country had a native name that predated the new one. Two of the nation's biggest cities — Chicago, from an Algonquin word for "garlic field," and Manhattan, from another Algonquin term, "isolated thing in the water" — had Indian origins.

The year had been especially busy for the twenty-sixth president, who took office after an assassin killed William McKinley in 1901. At home, Roosevelt fought the major trusts, making enemies of the richest men in the country. And when the Supreme Court ruled in 1904 that the president had the constitutional right to break up concentrations of great wealth that restricted competition, Roosevelt anticipated that J. P. Morgan and E. H. Harriman (the Alaska expedition sponsor) would use their power to deprive him of a second term. Abroad, Russia and Japan were in violent conflict over disputed territory; Roosevelt the warrior had been called upon to act as a peace broker. He was also guiding a treaty through Congress that would give the United States control of the Panama Canal Zone, a right-of-way to dig a fifty-mile-long ditch through a malarial isthmus. He had introduced a term into everyday public life — conservation — and was trying to get fellow Americans to see that the continent they now straddled was a fragile one, losing much of its physical character in the clamorous tumble into the new century. Though he was considered the most popular man in the country, Roosevelt had yet to face the voters. He was up for a full four-year term in mere months. But just now he had other concerns. Could Mr. Curtis do the family a favor? *Yes, Mr. President — anything.* Curtis had made a blue-cheese salad dressing earlier, and Mrs. Roosevelt loved it. She was, Teddy said in a characteristic word, *deeelighted!* Could he share the secret of the recipe? For lunch.

· · ·

Earlier that year, *Ladies' Home Journal* had named the winners of its Prettiest Children in America contest; the picture that Clara Curtis had submitted of a Seattle girl was one of the chosen few, selected from eighteen thousand entries. And just as the rescue of two distinguished easterners on Mount Rainier had opened a much bigger world to Curtis, this contest proved again that he had a knack for fortuitous serendipity. Walter Russell, who was to paint the prettiest children, had been fascinated by the Curtis portrait of the little girl; he had passed on the name of the Seattle photographer to the president. And so in June of that year, as Curtis was packing for another long season in Indian country, came an invitation to visit Oyster Bay, to photograph the Roosevelt children.

He traveled the length of the country, four full days by train, and then took a short boat ride from New York City to Long Island. In barely a decade's time, Curtis had gone from a homesteader's shack on Puget Sound to the summer White House on Long Island Sound. He and Roosevelt had friends in common: Gifford Pinchot, for one, whom the photographer had met on the Harriman expedition and kept in touch with. A patrician bachelor with a self-righteous streak, Pinchot was a top domestic adviser to the president and the nation's chief forester. Bird Grinnell was a longtime hunting buddy of the president's. The naturalist John Burroughs—one of the Two Johnnies on the Alaska trip—was so close to Teddy that the president would dedicate his next book to him. Good men all around, they agreed.

Curtis was instructed that his only duty, at first, was to get to know the children: to play with them, to make fires with them, to race with them, to dig clams with them, to tell them stories of the West. They were a kinetic bunch, riding horses around the grounds, whooping and hollering up the stairs, playing hide-and-seek around the orchard, the barn, the icehouse, the windmill, the pet cemetery. They buried each other—and the dog—in beach sand up to their chins, and the kids rode camelback-style on Curtis's shoulders. The biggest child, Teddy Roosevelt himself, was a believer in vigorous exercise. "I wish to preach, not the doctrine of ignoble ease," he said, but "the doctrine of the strenuous life." But that didn't mean he couldn't make it a game. At Sagamore Hill, the Roosevelt Obstacle Walk was led by the president, followed by Curtis and the children. It left everyone breathless on the veranda at sunset.

"I found them the most energetic, vital family," said Curtis. "They made me feel at home, in fact like one of the family." During the day, he foraged along the shore with Quentin, who was six years old, or rode ponies with Archibald, who was ten. The teenagers, Theodore Junior and Kermit, spent much of the time with cousins and people their age. And now and then twenty-year-old Alice would drop by. "Princess Alice," her family nickname, was a heartthrob for men of many ages, a high-spirited beauty. "I can be president of the United States, or I can control Alice," said Roosevelt. "I cannot possibly do both."

As thrilled as Curtis was to be allowed into the inner circle of the first family, and to be chosen to take pictures of the president's children, he had something else he wished to accomplish. In 1903, the studio had hired Adolph Muhr, a midwesterner well known for his own Indian pictures and a brilliant technician. It was a coup for Edward and Clara to bring Muhr into the fold, for he was the talent behind many of the Indian photographs of Frank Rinehart, an artist and photographer of some renown. Once in Seattle, Muhr would never leave the Curtis dynamo. His influence on Curtis was immediate and lasting. It was his finishing hand that made so many of the Curtis portraits of the past year memorable. Muhr was the first step in hiring a crew that could construct the Curtis blueprint. Young Bill Phillips, Clara's cousin, was already on the payroll, a full-time assistant. Soon, Curtis planned to add a field researcher, someone trained in ethnology, and a writer, someone who had practiced deadline journalism. He also needed an editor for the finished product, though he was still not sure exactly what form that would take —a book, several books, a permanent exhibition. He needed translators, dozens of them, in every part of the West. All of this would cost money that Curtis did not have. No matter how well his portrait business hummed along and how many individual Indian pictures he sold, the revenue could not begin to support the ever-growing undertaking. The Big Idea might sink him.

Looking for a benefactor, he had gone east for the first time in 1903, for an audience with experts at the Smithsonian Institution's Bureau of American Ethnology. In recent years, they had launched several research projects into Indian country and were gathering all manner of cultural artifacts for permanent storage in the capital. But in 1903 the Smithsonian came under fire in Congress for spending federal dollars on patronage hacks and glorified junkets. When Curtis arrived for a meeting that included William Henry Holmes, chief of the Bureau of Ethnology, they were in retreat. Curtis had been courting the Smithsonian for months with letters hinting at his grand scheme. And just what made a dropout from a one-room schoolhouse think he could get the nation's top ethnologists to back his project? *Balls.* Those who didn't try for the highest peak were doomed to the foothills. In that sense, Curtis had something else in common with Roosevelt, whose most famous words were an encouragement to take risks: "to dare mighty things, to win glorious triumphs, even though checkered by failure, than to rank with those poor spirits who neither enjoy much nor suffer much, because they live in that grey twilight that knows neither victory nor defeat."

Inside the red sandstone walls of the Smithsonian Castle, Curtis gave an exhaustive presentation to some of the nation's leading authorities on American Indians. His way inside had been greased by favorable words from Grinnell and Merriam. Curtis planned to document eighty tribes, he explained: all the people in North America still living somewhat of a "primitive existence." Eighty tribes? The figure made jaws drop; it amounted to one of the largest anthropological projects ever undertaken in the United States. He would make audio recordings of songs and languages so the words would never be lost, even if the tribes disappeared. He would write down their music so people could play it later. And finally, he planned to use a heavy, stand-up device that a few photographers were just starting to tinker with: a moving-picture camera. Moving pictures? *The Great Train Robbery,* the first narrative film, had recently been released. So lifelike. Curtis explained that he would use this camera to film the Yeibichai Dance of the Navajo. This last task struck the learned men at the Smithsonian as preposterous. Well-trained doctors of science had been trying for years to get close enough to the

Navajo to obtain pictures and interpretations of the Yeibichai Dance. It was impossible. In closing, Curtis insisted that for all the other work he intended to do, in the main his great undertaking would be a picture record—using only the finest and costliest finishing process—of the daily lives of the first Americans. And, of course, it was art as well, a subjective look, by the very nature of how and where he pointed the camera.

Though Curtis had impressed Frederick Webb Hodge, the top official of Indian affairs at the Bureau of Ethnology and the editor of *American Anthropologist,* the other authorities at the Smithsonian were unmoved. They rejected him outright. He would get nothing from the nation's foremost storehouse of its history and artifacts. They doubted that Curtis could ever pull off such an immense project, and they were wholly unimpressed with his credentials. For God's sake, he's *uneducated!* Curtis was clearly indignant at the setback, and it hurt.

More humiliation was to come. During the same trip, he went to New York in search of a book backer. Surely he would have no problem finding a major publisher. In Manhattan, Curtis outlined his plan to Walter Page at Doubleday. The editor gave Curtis a respectful listen. But Page was troubled, he told the upstart from Seattle, by how many Indian products were already on the market—books, portfolios, cards.

"Couldn't give 'em away," said Page.

That is, unless Curtis wanted to do something along the lines of Karl May's depictions of that hardy perennial, the Noble Savage. May was a German author who sold millions of books about Indians well before he ever saw one, or set foot in America. *No, no, no*—Curtis wanted realism, albeit with a humane touch, and he insisted that his published works be produced in a costly finishing and printing process. If that was the case, Page informed him, this collection would have to sell for a much higher price than normal picture books. How much higher? A typical hardback might cost $1.50. The multivolume Curtis books would have to fetch several hundred dollars, maybe $1,000 or more, just to break even. A thousand dollars: that's what the average American earned in a year. Only the very rich, and the largest cultural institutions and universities, could afford them. And even that high-end market might not be enough to support the publication. But see here, Curtis countered, his Indian pictures were unique—*look at them!* These portraits were not dime-store savages or cartoon maidens or Karl May fantasies. He intended to make publishing history. Sorry, Page said, there's just no audience for fine Indian pictures. With the rejections, Curtis could not build his team beyond Phillips and Muhr. Until he could find a deep funding source, all other hiring was on hold.

At Sagamore Hill, Curtis was unsure how the president would feel about his fascination with Indians. In his early writing, Roosevelt had been none too sympathetic. He called them "filthy" and "lecherous" and "faithless" in his volume of western history published in 1896. What he had seen of Indians during his ranching days, tribes decimated by disease and war, "were but a few degrees less meaningless, squalid and ferocious than that of the wild beasts with whom they held joint ownership." A decade earlier, he had been even more cruelly glib. "I don't go so far as to think that the only good Indians are dead Indians, but I believe nine out of every ten are, and I shouldn't inquire too closely into the case of the tenth." In almost every respect—personal hygiene, sexual relations, the worship of multiple spirits, the tribal approach to battle, preferring to ambush and raid instead of lining up in formation for a formal fight—the Indian way was appalling to the settled customs and manners that had produced the Roosevelts of New York City. But later, as a warrior colonel, with Indians among his Rough Riders who charged up San Juan Hill in 1898, Roosevelt for the first time saw natives who were heroic. He was moved by how fearless they were, riding into a blizzard of enemy fire on behalf of the American flag. As president, his views continued to evolve. Like everything else on American soil, Indians were in his care now, a tenuous trust relationship.

Still, Roosevelt was not a likely ally for Curtis. The photographer faced a tough dilemma: could a man whose dream was to humanize Indians persuade a man who was so dismissive of them to back his work? The question roiled Curtis while spending long days and intellectually stimulating evenings with the Roosevelts and their circle. Should he dare to ask the president to intervene? Was there something he could do to get the Smithsonian experts to change their minds? Or could he set Curtis up with one of his friends, a patron with deep pockets?

But first he had to humanize the first family. He shot pictures of the boys in a variety of settings: outside, in the library, at play, in serious thought. Quentin, the youngest son, looks pleading in his close-up, no easy smile, his eyes holding his emotion. After finishing with the children, Curtis persuaded the president to pose for him—a formal portrait. In it, Roosevelt is seen from the chest up, in dark suit, knotted tie, gray-speckled mustache, his pince-nez in front of his eyes as usual. But two things stand out: the light, showing one half of Roosevelt's face as if it were a waning moon, and the jawbone, which is stern but not forced or clenched in fighter mode. Those ferocious teeth, a favorite of cartoonists, are hidden behind a closed mouth. The president looks bookish, studious, pensive. Curtis loved the effect, and believed he had captured a Roosevelt seldom seen. When he developed the picture, he used a process reserved for less than one percent of his pictures: orotone. "The ordinary photographic print lacks depth and transparency," said Curtis in one of his brochures explaining the technique. But with orotone, even dull stones "are as full of life and sparkle as an opal." The image is printed directly onto glass and then backed with gold spray: a difficult and very expensive way to finish a photograph in 1904.

"My picture of the President is great," Curtis wrote Gifford Pinchot. "It is quite different from anything before taken and, I believe, will be considered by all who know him, a splendid likeness. I made no effort to re-touch up the face and make him a smooth-visaged individual without a line or anything to show character." Well! Pinchot could have popped a vest button at the brazen, breathless self-regard coming from the man the Indians called the Shadow Catcher, a name he had been given in Arizona. But it wasn't just self-praise. The social reformer and journalist Jacob Riis, a Roosevelt intimate, was equally impressed after he saw the print. "It is more than a picture," he said. "It is the man himself."

At the end of his stay with the family, Curtis opened his Indian portfolio to the president. He showed him the handsome Hopi men from Walpi, the giggly-faced Hopi women with their hair in those tight flower whorls, the Blackfeet praying in the high-plains heat. In the past few years, Roosevelt himself had traveled throughout the Southwest, seeing much of it for the first time. The Hopi and Navajo dwellings in the Curtis pictures—strong, well-built homes holding to cliffs—were anything but the dingy, transient tents and lean-tos of Roosevelt's earlier view. As part of his expanding knowledge of the country he governed, Roosevelt was starting to see the legacy of indigenous human life in the same way he saw the natural world—something that would be lost if present trends continued.

The *living* Indian communities were another story. Roosevelt was influenced by those who believed that tribal ties should be loosened, and natives eventually given full U.S. citizenship—assimilated, like recent European immigrants. The portrait of Chief Joseph, who had also posed with his mouth closed, eyes intense, caught the president's attention. After hearing Curtis out, Roosevelt said the project was a *bully* idea, and a noble one, important to America's lasting sense of self. Without being specific, he made a promise to Curtis in written form:

"No man could be doing anything more important," he wrote. "I will support you in any way I can."

In July of 1904, Curtis spent a frenzied few days with the joys of his home life: ten-year-old Hal, eight-year-old Beth and six-year-old Florence. The children hardly knew their father during the first years of the Indian project, Florence said later, but when he was around, the house was full of radiant sunlight. Stories, games, questions, tricks all flowed from the towering and peripatetic man. He renewed his vow to take the family—why not all of them?—on a long trip to Indian country. Soon. Appointments, requests and unanswered letters were stacked all over the house. They would have to wait.

He checked in with Muhr, running the technical side of the studio, fine-finishing the negatives Curtis brought home from the tribes. Muhr had never worked harder. "His example is so contagious," Muhr said of his boss, "that everyone connected with him seems fired by the same enthusiasm and imbued with the same energy and ambition." That contagion had spread to Ella McBride, the mountaineer Curtis had met on Rainier a few years earlier. Curtis had talked her into leaving her teaching job in Portland and moving to Seattle, where she became indispensable behind the camera at the studio. She also lived in the Curtis home, and was like a second mother, the girls said later.

Out the door Curtis went again. For the rest of the summer and into the fall Curtis worked at breakneck speed, bouncing all over the Southwest with a small entourage, usually including a few translators, and Phillips. In New Mexico Territory, west of Albuquerque, he arrived at what was the oldest continuously inhabited city in the United States, nine hundred years. Descendants of the Anasazi, the people had built a community on a mesa seven thousand feet above sea level and named their fortress Acoma, a word that means "the place that always was." Curtis found Acoma in the high-desert air just as he had found Supai in a basement next to the Colorado River—a cluster of people living in a remarkable redoubt, forgotten by the rest of the world. After dealing with Europeans of one sort or another for three hundred years, Acomans were cautiously accommodating.

Curtis was taken to the top, where women drew their water from a deep well and balanced the painted earthen jars on their heads. He climbed ladders to houses of sun-blasted rock. He was shown the cliffs where the natives had rolled giant boulders down on enemies—white, red and brown. They worshiped Jesus and the sun at Acoma, in equal measure, "a positive argument that a people can be loyal followers of two religious creeds at one and the same time," Curtis wrote in *Scribner's*, which published several large spreads of Curtis's photojournalism. Their prize possession was a silver-crowned cane given them by Abraham Lincoln as a reward for loyalty to the Union. Curtis heard of the three-day battle with Don Juan de Oñate's conquistadors in 1598, the worst blow in the history of Acoma. The Spanish burned homes, raided food supplies, threw men from the cliff and marched the surviving stragglers off to a makeshift prison in the valley. There, Oñate pronounced them guilty of violating the Act of Obedience and Homage, though most had never taken the oath Spain had forced on the natives. For punishment, every man over the age of twenty-five was to have one foot cut off; those younger were sentenced to slavery. Nearly two centuries passed before the Sky City of Acoma regained its preinvasion population. But people never entirely deserted the rock. They had been written off, like Indians in general; in obscurity, they eventually thrived.

Over several days, Curtis hiked up and down the winding, narrow passage to the summit village, a footpath of rock polished by wear over ten centuries. He shot *At the Old Well of Acoma*, one of his most Edenic still lifes, showing two veiled young women gathering water with their intricately painted vases. Calm pools of water always brought out the painterly side of Curtis. Near the base of the mesa looking up, he did a different kind of day-in-the-life, called *The Old Roadway of Acoma*. Like Georgia O'Keeffe, another artist who found renewal in New Mexico, Curtis loved the light in the Land of Enchantment.

Back in Arizona, Curtis went to see his friends in the Hopi Nation, and predictably, the high priest Sikyaletstiwa again rejected his request for entry in the Snake Society. For The Man Who Sleeps on His Breath, this was the third visit to the Hopi. He could watch. He could shoot pictures. And, in a step closer, this time he was invited to climb down into a kiva where priests tamed rattlesnakes in advance of the ceremony. But he could not join the men who performed the ritual.

The Hopi were amused by the latest device to emerge from the worn wagon Curtis had hauled to the high desert: a moving-picture machine. He set up the camera on the roof of a house and captured the choreography of the last days of the Snake Dance. It had been twenty-five years since young Ed Curtis canoed the waterways of Minnesota with his father, the colicky preacher spouting evangelical Christianity, a faith that never caught on with the boy. In the Hopi church of the outdoors, though, Curtis felt something stir in his soul. "Hopi have become a spiritual crossroads in my work, a still place in the middle of the continent," he said. "These events are beyond words."

His best work that year was with the Navajo, as he roamed over their 14,000-square-mile reservation under the sandstone spires of northeast Arizona. Like many who spent time with the Diné, Curtis was impressed by their silver and turquoise jewelry, their weaving and their colorful sand paintings. "As the chief human touch of the great southwestern desert, the Navajo are the artist's joy," Curtis wrote. He learned, by watching and through translators, that most Navajo families lived in three homes: a summer residence with a big garden; a stone house in a cliff above a wash, where freshets of water were captured for irrigation; and a hogan, usually built of clay, rock, mud and reeds, rounded at the edges. Polygamy was common, but women had superior property rights, owning sheep and the houses. A man who deserted his family would be destitute—a powerful incentive to stay married.

Threats to these domestic patterns came from federal agents, who were trying to dismantle Diné culture in the name of promoting civilization, and from Catholic missionaries, who were up to the same thing, though using a spiritual carrot instead of a government stick. Defying the doubts of the Smithsonian authorities, Curtis learned enough about the Yeibichai Dance to write up an explanation in his notebook, detailing what happened on each of the ritual's nine days. If only, Curtis mused at one point, the average visitor could experience the sensation he felt after the sun went down in the Navajo Nation: "There he is in touch with the stillness of the night under the starry sky and sees before him, in this little spot lighted out of the limitless desert, this strange ceremony of supplication and thanksgiving."

The highlight was Canyon de Chelly. Like Acoma, this stone-walled cavity had known human habitation for at least ten centuries. Though the valley floor was nearly six thousand feet above sea level, the weather was moderate enough year-round to make the canyon the garden spot of Navajo land, where rock, sun, wind, water and the ages had produced one of the world's singular places. A haunt of history hung over the cinnamon-colored gash in the earth—those Anasazi, who had left so mysteriously in the mid-1300s, their well-kept stone houses intact, and those charred stumps of the once magnificent peach orchards that Kit Carson had burned to the ground when he starved the Navajo into submission in 1864. Just as he had seen the hunched figure of old Princess Angeline as an emblematic native of the land, Curtis saw the Navajo in sync with Canyon de Chelly. On horseback, they were dwarfed by cliffs rising a thousand feet above them and by a limitless empty sky. Being there, he understood why no one had bothered the Navajo for so long. The canyon was impossible to see from afar; it revealed itself only when you were actually upon it.

Curtis titled one picture *Sunset in Navajo Land*, another *Cañon de Chelly*. But a single long-view photogravure defined the entire Curtis enterprise: *Vanishing Race*. Seven Indians, perhaps of the same family, are on horseback, trailed by a dog, moving across the canyon floor, no faces visible, a bare human and animal presence against the monolithic rising walls. They appear tentative, on their way out, while the rock is forever and immutable. The title served his theme, but was dishonest to the Diné. No tribe in America, save perhaps the Sioux, had more people at the time, and no tribe had a bigger land base for a reservation. Their isolation had been their salvation; for centuries, no one else coveted the prickly ground they inhabited. And yet Curtis feared for their future as much as he worried about the dwindling cadre of Havasupai living near the Grand Canyon.

He shot more than six hundred photographs on that excursion. "My late trip to the southwest has been a successful one," Curtis wrote his friend Professor Meany, the only man in Seattle who could appreciate the enormity of Curtis's task. "In no former trip have I accomplished so much in so short a time." He dashed off a letter to Gifford Pinchot, mindful of the possibility that the president's confidant would pass the words on to his boss in the White House. "One of the hardest trips that I have ever made," he wrote the forester, "met with more trouble from rains, accidents, that sort of thing than I have in my work heretofore, but withal, succeeded in getting a very large amount of splendid new material." At home, he was given the kind of press adulation reserved for expeditions to the North Pole.

A SEATTLE MAN'S TRIUMPH

Curtis's ally and publisher Alden Blethen continued to be supportive, ordering up multiple-page treatment for the photographer's work, with six-column headlines such as the one above. The local kid had shown those eastern elites. "And he went to Arizona, and he stayed just long enough to accomplish that which Uncle Sam, with all his power and authority, had tried for two decades to do and failed," Blethen's *Seattle Times* reported. Three times in 1904, the paper devoted full-page features to Curtis, displaying his Canyon de Chelly pictures, referring to him in one headline as "Explorer, Clubman, Photographer, Historian and President's Friend."

Of course, Curtis couldn't help rubbing it in with the men of the Smithsonian, though he tried to be diplomatic. He still hoped to win their backing, after all. "The longer I work at this collection of pictures the more I feel of their great value," he wrote in late October to Frederick Webb Hodge, the most sympathetic of the Smithsonian's Indian experts. Hodge himself had been to many of the places in the Southwest that had stoked Curtis's passion. A year earlier, when the photographer had begun a correspondence with Hodge, he tried to get him to see the inevitability of the Curtis design. "In the beginning, I had no thought of making the series large enough to be of any value in the future, but the thing has grown so that I now see its great possibilities, and certainly nothing could be of much greater value. The only question now in my mind is, will I be able to keep the thing long enough and steady work, as doing it in a thorough way is enormously expensive."

There was the nightmare—a sleep-destroying one at that. Curtis would soon be broke. He had spent thousands of dollars of his own money, depleting what savings he had and taking everything he could from the studio to finance four years with the Indians, dating to the Blackfeet summer with Grinnell. What was coming out now as finished photogravures could not begin to cover his costs. Meekly at first, and then more aggressively as his situation worsened, he lobbied Meany to arrange a loan from his wealthy Seattle friends, something to get him through another year or two of fieldwork. How much did he need? Curtis equivocated, then arrived at $20,000. Such a figure. But Meany went to work around town, capitalizing on the good press.

Clara was getting frantic. She did the books, and knew more than her husband that they were headed for disaster. The months apart had nearly made them strangers to each other. They now fought over Edward's absences, over the direction of his work, over child-rearing decisions and schools, and all the social events she had to reject while her husband was feted by presidents and scholars. But mostly they fought over money. It was his load to bear and hers to live. The partner who'd followed her love across the sound at age seventeen, who'd spent many moonlit nights in alpine camps with him, was losing her husband to something bigger than both of them.

Curtis had to find a benefactor soon, or the entire enterprise would fold just as it was entering its most productive period. He wrote Merriam, Pinchot and Bird Grinnell, his powerful allies in Washington. He wrote the National Geographic Society, the Washington Academy of Science and the mogul who had given Curtis his first big break: railroad titan E. H. Harriman. All were sympathetic, supportive and full of praise, some of it over the top. Yes, they agreed, he was on to something masterful—keep at it! None put up a dime.

Teddy Roosevelt was his last best hope. Curtis sent recent Indian pictures to the president in December of 1904. A landslide election in November had kept T.R. in the White House; he won 34 of 45 states over a hapless Democrat and a Prohibition Party candidate with the unfortunate name of Silas Swallow. Two days after Christmas, Curtis got a letter from the president—labeled "personal"—thanking him for the pictures and praising the work, particularly one Navajo portrait. "Mrs. Roosevelt was as delighted as I was with that remarkable Indian picture," Teddy wrote. "My dear sir, how are you able to do such work!"

How, indeed. Curtis was the toast of those who looked upon photography as an art form, not an easy crowd to please, prone to mumbled pretentions and caustic insecurities. This circle followed Alfred Stieglitz, the alpha male of sophisticated photography, who had lavished praise on the Shadow Catcher. And Curtis was held in equally high regard by those who saw in the emerging field of photojournalism an incalculable archival tool. Like Curtis, the great portrait photographer of an earlier era, Mathew Brady, had abandoned a prosperous private business framing faces of the famous in order to document an American chapter, in his case the Civil War. Photography, Brady said, could be "a great truthful medium of history," but also like Curtis, he posed his warriors in positions that suited his views. Curtis was old-fashioned in one sense, sticking with cumbrous, fragile, heavyweight and dangerous glass-plate negatives when easier ways to take a picture were available. But in other photographic realms he embraced cutting-edge technology well ahead of his contemporaries. That same December of 1904 Curtis rented out a large hall in Seattle and mesmerized the audience with hand-colored lantern slides and moving pictures of Indians of the Southwest. The film prompted members of the audience to jump from their seats in fear. The Portland *Oregonian* raved about the "New and Remarkable 'Motion Pictures' of Snake Dance and Other Mystic Ceremonies."

Alas, though Roosevelt could move trainloads of dirt and make water travel uphill by building a canal in a pinch of Panama land that had bankrupted the French, the imperious and strong-willed leader of the Western Hemisphere could not find someone with enough money to keep the Curtis Indian project alive. What he did for Curtis in the last days of 1904 was to connect the photographer with Francis Leupp, his commissioner of Indian affairs. Leupp could give Curtis a pass to photograph many of the rituals that Leupp's Indian agents were trying to shut down. Curtis charmed him, and in short order they were close. In the new year of 1905, Leupp invited Curtis to Washington for Teddy's inauguration in March. Many prominent American Indians—Geronimo of the Apache among them—had been asked to lead a parade past the Capitol on the day Roosevelt was sworn in.

Curtis rose from a short, sleepless night to greet the cold air of March 4, 1905, Inauguration Day, in Washington, D.C. He was staying at the Cosmos Club, once the Dolley Madison House, which had a reciprocal relationship with his own Rainier Club in Seattle; he had done a show of his colored lantern slides for members earlier in the week. He was barely into his second cup of coffee when a well-dressed older man from the club approached him with a request.

"Mr. Curtis," he said, "I would like to see an Indian and talk to him."

That so, Curtis mumbled. *What else was new?* It was the kind of request he got all the time, but especially in the East, where he was often treated like a travel agent with a limited number of visas to the Indian world. Curtis asked the man his business. He was a scholar—of Indian studies. But like Karl May, that popular novelist of Indian stories, this expert had never made eye contact with his subjects.

"I have written about the Indian for scientific magazines all my life and I have never seen one. I would like to learn about their life and logic."

Curtis stormed outside. Here he had spent more time with native people than any of these so-called experts from the capital and he could not find a single financial backer. Yet this man—he made his living writing about Indians and had never seen one. He rushed off to the White House, where he had an appointment to photograph six tribal leaders. Snow patches covered the lawn, and Curtis shivered as he set up his tripod in an icy drizzle. The Indians who assembled on horseback wore feathered headdresses, some trailing down to their ankles, and were not in much of a mood for prolonged posing. The man in the middle, wrapped in a plain red army blanket, looked the most puckered and least amused: Geronimo. Curtis had met the leader of the Chiricahua Apache a few days earlier, at the Indian commissioner's invitation. Geronimo was seventy-five, and the fire had yet to leave his eyes. "The spirit of the Apache is not broken," Curtis wrote after spending time with him.

Born near the Gila River headwaters in New Mexico, Geronimo became a warrior after his wife, three small children and mother were slaughtered by Mexican soldiers in 1858. He would fight Anglos and Latinos of various uniforms for the next twenty-eight years, and take many wives. Among the Apache, though he was never a chief, he had mythic standing: it was said he could walk without leaving tracks, and defy bullets, injury and capture. He could make himself invisible. Near the end of his resistance, chased by five thousand troops—one fourth of the standing army—his followers numbered no more than thirty-six, for the raiding, nomadic Apache had many enemies, including other bands of the same tribe. His surrender in 1886 marked the formal end of organized military resistance by Indians to their conquerors.

After being captured, Geronimo was incarcerated at camps in Florida and Alabama. In old age, relocated to the compound of Fort Sill, Oklahoma, Geronimo became a celebrity of the new century, the last of the "wild Indians," now professing to embrace the pickled tenets of the Dutch Reformed Church. Though in the slow-motion harmlessness of his old age, Geronimo needed government approval to leave the fort;

he remained a prisoner of war for the rest of his days. President Roosevelt gave him permission to tell his life story to a writer, S. M. Barrett, and to attend the St. Louis World's Fair in 1904. At the exposition, he sold autographed photos of himself for twenty-five cents apiece, keeping a dime in profit. On good days, he cleared two dollars.

In the life of Geronimo, Curtis saw much of Chief Joseph, and also a cautionary tale against Indian assimilation. The stories of clinging to the last bit of independence, of elusive escapes and long, dreary imprisonments in a strange land, were not unlike those of the Nez Perce leader. Still, Curtis was in Washington to take pictures, not to redress old wrongs. His outrage would have to be conveyed through his camera. In fashioning Geronimo's portrait, after persuading him to pose in a separate sitting, Curtis resolved to transmit the truth of a hard man who would give up nothing for sympathy. He photographed him staring into the lens, bonnet on his head, clutching a spear. In that picture he looks shrunken, lost. Then he captured another man: Geronimo in profile, his entire upper body wrapped in a rough woolen blanket. This Geronimo is without a single bit of jewelry or ornamentation, and with only a simple cloth headband, as he used to wear in his youth. This Geronimo is a face—barely half of one—that is deeply lined, just like old Angeline. His brow is furrowed, his chin clenched. He looks away from the camera in a defiant snub for all time. *Go to hell!*

Not long after the inaugural, the pictures of the Roosevelt family at Sagamore Hill appeared in *McClure's Magazine*. The president liked them so much he would use them in his autobiography. The fuss around the first family photos reinforced Curtis's reputation as the premier portrait photographer in the United States. At the same time, he basked in a prolonged run of national publicity in magazines and big-city newspapers about his Indian work, matching the kind of press he was getting back home. Bird Grinnell's piece in *Scribner's* set the tone:

"It is easy to conceive that if Curtis shall have his health, and shall live for ten years, he will then have accumulated material for the greatest artistic and historical work in American ethnology that has ever been conceived of," he wrote. "I have never seen pictures relating to

Indians which, for fidelity to nature, combined with artistic feeling, can compare with these pictures by Curtis. Today they are of high scientific value. What will they be a hundred years from now when the Indians shall have utterly vanished from the face of the earth?"

Gilbert H. Grosvenor, the first full-time editor of *National Geographic Magazine,* was equally effusive. "He gave our Geographic Society the most wonderful exhibition last night I have seen," he wrote in a letter to a friend. "We had about 1,000 people and they just sat and clapped and clapped. He showed about 130 pictures and they applauded nearly every one, though our audiences are usually very staid."

For all of the adulation from men in high places, Curtis still could not get the financial backing he needed to continue. Meany was having trouble finding enough donors to bundle a loan. More publicity would help, he suggested. The favorable press seemed without limit; time was something else.

"As you were so good to say that I might write you in regard to this Indian work, I am losing no time in availing myself of the privilege," Curtis wrote to President Roosevelt, on a dare and a prayer, while in Washington, D.C., for several exhibitions in late 1905. "Trusting I am not asking too much and again thanking you for your great interest in the work." He requested a letter of introduction to Andrew Carnegie, one of the few tycoons on good terms with Roosevelt and who was planning to give away most of his fortune. Roosevelt didn't know Carnegie well enough, and also considered him somewhat of a pain in the ass, always with the little nag notes to the president. Other rich men in the country despised Roosevelt, the Republican who had raged against "malefactors of great wealth" and waged court fights to break up their monopolies.

"There is no man of great wealth with whom I am on sufficient close terms to warrant my giving a special letter to him," Roosevelt replied, understating the obvious. "But you are most welcome to use this letter in talking with any man who has any interest in the subject." He continued with a stream of superlatives: "I regard the work you have done as one of the most valuable works which any American could do . . . You are making a record of the lives of the Indians which in another decade cannot be made at all, and which it would be the greatest misfortune, from the standpoint alike of the ethnologist and the historian, to leave unmade. You have begun just in time, for these people are at this very moment rapidly losing the distinctive traits and customs which they have slowly developed through the ages."

It was a gold standard of a letter. The leader of the United States at the peak of his popularity, a prolific author as well, had written an endorsement for a project that was vital to the nation. Curtis read the reply as he prepared for another beggar's trip to Manhattan in the chill of winter, his last chance to find a way to fully inflate the Big Idea. He would try to win the indifferent heart of the richest man in the world, so called, though he was told that a note on White House stationery would not help—and would probably hurt.

Theodore Roosevelt, 1904. Curtis was invited to the president's family estate at Sagamore Hill to take pictures of the children. He talked Roosevelt into a sitting as well, and both men loved the resulting portrait.

Fun in the sand, 1904. Curtis was told to play with the kids at the summer White House. He helps bury a compliant dog with, left to right, Quentin, Archie and Nicholas Roosevelt.

At the Old Well of Acoma, 1904. Curtis made several trips to the Sky City of Acoma, New Mexico, the oldest continuously inhabited town in the United States. The cisterns here caught the eye of Coronado when the Spanish arrived in 1540.

6

IN THE DEN OF THE TITAN

1906

WITHIN THE SHORT ARC of Edward Curtis's life to date, the
United States had gone from a scruffy nation of farmers and
Main Street merchants to the foremost industrial power on the planet,
and done so without a central bank. But while there was yet no Federal Reserve, there was the colossus of J. Pierpont Morgan, a crow-eyed
collector of art, railroads and women, who made his fortune by timely
bets on the most desirable commodities of the age. Morgan was no
bootstrapper; there was no Horatio Alger in his story, this product of
the best schools in the East and Europe. Morgan came from money and
comfort, and converted a family stake into monopolies and a regal life.
Napoleon was a personal hero; Morgan studied his military moves and
matched them on the financial field. Having more money than anyone
else meant the House of Morgan could spring when others were crippled, lend when rivals were barren of funds, own politicians without directly paying for them. Morgan was a predator with a plan, and largely
bloodless. He took the competition out of railroads, corralled chaotic
suppliers of electricity into the smooth-running trust of General Electric and shaped U.S. Steel to become the world's first billion-dollar cor-
poration. At the height of his powers, he was compared to Alexander
the Great by a scholar at Yale, and disparaged as "a beefy, red-faced,

thick-necked financial bully" by the progressive senator Robert M. La Follette. At the age of sixty-eight, with few financial castles left to conquer, Morgan was drawn to high Renaissance art and mistresses who knew how to make him laugh. He had six homes, and was getting ready to open a palace of marble to house his treasures next to his main residence, an imposing brownstone at 219 Madison Avenue in Manhattan.

Morgan conducted business a few miles downtown, in the heart of a financial district that was largely an ecosystem of his own making. His white marble lair at 23 Wall Street was to global capitalism what the Vatican was to Roman Catholicism. At the six-story building—known as "the Corner," just across the street from the New York Stock Exchange—Morgan received monarchs, heads of state, senators, congressmen and silk-vested sycophants from all areas of moneymaking. Women were allowed to enter the inner sanctum but once a year, a formality designed to show that Morgan had a touch of enlightenment. Morgan was thinking of razing the building and replacing it with a neoclassical limestone fortress, daunting and impenetrable to outsiders.

It was at the entrance of 23 Wall Street that Edward Curtis presented himself on the twenty-fourth day of January 1906, with a last-chance plan to keep his Indian project alive. Within a few months, Morgan would be spending most of his time at his new library, at the corner of Madison and Thirty-sixth Street. The manse next door, Morgan's home, had been the first in New York to be entirely illuminated with electric light. By contrast, the library was an homage to antiquity: it was built using the ancient Greek technique of fitting massive marble blocks one atop another—precision construction using almost no mortar. Nothing could be more costly. During the design phase, he had made so many demands that his architect, Charles F. McKim, suffered a nervous breakdown. Inside, visitors would pass through a pair of bronze doors into a rotunda with curved walls of mosaic panels. The apse was based on Raphael's design for the Villa Madama in Rome. The ceilings throughout the library were clouded with narrative art. The den was stuffed with more carved stone, more masterpieces, and its ceiling woodwork was chipped from its anchor in a fifteenth-century Tuscan palazzo. Directly across from the study, where the architect had wanted high windows to let in light on his creation, Morgan walled off the space so he could hang another acquisition: a huge, four-hundred-year-old tapestry titled *The Triumph of Avarice.*

A long letter from Curtis had arrived in advance of the photographer's appointment. Despite his desperation, Curtis conveyed his usual breezy brio. "When I call to see you tomorrow afternoon, you can see what I am like." He then went on to the significance of the task; no use throat-clearing. "As to the artistic merit, it must speak for itself, and no one can be a better judge of that than yourself." A pinch of flattery—of course. Morgan was the president of the Metropolitan Museum of Art and the foremost market force in that high cultural realm; he could indeed judge for himself. But just in case: "I feel the work is worthwhile and as a monumental thing, nothing can exceed it." And then a cut to the chase: "I have the ability, strength, and determination to finish the undertaking, but have gone to the end of my means and must ask someone to join me in the undertaking and make it possible for all ages of Americans to see what the American Indian was like. Whatever the outcome of our meeting, let me now thank you for your courtesy in allowing me to bring the matter before you."

Morgan had only the vaguest notion of what an American Indian was like, but few people had so altered the destiny of the tribes as had the lion of Wall Street. He had gone west for the first time in 1869, not long after completion of the transcontinental railroad. At a stop in Nebraska, young Morgan and his wife, Franny, ran into a group of Pawnee Indians—"horrid-looking wild creatures with no clothes to speak of," as a member of their party recalled. When a native approached Morgan, he beat a hasty retreat to his private rail car. Later, Morgan's consolidation of the railroads, eventually joining corporate cause with E. H. Harriman and James J. Hill, led to a growth spurt that created the largest rail network in the world. In a short time, the buffalo prairies and game-rich valleys of the open West were laced with steel roads, servicing all manner of newcomers and prospectors of property. Buffalo Bill Cody got his start killing bison for railroad crews. The tribes knew they were doomed when the smoky exhalations of the iron horses filled the skies of the Great Plains, for an obsidian-tipped spear could bring down a five-hundred-pound buffalo, but it was worthless against metal-hulled trains carrying immigrants to Indian country. In a single decade, the 1880s, more than seventy-five thousand miles of track were tacked to the ground, and nearly three million people moved west.

No sentimentalist in business, Morgan did have a soft spot for beautiful things, whether on canvas or fitted into a tailored dress. No art-rich estate or château in Europe was safe from his wandering buyer's eye. In 1898, he spent $300,000 on *The Progress of Love*, fourteen decorative panels by Jean-Honoré Fragonard, commissioned in 1771. Three years later, he bought a fifteenth-century Raphael (a Perugian altarpiece) for $400,000 — at the time, the most expensive art purchase in the world. He topped himself again in 1902 when he paid $700,000 for the contents of a British squire's private library. Books were particularly appealing to Morgan, a bibliophile with a taste for big names. He owned a first edition of Milton's *Paradise Lost*, a vellum Gutenberg Bible, original copies of the Declaration of Independence and the fussed-over manuscript of *A Christmas Carol*, the Charles Dickens classic written in 1843. These treasures were all bound for the new library.

Edward Curtis wanted nothing more than to be part of Morgan's collection. In his advance letter, he outlined the project: "The plan in mind is to make a complete publication, showing pictures and including text of every phase of Indian life of all tribes yet in a primitive condition, taking up the type, male and female, child and adult, their home structure, their environment, their handicraft, games, ceremonies etc.; dividing the whole into twenty volumes containing fifteen hundred full-page plates, the text to treat the subject much as the pictures do, going fully into their history, life and manners, ceremony, legends and mythology, treating it in rather a broad way so that it will be scientifically accurate, yet if possible interesting reading."

The last line was central to the Curtis task. Yes, he was creating something scientific, something artistic, something that would withstand the ages, something that must be *done now!* But as a self-educated product of a new middle class with broad tastes, Curtis also wanted his work to be read outside the claustral realm of academia. He was not doing this to be praised by the small circle of Indian scholars, though he certainly wanted their approval. Most everything scholarly on the subject, he implied, was tedious, if not damn near impossible to read.

Now, to the money: "It has been estimated by publishers that a work of this nature would have to sell at five thousand dollars a set, and that one hundred sets could be disposed of in this country and abroad. To finish the field work will require five more years at an approximate annual expense of $15,000 for the five years — $75,000." There you had it, what every businessman looks for: the bottom line. Twenty volumes. Five years to complete. And $75,000 total. It would be not only one of the world's costliest literary projects, but the rarest of books: the total print run would be a hundred sets.

Curtis mentioned in closing that he had already spent $25,000 of his own money, and that while his bankbook was empty, he still had his life to give, and was willing to put it up as collateral so that Morgan would never lose a penny. "To further safeguard the patron of the work, I could insure my life . . ."

The next day, Curtis presented himself in the afternoon to make his case in person. He had gotten this far — that is, through the bronze doors of 23 Wall Street — because of his connections, though not the political ones. President Roosevelt was a liability. It was no secret, as T.R. had mentioned in his letter to Curtis, that the "man of great wealth" despised Roosevelt, and the feeling was mutual. When the United States first went after Morgan's railroad trust in 1902, the mogul thought everything could be settled by gentleman's agreement. "If we have done anything wrong, send your man to my man and they can fix it." Roosevelt replied, "That can't be done." Two years later, the Supreme Court ruled for Roosevelt, and the monopoly was broken, though Morgan seemed not to suffer in the least. Another man of wealth was Pinchot, the forester and top Roosevelt adviser who had inherited a private fortune made by his grandfather in the timber industry. Pinchot also hated Morgan. And Pinchot, while encouraging Curtis, had turned down the photographer when he asked for a $7,000 loan. A better ace in the hole for Curtis was the leader of the Alaska expedition, E. H. Harriman. Not only was Harriman a Morgan partner in the railroad consolidation (after years of being at each other's throats), but he had spread his patron wings wide, in Morgan's same circles. The year before, Harriman had arranged for a New York show of Curtis's work, and invited the influential critics and patrons in the city to view rare pictures of the "curious rites, ceremonies and customs" of Indians—a bit of a carnival come-on for the New York elite. It cost Curtis $1,300 to rent the ballroom at the Waldorf-Astoria Hotel. Hundreds of the city's swell set turned out, and sales were brisk. Among the admirers was Louise Satterlee, Morgan's daughter. The critics raved, elevating his work to a national cause célèbre. "We are painting our plains, protecting our forests, creating game preserves, and at last—not saving the existence of our North American Indian, the most picturesque roving people on earth," declared the *Craftsman*, an influential photography magazine. "Just one man, an American, an explorer, an artist with the camera, has conceived and is carrying into execution the gigantic idea of making a complete photographic and text record of the North American Indians so far as they exist in primitive conditions today."

Harriman and Morgan's daughter had gotten Curtis close to the great man. But to gain an audience with him, Curtis would have to pass through one more person: an olive-skinned, sly-witted twenty-two-year-old from Princeton who had been hired to oversee Morgan's library and all the literary acquisitions, Belle da Costa Greene. An expert in illuminated manuscripts, she had charmed her way into New York's art circles, and left some men speechless in her wake, with her green eyes and body-hugging clothes. "Just because I'm a librarian," she once said, "doesn't mean I have to dress like one." Morgan was instantly taken, hiring Greene in 1905 and granting her extraordinary powers for one so young; she was given the kind of access to his world that no other woman had. If Greene did not like a manuscript, or increasingly, a work of art, Morgan would pass on it. She pretended to be somewhat aloof in Morgan's presence, feigning resistance to the lure of his charm and vast wealth, joking that she was the only woman who was not "a willing candidate for the harem." She told everyone she was of Portuguese stock, and hinted at distant royal blood. Curtis was also impressed by her beauty and exotic background. But he did not know

—nor did Morgan—that virtually everything about her biography was a lie. Her real name was Belle Greener, and she was the daughter of a prominent black family from Washington, D.C., unrelated to any kind of European royalty. She never spoke of her father, though he was the first African-American graduate of Harvard. Light-skinned enough to pass as white, Belle slipped out of one racial outfit before her twenty-first birthday and dressed herself in another. The new woman, complete with a package of made-up anecdotes to fill out the narrative, was in place when she found work at the Princeton Library, and was refined over the years as Morgan's aide in New York.

After preliminary discussions with Greene, following a favorable response to his introductory letter, Curtis was ushered in to see Morgan. As he had clambered over a glacier to rescue two strangers on Mount Rainier; as he had descended a ladder into a Hopi kiva thick with rattlesnakes; and as he had sailed to Alaska with some of the nation's best minds, five years after he was picking berries and digging clams, Curtis walked in, certain he could make his way. He was an interpreter, after all, a bridge between worlds, and he could find common ground with a financier who talked in the language of Wall Street as well as he could see why an Acoma native lived atop an eight-hundred-foot-high rock in the Southwest. But, for a moment, he was caught off-guard.

Curtis was prepared for the man's intense gaze—made famous in the best-known picture of Morgan, a 1903 portrait taken by Edward Steichen that captured a laser stare that could crack open a bank vault. And New York associates had given him tips on the Morgan conversational style. He was not known for being profligate with words, urging one and all to get to the point. But what Curtis was not ready for was the man's appearance: Morgan was grotesque-looking. As beautiful and radiant as Belle da Costa Greene was on first impression, Morgan's outward projection was at the other extreme—repulsive, shockingly so to those who had never met him. The forks of thinning, bone-colored hair, the ascot, the watch fob, the slow-burning cigar, the mahogany walking stick: familiar, and expected. But the eyes of a visitor were not drawn to the accessories of J. P. Morgan; they were pulled directly to his face. His oversized nose was severely mottled and inflamed. It was like the fog light of a ship, making it impossible to turn away. Morgan suffered from rhinophyma, which the best doctors could do nothing about. Women friends had suggested makeup and other cosmetics, but Morgan, after nearly twenty years of living with his condition, had stopped acting as if he cared. In old age, the rhinophyma had turned Morgan's nose into "a hideous purple bulb," as his biographer Jean Strouse wrote, and was the subject of constant comment by all who came in contact with him. "Pierpont's face is now too terrible to look at," said one friend, the historian and writer Henry Adams. "The nose has spread."

"Sit down," Morgan directed Curtis. Face stern. No smile. Hands together as he sat at his desk in a room of buffed teak paneling. The sunken eyes of the financier focused in on the photographer. Curtis had barely spoken his first words when Morgan interrupted him with a dismissive wave of his hand. "Mr. Curtis, there are many demands on me for financial assistance."

Yes, Curtis said, he understood. As their mutual friend E. H. Harriman had explained. As Morgan's own lovely daughter Mrs. Satterlee had implied. Again Curtis went over the plan, before he jumped to his next argument. He had given Morgan an additional document, a list of estimated annual expenses. Hotels. Money for translators and money for his subjects. Food for the crew. Food for the horses and mules. Rail tickets. Salaries of three assistants: an editor, a writer in the field and an ethnologist. The Indians would have to be paid every bit of the way. But as for Curtis himself, he would work for free.

Free! Morgan said nothing at that, but this was as far as Curtis would go. He would be reimbursed—he hoped—from sales of the twenty complete volumes. They would be priced at $5,000 a set, and Curtis would have to hustle the subscriptions. Morgan himself would get twenty-five sets for his new library, or to distribute to various museums and universities—an impressive gift, yes? Also, hundreds of original photogravures would go to Morgan. So, for all the hours on the reservations, all the days on trains, the months of searching for subjects, interviewing, photographing, the seasons spent squinting into the sun, shivering in the snow and straining in a darkroom—for all of that, Curtis would get nothing. But Morgan raised not an eyebrow.

Curtis tried another tack, a way to Morgan's wallet. Here was the thing: this project matched Morgan's passions. How so? Think of it this way: the Curtis Indian creation would be a publishing sensation. The Vatican, the monarchs of Europe and the kaiser of Germany would want sets. For Morgan it would be an ideal addition to the collection of a man who owned medieval icons, antique Chinese porcelains and the famed Indian Bible, printed in 1663, the first time Scripture was published in a Native American language, Algonquin. What Morgan desired was to have that which no one else could possess. As he himself had said, the most expensive words in the world are *unique au monde*.

Yet Morgan was unmoved. "I will be unable to help you."

Had Curtis stood up and walked out, as rejected suitors to Morgan's money usually did, that would have been the end of it. Meany's loan was still a pipe dream. Clara cried that the family would soon be in the poorhouse. And even an exhibition at such a tony showcase as the Waldorf-Astoria, selling Indian pictures to the New York rich, barely covered the cost of renting the room. But instead of turning to leave, Curtis sat in place and went on the offensive. He opened his portfolio and spread the pictures on the desk of the king of Wall Street. Here was the Walpi warrior. Here was the Chief Joseph portrait so loved by Teddy —um, the president. Here was the old well at Acoma. Here were the salmon people of Puget Sound. The more the rich man saw of the pictures, the more he seemed touched. These faces were as much a part of the American landscape as a Hudson Valley promontory. Did Morgan think the country could afford to lose this piece of its past? And, more cynically, benevolence could do wonders for Morgan's image. Roosevelt had made the wealthy out to be heartless bastards, the lot of them, and the progressive mob wanted them taxed at an annual rate of 50 percent or more. These people, many of them Republicans with personal fortunes of their own, were calling for the creation of an income tax, of all things—the audacity. If Morgan agreed to sponsor something historic on behalf of a downtrodden native class, it would do quite a bit for his reputation. See, the rich aren't so hollowed-out inside. How much longer did he have to live? And what, truly, would outlive him? What would be his legacy? All the carved stone in his library?

One more picture did the trick. This portrait, titled *Mosa*, shows a Mojave girl in early adolescence. She is a face-painted beauty with a careless gaze, skin as smooth as a bar of soap—just the jewel for Morgan the collector. He loved the picture, and it sealed the deal. Very well:

"I will lend financial assistance for the publication of a set of books illustrated with photographs such as these," Morgan said. Yes? More Mosa, in other words. Curtis assured him there were many more Mosas where that came from. Now, had Curtis heard him right? A deal was done, just like that? Indeed he had. "My staff will take care of the financial arrangements."

Morgan agreed to the $75,000, spread over five years—for fieldwork only. The money for publication, the printing and binding, would have to come from those willing to pay the subscription for the complete twenty-volume set. And $5,000 was too much to ask. How about $3,000 for a set printed on thick etching stock, and $3,850 for Japanese tissue? And instead of one hundred sets, why not try to sell five hundred sets? A superb idea! The books must be bound in lustrous leather. Of course! Beautiful to behold, a thing of great artistry. Done! There remained one quibble about the text. Rather than hire some eminent scholar for the prose narrative, or a ghostwriter with many books already published, why not have Curtis write it himself? After all, who better knows the Indians? He had promised in his outline to produce "interesting reading," had he not?

"You are the one to write it," Morgan said. "You know the Indians and how they live and what they are thinking."

They shook hands. The photographer gathered up his material, closed his portfolio, turned to leave. "Mr. Curtis," Morgan said in closing, "I like a man who attempts the impossible." By then, Curtis had forgotten about the nose.

For days, Curtis strolled on air. No January looked so good. No city so great as New York. No man so wonderful as J. Pierpont Morgan. "I walked from his presence in a daze," he said. Yes, $75,000 was a trifle compared to the nearly ten times that amount Morgan had spent on the musty book collection of a Brit. But to Curtis it was everything—his life work, his future. Clara was with him, getting a rare chance to share a triumph with her husband. For the moment, he did not care about the details of selling individual sets, on spec, for an amount equal to three times the annual wage of an average American. Nor did he seem concerned that he had cut himself out of a salary. What he rejoiced at was the assurance of $15,000 a year, enough to bring the Big Idea home and establish himself among the greats who strived to capture human images for posterity.

MORGAN MONEY TO KEEP INDIANS FROM OBLIVION

Morgan got the kind of press he wished for, the historic irony lost on the daily papers. But before the headlines, Curtis told Roosevelt of his triumph.

"I congratulate you with all my heart," the president replied in a short note. "That is a mighty fine deed of Mr. Morgan." And to this Roosevelt added a surprising request. His daughter Alice, the most celebrated young woman in America, would be marrying shortly. Yes, Curtis knew: it was in the press every day, the upcoming nuptials between a handsome congressman, Nicholas Longsworth, and Princess Alice. Roosevelt asked Curtis if he would photograph the event. Everyone in the country would want a look, and what they would see would be filtered through the lens of the Shadow Catcher.

Near the end of the summer, after Morgan's first check had been cashed, after the wedding pictures of the first family had gone out to wide acclaim, after Curtis had put together a staff of top-drawer talent, the photographer wrote Roosevelt to ask a favor of his own. He was deep in Indian country, composing a note from the Hopi homeland. The work had gone very well, he reported: he expected to publish the first two volumes within a year. He'd made a major breakthrough with the Apache. He was closer than ever to the Hopi. And he felt he knew enough about the Navajo to tell a word-and-picture story without precedent. He was fascinated by the Zuni; the pueblos of New Mexico Territory were a photographer's dream. He wondered if the president would be willing to write an introduction to the work, something along the lines of the earlier letter of endorsement Curtis had circulated while looking for a benefactor. "Pardon my crude way of saying it," Curtis wrote, "but you as the greatest man in America owe it to your people to do this." Such nerve. But Roosevelt couldn't resist. He replied from Sagamore Hill, saying he was honored that Curtis had asked him to pen a few words on his behalf.

"Now I so thoroughly sympathize with you in your work that I am inclined to write the introduction you desire," Roosevelt wrote. "But how long do you wish it to be and when do you wish me to have it ready for you?"

The year closed with Curtis at his happiest. He not only had the patronage of the most powerful banker on the planet, but the president of the United States was working for him as well. For free.

Stare of the titan: J. P. Morgan, 1903. Edward Steichen's famous portrait of the richest banker in the United States, taken three years before Morgan agreed to back the Curtis project. The light glinting off the armrest was seen by many viewers as a knife.

Mosa—Mohave, 1903. This is the picture that won over Morgan, who at first was reluctant to help Curtis.

Belle da Costa Greene, gatekeeper of the treasures of the Morgan Library. Greene kept her personal life secret, shedding one racial identity for another.

7

ANGLOS IN INDIAN COUNTRY
1906

W HEN HE RETURNED to the White Mountain reservation
in late spring of 1906, Curtis was determined to stay until he
could decipher the inner lives of the Apache. He had with him a paid
crew this time, and enough cash to be a bargaining force among people who had shunned him earlier. He would not leave, he insisted, until the Great Mystery was evident in his pictures and understandable in
his words. Three days out of Seattle, he arrived at the rail stop of Hol-
brook, a dust-choked trading town along the anemic Puerco River, just
downslope from the Apache homeland in the mountains of eastern Arizona Territory. Though the days were long under the glare of an un-
blinking sun, winter still had a grip on snow-covered peaks of ten thousand feet or more. Roads were half built, washed out in places, mere
rumors in others. Six years before Arizona became a state, portions of
it were terra incognita to the outside world. In advance of the trip, Curtis had written the Smithsonian wondering if someone could send him
"an available map there in Washington which gives a good detail of that
country."

Upward the Curtis party marched, a dust cloud around a wagon
pulled by four horses, upward to piñon-covered prickly ground,
through an area known as the Petrified Forest, winding and stumbling

in search of faces to fill Volume I of the series that would soon be for-malized under the title *The North American Indian*, with an office (for selling subscriptions) in New York, at 437 Fifth Avenue. For the first book, Curtis had chosen the Navajo and the Apache, two tribes that had most enchanted, and eluded, him.

Curtis did not lack internal fuel: he wanted to show Morgan and Roosevelt that he could live up to their trust, but he also wanted to prove to the credentialed Indian experts that their ignorance was stupe-fying.

"You are going to get something that does not exist," an Indian scholar had told Curtis in Washington, D.C., a few months earlier. "The Apache have no religion."

"How do you know they have no religion?" Curtis replied.

"I spent considerable time among them, I asked them, and they told me . . . You're wasting your time."

The money from J. P. Morgan allowed the photographer to stock his project with a first-rate posse, building his team one at a time in the months after leaving Manhattan. His closest aide was an ex–newspaper-man of multiple talents, William E. Myers, who was twenty-eight years old when he fell under the spell of the Shadow Catcher in 1906. Like his boss, Myers grew up in the Midwest; unlike him, he had a pedigreed ed-ucation, majoring in Greek on his way to graduating with honors from Northwestern University. He spoke several languages, and had been raised in a middle-class family that valued learning. An uncanny lin-guist, Myers had an ear for the nuances of speech and dialect, which was vital to the groundbreaking work that Curtis aspired to do. In ad-dition, his swift shorthand proved invaluable in taking down words for the dictionary-like glossaries Curtis was pulling together of languages that were falling out of use. Myers had taught school in the Midwest, then worked at the *Seattle Star*, a gritty daily, before signing on with the open-ended adventure of Edward S. Curtis. "To the Indians, his skill in phonetics was awesome magic," Curtis wrote of Myers. "In spelling, he was a second Webster." Equally important, he had the stamina and sta-ble personality for a project that would allow no room for a private life, let alone sleep.

Myers was two years older than Bill Phillips, who had been working for Curtis since his student days at the University of Washington. Now twenty-six, Phillips had become a jack-of-all-trades for the Indian enterprise. He would find translators, arrange for food and transport, set up portrait sessions and locations for outdoor shoots, smooth disagreements and take copious notes. Phillips was in awe of Curtis, impressed by the audacity of his leaps to the upper reaches of American society and by the vision of the Big Idea. Rounding out the traveling crew was at least one translator, depending on the tribal band, and a steady cook named Justo, who had the added skill of being a horse wrangler.

Outside the field team, Curtis made one other hire that year, a plum for him: Frederick Webb Hodge, a Smithsonian ethnologist and scholar of American Indians. Curtis had been courting him for three years. English born, Hodge was trained as an anthropologist and historian but did his best work applying authoritative polish to other people's words. He was forty-one when he agreed to become the long-term editor for Curtis, at $7 per thousand words. He would also keep his day job at the Smithsonian, where he was overseeing *The Handbook of American Indians,* considered the definitive guide in the field. Unlike other Washington experts, Hodge had visited tribal lands — Acoma, the Navajo reservation, the Zuni Nation — many times. To have the prose of a self-educated photographer acquire the imprimatur of Hodge assured Curtis that the most ambitious literary undertaking of the new century would not be easily dismissed in learned circles.

Finally, Curtis had with him a wide-eyed and worshipful twelve-year-old boy, his son Hal. He rode on horseback beside his towering father, ahead of the wagon. He delighted in watching Curtis orchestrate the field team — "directing the activities, looking after the welfare of everyone" — and was brought into the larger discussion of how to extract the secrets of the Apache. In all, it was a boy's dream.

The two-million-acre Apache reservation presented itself to the Curtis party as a wave of mountains and high mesas, much of it forested in oak and cedar, pine, cottonwood, alder and walnut, with cacti throughout. The lowlands looked jungled to Curtis, a profusion of wild grapes and vines, more like parts of the Cascade Mountains than the whiskered tablelands of central Arizona. This June, the wildflowers had opened to a chorus of bright color, the columbines in full-throated blossom. Curtis followed a wagon trail through Black Canyon, a valley of thick-armored oaks that led to a protected fold of land forking left. Most of the tribe of about two thousand people lived near the head of the canyon, in a village called White River.

The Curtis party settled in. Their task was to soak up a culture— legends, quirks, habits, history, diet, sex life, songs, myths and religion. In the first few days on Apache land, Curtis got sick and was confined to camp, frustrating him. It did nothing to dampen his resolve. "I have unfortunately been ill," he wrote Hodge. "But one thing is certain: at the time I quit the Apache reservation, there will be a good many questions answered as to the inner life of the Apache."

The tribe was under siege by government agents, who had jailed some of the medicine men for practicing their rituals. Freedom of religion was cherished as a sacrosanct American right—everywhere, that is, but on the archipelago of Indian life. What Curtis wanted, to watch and record the Apache praying in their customary way, could make him an accomplice to a crime. At the same time, natives who worked with him were seen as traitors to their own people. "Old friends looked the other way," Curtis wrote. "One of my former interpreters, learning of my purpose, declined to have anything to do with me, declaring he was not going out in search of sudden death." His strategy, as before, was to appear indifferent, "to be just a sucker furnishing the food and paying for the privilege—perhaps in playing that part I was a natural." Still, the enterprise had money in a poor land, no small thing. Curtis drew into his orbit the cautiously curious and those looking to earn something. And at night, women, too, came to the camp, and Curtis was tempted.

"Some of the maidens needed no sales argument," Curtis wrote. He was unsure if this was a trick—a way to get him arrested—or prostitution, or something in between. Apache mothers arrived in the dark with their teenage daughters and drew erotic pictures in the sand—come-ons that indicated the kind of sexual romp that awaited him. Curtis kept his professional distance from the women, he wrote, while doing everything he could to get close to those who knew the religious secrets. He recognized some of the medicine men from his previous work; the incantations were also familiar. But over and over again, when Curtis asked questions about certain words in the Apache language, he was rebuffed with a single refrain:

"We don't know."

Then what about a symbol, he would ask—why was it drawn in such a way?

"To make it look pretty."

At night, staring at the starry infinity of the Arizona sky, young Hal wondered about the Indian explanation for the twinkling overhead. Inspired by his father, he said, "I will get the Indian boys to talk with me about all of this." But he had no more luck than did his dad.

By July, after six weeks in Apache country, Curtis had little to show. "We had only succeeded in building up a wall of tribal reticence. Every member of the tribe understood that no one was to talk to us, and a delegation of the chiefs had visited the Indian agent in charge, demanding that I leave the reservation."

Facing banishment, Curtis promised to close up shop soon—but kept the departure date uncertain. "Maybe today. Maybe tomorrow." At the same time, he narrowed his quest to a single medicine man, named Goshonné. In the predawn darkness Curtis and a translator crawled through the brush to spy on Goshonné as he chanted. It was beautiful, a morning prayer that moved Curtis. He went again and again to listen. Though Curtis was a religious voyeur on his stomach in the dust, he felt his actions were justified because the world had so miscast Apaches as pagans. One day, at the close of prayer, Curtis sprang from the bushes and revealed himself. Goshonné was upset, angry and threatening— how dare this white man spy on him? He was a respected elder, and also had spent time in jail for openly practicing medicine man pharmacology.

Curtis expressed sympathy. He had watched Goshonné to learn from him, not to report him. He raged against the Indian Religious Crimes Code, a cultural bulldozer scraping away centuries of tradition. And, in a naked appeal to Goshonné's needs beyond the spiritual realm, Curtis offered a sizable financial prize for the medicine man's knowledge. Over cigarettes, the two men talked for several days. Near the end of their negotiations, Goshonné took frequent steam baths and plunges into the White River. Curtis wondered: what was *that* about? Goshonné explained that he was trying to cleanse himself. For Curtis, this was a good thing: it meant he was getting ready to share insider knowledge with an outsider. In the end, it was not the force of Curtis's personality that nudged Goshonné along; it was the cash.

A few days earlier, for a substantial fee, Curtis had been allowed to take pictures of a deerskin scroll holding symbols of the Apache creation myth—a page from a bible, essentially. This was a huge step. But only a medicine man could explain the drawings on the skin. When the deal with Goshonné was completed, he took Curtis and a translator to a secluded place in the woods and talked for half a day, answering their questions in a slow and deliberate manner. Curtis made audio recordings and filled several notebooks. Back in camp, he was gleeful: the tribal secrets—a complex and lengthy description of how the world came to be—were out.

In addition, Curtis learned many everyday things from his stay. A full-blooded Apache never took a scalp. Their language, an Athapaskan dialect, had no profanity. The Apache feared the dead, for ghosts could exact revenge. Their diet was mixed—piñon nuts, acorns, mescal pulp, juniper berries and the fruit of the prickly pear cactus, supplemented by protein from wild turkey, antelope, deer, rabbit, quail. Eating bear or fish was forbidden. Water containers were made of woven sumac coated in piñon gum. Tribal government was weak or nonexistent. The medicine man had more influence than anyone, and was a keeper, until death, of the skin that explained how people came to be. After this season with the Apache, what Curtis wanted the world to know was the opposite of what he had been told at the Smithsonian, which was peddled in almost any story written about the tribe. "The Apache is inherently devoutly religious; his life is completely molded by his religious beliefs," Curtis wrote in his first volume of *The North American Indian*. "From the morning prayer to the rising sun, through the hours, the days, and months—throughout life itself—every act has some religious significance."

The breakthrough with Goshonné opened the way for the pictures. At last—faces. *Apache Girl*, bare-shouldered, her skin just above the nipple of her left breast exposed to soft light, was memorable. *Das Lan*, a medicine man who was a rival of Goshonné's, posed for Curtis with a scholarly stare. *Alchise* is a thin-faced, cerebral-looking Apache chief in early middle age, his face illuminated by midday sun. *Bathing Pool* and *By the Sycamore* show people as an integral part of the land. Depicting a woman harvesting food, *Cutting Mescal* is a Southwest version of Curtis's *The Clam Digger*. A motion-blurred platinum print, *Before the Storm*, is extraordinary for the multiple messages in the frame: four Indians on horseback moving away from the camera, a lone face looking back, a foreboding sky overhead, wind-rustled yucca plants in the foreground, all shot from a low angle. And the trophy that Curtis most wanted the public to see: *Sacred Buckskin*, which was hand colored in the finish.

"I think I can say that the Apache work has been quite successful—far more than I had hoped for," Curtis wrote Hodge. But it came at a price. In trying to extract secrets of a religion for a public that doubted whether the Apache even had one, Curtis had disrupted the sacred rhythms. Just as Curtis was packing to leave the White Mountain reservation, Goshonné showed up in camp. He was twitchy, breathless, ashen-faced, angry at himself and at Curtis. The outsiders' mood darkened immediately, from triumph to edgy second-guessing.

"I am sorry I talked," said Goshonné.

"Why?"

"Spies watched us and know my words have gone to the white man. My words are on the white man's paper and I cannot take them back." Curtis tried to reassure him; he would never reveal that it was Goshonné who had collaborated. No, no, Curtis did not understand—the word was already out about the medicine man's role. They knew. Goshonné trembled, visibly afraid, cursing himself for betraying his people and their gods.

"My life will be short," he said over and over, shaking his head, his fists clenched. "All the medicine men have said it."

Not long after Curtis returned to Seattle, after he had brought the faces of the Apache to life in his studio, he received word that Goshonné had died an early death, cause unknown.

North, about fifty miles from the Apache village, Curtis steered his covered wagon into Gallup, New Mexico Territory, answering the call of a long-delayed family obligation. Curtis had been on the road constantly since he set off with the Harriman expedition in 1899. Even by the standards of the late exploration era, when men would leave their loved ones for years at a time, Curtis was an absentee father and husband. When he dropped by his home in Seattle, Clara would greet him with silence or forced indifference, the children remembered. Questions about his fidelity followed.

Curtis admitted to having a mistress, an insatiate one — *The North American Indian*. Everything else was secondary. He certainly shared with Alfred Stieglitz an obsession with perfection. "Nearly right," Stieglitz once said, "is child's play." But Curtis wanted to be a father, as evidenced by his attempt to bring the children to him, even if he couldn't go to them, even if he was not there for birthdays or by a bedside when a child fell sick. Clara the teenager had nursed Curtis back to health after he mangled his back. Clara the woman had been mother to three children, the keeper of schedules, the provider of clothes and food, getting them all off to school, doctors' appointments and baseball games, all of it. Clara the manager had held the studio together on nights when bill collectors came calling and days when *tout* Seattle wanted a tour. And she had to put up with the questions from friends and neighbors. *Where is he now?* At times, she didn't know. Was he in Montana with the Crow, or in the Dakotas with the Sioux, or in Wyoming with the Assiniboin? And how was the Curtis clan going to make ends meet while the Shadow Catcher worked for free and the portrait business languished?

He offered reassurances, a kiss on the cheek, a hug for each child, and then, as always, rush rush rush out the door and down to the train station, away to other families.

Throughout 1906, Curtis tried to save his marriage. The magnificent early months of that year—the meeting with Morgan, exhibitions in Washington and New York, parties with well-heeled lovers of his "art," the wedding of Alice Roosevelt, a lecture in Pittsburgh at the Carnegie gallery, a trip to Boston to set up copper-plate engravings by John Andrew & Son—had all been with Clara. They shared those best of times; she was in on the creation, the act of becoming Edward S. Curtis. He had shown her the part of his world that included the East Coast power brokers. And now, as he greeted Clara and the children at the train terminal in New Mexico, he finally had a chance to show her the other part of his life.

By horseback and wagon, the Curtis family and *The North American Indian* entourage traveled from Gallup over barren terrain, through the high reaches of a stubby piñon forest, then to a treeless desert, past mesas and over arroyos, to the town of Chinle in the heart of the Navajo Nation. The mobile family photography project was weighted down with tents, bedding, food, cooking stoves, a typewriter, hundreds of reference books, trunks of clothes, a motion-picture camera and the small glass-plate equipment now used by Curtis for his 6½-by-8½-inch cameras. His road load was about a thousand pounds, and his animal team comprised eight horses. In Chinle, perched on the edge of Canyon de Chelly, Curtis met up with the trader Charlie Day, who grew up with the Navajo and was fluent in their language. Day chafed at the way officials from the Indian agency were treating his neighbors. As with the Hopi, Apache and Blackfeet, people in this most populous of Indian nations, living on a reservation about the size of Virginia, were jailed, sometimes without trial, for the crime of practicing native life at its fullest. At the same time, they were encouraged to become dependent on a government that did not have their best interests at heart. Day wrote President Roosevelt to complain. And when Curtis approached him for a second season as translator, Day told Curtis to get written permission before he agreed; he was worried they would be arrested.

Curtis tried a preemptive move: he used his influence with Francis Leupp, the commissioner of Indian affairs, to arrange letters of transit, sent by telegram. Once these documents arrived, Charlie Day and the Curtis party moved down into the thirty-mile-long Canyon de Chelly for an extensive field session. Day had been appointed by the U.S. Department of the Interior as a guardian of Anasazi treasures, and knew every wrinkle of the canyon. Vandals and thieves were actively chiseling away the centuries of life left behind in the cliffs. The stone apartments cut from the rock, so well preserved by the protective canyon walls, looked as if their inhabitants had gone only days ago.

Curtis already had much of the material he needed for the Navajo section of Volume I; a picture he had taken of Indians moving through the canyon two years earlier was being hailed as a masterpiece. When John Ford went to Monument Valley some thirty years later to shoot the first of his greatest westerns, he was building on the images Curtis had produced in the Navajo living room: people dwarfed by cloud-piercing rock walls and spires in the open West. On the 1906 trip, Curtis was looking for just enough to fill out the rest of the first book, with Day helping to find subjects. "We made camp in an oasis under cottonwood trees," Curtis wrote, and then cast about in search of faces that matched the terrain.

The sky was alive on those summer days. Afternoon temperatures of 105 degrees were broken by electric storms and flash floods, the warm-season monsoons of the Southwest. For the Curtis family of five, together at last in common purpose, the hours went by at a pleasant pace. Florence was impressed by her father the cook, who would procure fresh-butchered lamb from the Navajo and grill chops and corn over an open fire. With this meal he usually served squaw bread made by people in the canyon. On days when Justo wasn't up to it, Curtis would prepare a big feast from scratch for the entire team, including any natives who happened to be around. Their camp was always full of Navajos, the women in rippling skirts and blouses made of velvet, the men with bright scarves and thick, buckskin-soled shoes. "The Indians laughed inside and out," Curtis said, reflecting the joy he felt. Several hundred people lived full-time in the canyon, tending to gardens watered by freshets from the thunderstorms, while others moved through season-ally, in search of forage for sheep.

The Curtis children were fascinated by the turquoise jewelry makers, the rug weavers, the sheepherders, the storytellers, the colors and sounds of the canyon, with its sun-burnished walls of stone, the flanks streaked ocher and rust from the mineral-rich water. The girls wore sun hats and frocks; Hal was dressed like a cowboy. They rode mules and horses, collected horned frogs and small lizards, chased jackrabbits. They climbed the cliffs with Charlie Day and their father to get a peek at those haunted stone neighborhoods which had been abandoned eight hundred years earlier, and tried to decipher petroglyphs, some dating back nearly three millennia. In their eyes, the Shadow Catcher was the field general of all human activity in Canyon de Chelly. He worked the audio recording machine, with Myers taking shorthand. Songs, legends, words were catalogued. Curtis spoke enough of the language to force a smile from an old native. As a horseman and a cliff climber, he was a springy athlete. And the things that went on in the heat of the afternoon inside the tent—a makeshift studio—were magical.

He took pictures not just in the low-angled light of dawn and dusk, when "nearly right" was easy enough. Each hour of the sun could produce a different effect. He waited for opportune weather. And he never used a flash, at least not in the Southwest. "Conditions cannot be changed," Curtis explained. "I must fit myself to them."

One day in August, the canyon suddenly emptied of Indians, and a stillness fell over the big crack in the earth. Charlie Day told the family to stay close to camp and await his word. At night, the children heard chants bouncing along the thousand-foot-high walls around them. The chants lasted till dawn, though they saw no people. Curtis was at a loss to explain. When Day returned late at night, he said they were in trouble—they, the Anglos. A woman was trying to give birth not far from the Curtis encampment, but it was going badly. She was deep in labor, in terrible pain, bleeding profusely, but the infant would not emerge. Medicine men were summoned. They tried traditional remedies, to no avail. Then the Indians diagnosed the problem: it was the presence in the canyon of white people taking pictures. Curtis immediately woke his family and started heaving gear into the wagon. He told them they must leave immediately.

Groggy children snuggled in the wagon, their mumbled questions met by a shush from their father. Horses were hitched in the dark as the chanting continued. *Flee,* Charlie Day ordered—quickly and quietly, and do not make contact with anyone along the way.

"Pray the baby will live," said Day. "There is no power on earth that will save you and your family if it should die."

He was exaggerating, surely, but as a cautionary measure. For the first time in nearly eight years of concerted forays into Indian country, Curtis felt helpless and afraid, at the mercy of his photo subjects. The family rode out of the canyon, a long, tremulous climb, and made their way to Chinle, where word came through Day's contacts that the baby had lived. But what had started so blissfully for the family now broke down in a prolonged spat between Curtis and his wife. The children's lives had been put at risk. How could he have done that? Great Mystery indeed. What did he really know about these people? Curtis had no answers; it was a freakish thing, forget it. They would reassemble again in another part of Indian country, next year, and the year after. Let's not let this one episode ruin the good days. But Clara was adamant: never again would the entire family travel to Indian land. With the start of school approaching, Clara and the children left for Seattle. Curtis stayed behind.

"Everything has to be kept on the move," he said.

On to Third Mesa, in the Hopi Nation, where Curtis was in search of the Snake Society once more. Crossing scabbed and pockmarked tableland in late summer was full of peril. Washes, often bone-dry, could fill with red water in a flash, enough to float the wagon. Coming from the maritime Northwest, where rain fell as soft and persistent mist, Curtis was not used to such muscular meteorological mood changes. "The rain pours down," he said. "What was an arid desert when you made your evening camp is soon a lake . . . And then comes the sand storm. No horse can travel against it. If en route you can but turn your wagon to one side to furnish as much of a wind break as possible, throw a blanket over your head and wait for its passing. It may be two hours and it may be ten." Overall, though, joy outweighed the misery. And when he arrived at Old Oraibi, after a half-dozen previous visits, Curtis was greeted with smiles from familiar faces—and a major piece of good news. On an earlier trip he had been allowed to film the Snake Dance from a rooftop. Now Sikyaletstiwa agreed to let him participate in that most important, extended prayer for water. He could go with the priests to the fields to gather diamondback rattlesnakes, bring them to a kiva and tend them, and be a part of the culminating dance.

There was some calculation on the Hopi side. It had been a summer of unrest, with missionaries stepping up pressure to end the ritual and send Hopi children to a Christian school. As it was, the Tewa and Hopi people who lived on the reservation felt overwhelmed—and certainly surrounded—by the much larger Navajo population. Enlisting Curtis, at the height of his influence, could help the cause of the traditionalists. During his visit in 1905, Curtis had heard that members of the tiny Havasupai band to the north were dying of hunger. He promptly sent word to Commissioner Leupp in Washington, and starvation was averted (though tribal members continued to die from measles).

Curtis agreed to meet all requirements, and to perform his duties without balking. First came days of fasting, to purify himself. Then the priests stripped and painted their bodies in preparation for the snake hunt, which lasted four days. Those early hours in the field, Curtis faced a trial that would reveal the depth of his dedication. As the new priest, Curtis was told that he had a special task: to wrap the first captured snake around his neck. It was tradition, or so they told Curtis. The Indians picked up a big rattler and extended it to him. The snake hissed and bared its fangs, the scaly skin touching the sun-bronzed neck of Curtis. He remained motionless, steeling himself for the tightening around his throat, trying not to scare the rattler into biting him. After a few long minutes, the snake uncoiled and was removed from his neck. Curtis had passed his first test.

What he knew already was that the actual nine-day ceremony wasn't so much a dance, as it had been advertised by outfitters and the rail lines that brought tourists to witness the public part of the spectacle, but "a dramatized prayer," in Curtis's words. To the Hopi, snakes were messengers to the divine. The priests of the Snake Dance order were the facilitators. In the kiva, the curling and hissing rattlers were washed to make them clean for the Hopi prayer. For nine nights, Curtis slept within a few feet of the snakes, either in the kiva or on the rim of the dugout home. On the day of the big dance, a congregant smeared paint on his cheeks, his forehead, his neck, chest and back. He removed all his clothes and dressed in a simple cloth covering his genitals. Crowds massed along the edge of the village, tourists and natives, ten deep in places. The snakes were lifted from the kiva to a central place. The crowd moved in tighter. Priests began to dance, picking snakes as partners, singing prayers and incantations. Curtis, waiting in the wings, held back, hiding from view. At the last moment, he balked. He knew the audience was stocked with missionaries and government agents; he could tell by looking at them, taking notes for possible prosecution. He recognized Anglo faces. His presence, the great Shadow Catcher, the first white man ever allowed to participate as a priest in the Snake Dance order, would be widely disparaged in official circles and reported in the popular press. After six visits, over six years, studying and photographing every part of the ceremony, getting to know the religious leaders and then becoming a priest himself — at this culmination of his quest he worried that, should he take the final step, he might undermine the most significant event of the Hopi religion.

"I was fortunate enough to be able to go through the whole snake ceremony," he wrote his editor Hodge, ". . . in fact doing everything that a Snake man would do except take part in the Snake dance. The only reason I did not do this was because I feared newspaper publicity and missionary criticism." He was also troubled by the earlier events of the summer. What had happened to Goshonné, the Apache medicine man, after he had spilled the secrets of the tribe's creation myths, and the scare of the last day in Canyon de Chelly, had told Curtis much about the balancing act of his work. He had gone deep into the culture of a people that Americans had never understood, deep enough to realize — even at this moment of triumph — that there were places where he did not belong.

Before the Storm—Apache, 1906. In the arid high country of Arizona Territory, Curtis spent many months trying to capture Apache moments. Told the Apache had no religion, he was determined to prove otherwise.

8

THE ARTIST AND HIS AUDIENCE
1907

CURTIS WINCED AT the stabbing questions of a writer facing the most terrifying of prospects: a blank page. Where to begin? How to tell the story? What exactly was he trying to say? Had his sole job been the photographer assembling an epic of images, it would have been much simpler. But words were something else. He'd been published in *Scribner's*, yes, and a handful of other magazines, and had given enough lectures to be confident he could hold an audience rapt. With the first book, he had to reach for something sturdy and authoritative, and that realization brought on writer's block. As Morgan had said, he was best suited to put down the words; he was the "photo-historian," so called by the newspapers, a dual responsibility — too much, perhaps. He forced pen to paper now under the lengthening shadows of thick oaks in Arizona, late in a season that had taken him from the Apache homes in the White Mountains to the Jicarilla Apache communities in New Mexico, with numerous other stops in between.

THE NORTH AMERICAN INDIAN
Being a series of volumes picturing and describing
the Indians of the United States and Alaska, written,
illustrated and published by Edward S. Curtis.

That was easy enough. He gave credit to Roosevelt, Hodge and J. P. Morgan on the title page. Myers, Phillips and Muhr were thanked inside. He noted that "the task" had its inception in 1898. But enough explaining and thanking; no one cared how the milk got to the porch. Once more—where to begin? So much to tell. So much to show. As a distraction, Curtis dashed off a letter to his patron, without mentioning his labor pains. "All goes well with the field work, and a year from now should see the first volumes completed and off the press." Oh, to be on the other side of the creation, looking back. He added a statement of intent, just enough to give Morgan a flavor of what was to come. The work would surely be "scientific" (that word again) but "not dry," as everything that came before it, by implication, had been. Was such a hybrid even possible? Above all, as he had explained to Morgan at 23 Wall Street, his ambition was to do something that might be worthy of display alongside the scribbled baubles in the banker's manuscript collection. Those literary treasures had just been moved into Morgan's new library, an interior space so stunning the London *Times* had called it "one of the wonders of the world" and compared him to Lorenzo the Magnificent, the Medici benefactor.

Morgan had other things on his mind. He was preparing for a six-month trip to Europe, a leisurely pursuit of some of the very Florentine masterpieces commissioned by Il Magnifico himself. As he was set to go, the stock market tanked. It was nothing he hadn't seen before. After hitting a high of 103 in the early part of 1906, the Dow Jones Industrial Average fell about 20 percent, and a recession knocked millions of people out of work. A scheme by copper barons to control that market was collapsing, forcing other commodity prices down. Morgan's riches had been made on superb timing: buy low in a panic, sell high in a bubble, look for efficiencies; why have two rail companies operating a line to Buffalo when a consolidated single one would do? Morgan had stakes in most of the troubled markets but, nearing his seventieth birthday, was inclined to take the long view. He sailed for Europe.

Curtis started in again with the introduction for Volume I, his muse arriving at last from the outdoors. "At the moment, I am seated by a beautiful brook that bounds through the forests of Apache land. Numberless birds are singing their songs of life and love. Within my reach lies a tree, felled only last night by a beaver . . ." That felt right: the words, like the pictures, must spring from the earth itself. "Nature tells the story," he continued, the light from his candles receding, wax falling to the tent floor. Though he would herewith record group histories, as one might explain Viking clans and their many battles, the goal of this narrative of small nations was to tell them from the point of view of the land and the Indian.

"It is thus near to Nature that much of the life of the Indian still is; hence its story, rather than being replete with statistics of commercial conquest, is a record of the Indian's relations with and his dependence on the phenomena of the universe—the trees and shrubs, the sun and stars, the lightning and rain—for these to him are animate creatures. Even more than that, they are deified . . . While primarily a photographer, I do not see or think photographically; hence the story of Indian life will not be told in microscopic detail, but rather will be presented as a broad and luminous picture."

Snow forced the Curtis party indoors in the final days of 1906, a year when he had been away from home for nine months. In the last few weeks of their fieldwork, the team had gone to Montana and the Dakotas to hire translators, and then returned to the Southwest for a tour up the Colorado River by primitive steamship, starting in the Mojave Desert. That end-of-year sortie was an examination of small desert tribes that would appear in Volume II—Pima, Papago, Yuma and related bands, scattered and largely landless, but bound by life under a broiling sun. Some of the people looked as desiccated to Curtis as a field that had not seen rain for months.

In Arizona at year's end, Curtis rented a couple of boarding rooms and holed up with Myers and Phillips for a winter of writing and sorting pictures. Away from saloons and cities, restaurants and churches, sporting events and family dinner tables, the Curtis party would have few distractions. "Not even our family knew our whereabouts," Curtis wrote to Morgan. The mail came a few times a week. Curtis cooked and went for walks. They labored over language and images, filling out and refining Volume I, drafting and sketching Volume II. Curtis was helped immensely by the economical prose that Myers had picked up as a newspaperman in the factories of early-century journalism, which allowed no room for writer's block. Myers found the words when Curtis could not. And he respected a deadline. When something was ready to be released from the Arizona cloister, it was sent to Washington, where Frederick Webb Hodge edited and vetted. The western crew worked for nearly three months, usually seventeen hours a day, no time off, not even Sundays. After some debate between Curtis and Hodge over how many of the crimes against Indians would be detailed, if at all, Curtis stuck with his initial vow not to rehash the woeful history. Still, after seeing so much of Indian country in decline, he could not resist a dig or two.

"Though the treatment accorded the Indians by those who lay claim to civilization and Christianity has in many cases been worse than criminal, a rehearsal of those wrongs does not properly find a place here," he wrote in Volume I. He saved his loftiest passages, as in his magazine journalism, for native spirituality. "Ever since the days of Columbus the assertion has been made repeatedly that the Indian has no religion and no code of ethics, chiefly for the reason that in his primitive state he recognizes no supreme God. Yet the fact remains that no people have a more elaborate religious system than our aborigines, and none are more devout in their performance of the duties connected therewith. There is scarcely an act in the Indian's life that does not involve some ceremonial performance or is not in itself a religious act."

Hodge loved the introduction, changing very little, but insisted on accuracy for things such as accent marks and pronunciation guides. His many queries on small details sent Myers shuffling through the field notes and audio recordings, and shooting questions to academics who were willing to help. Approval also came from President Roosevelt, editor without pay in the employ of Curtis. The president particularly liked the general theme, which Curtis brought home in the final words of the introduction—a justification for the manic pace of his life over the past nine years.

"The passing of every old man or woman means the passing of some tradition, some knowledge of sacred rights possessed by no other; consequently the information that is to be gathered, for the benefit of future generations, respecting the mode of life of one of the great races of mankind, must be collected at once or the opportunity will be lost for all time. It is this need that has inspired the present task."

In New York, starting in the spring of 1907, Curtis went hat in hand to solicit subscriptions from wealthy American institutions. He hated this drudgery—begging from the rich. There was the question of his background. Where had he gone to school? Who was his father? Are you sure Mr. Harriman will vouch for you? And just how involved is Mr. Morgan? In Manhattan, he was not the Shadow Catcher cajoling snake handlers and looking for faces in a storm. He was a salesman, a huckster of a grand history but huckster nonetheless, expected eventually to sell a full five hundred subscriptions. To date, he had commitments for only a few dozen. He needed $3,000 for each twenty-volume set, exact publication dates to be determined later. That price, of course, was the low end. But if the culture brokers shared his sense of urgency, as some of them said they did, they did not extend it with their checkbooks. Time and again, the door was closed in the photographer's face with the same response: he had the backing of J. P. Morgan, what more could he need? Let the world's richest banker pay for everything, as he had promised, yes?

It helped little to explain that Morgan's money financed only the fieldwork. And even that, it was already clear after less a year, would not be enough. A single month in Arizona had cost Curtis more than $5,000. Worse, it was not a good time to persuade the rich to unburden themselves with philanthropic ventures. Indians, *gad*—interesting, to a point. Stocks fell steadily through the first months of the year, after a selloff in the previous quarter. Commodity markets continued to collapse. Brokerage houses, having made speculative bets on margin, closed down. Interest rates soared. The economy ground to a halt. It was, in the parlance of those episodes when capitalism got very sick, very quickly, a panic. The one in 1907 was called the Bankers' Panic.

"Things here in New York are strictly Hell," Curtis wrote Professor Meany in Seattle, "and what the future is to be no one seems to want to guess. The book building, however, is moving along nicely."

Curtis was already obsessing over the subject of the next volume: the Sioux. Big parts of Minnesota, the Dakotas and Montana had been shaped by the many bands of the defiant Sioux, bison hunters and warriors who gave nothing to the easy-sketch historians trying to romanticize them at century's end. Curtis had started working with the Sioux in 1905 — "they got into my brain and I cannot shake it off." While on the northern plains, he had picked up a considerable amount of first-hand information about the final battle of George Armstrong Custer. What he heard from the Indians did not match the story that had made him a doomed hero among whites. The Sioux and the Crow — one tribe attacking Custer's men, the other serving as scouts for him — who had survived the Battle of the Little Bighorn in 1876 had valuable eyewitness accounts to impart. Nobody had done an exhaustive retracing from the Indian view.

It had been while walking the Custer battleground in 1905, following in the steps of those who took scalps and those who gave up scalps, that Curtis kept hearing of a man, Alexander Upshaw, who had a strange hold on people in the region. A full-blooded Crow, Upshaw was educated at Carlisle Indian Industrial School in Pennsylvania, the rough finishing institution for natives and the place where Curtis had first met Geronimo. After his graduation in 1897, Upshaw was hired as a school-teacher at the Indian school in Genoa, Nebraska, but did not feel comfortable as a man of two worlds. Thereafter, he never stayed long in a job; by his thirtieth birthday he was back among his people on the Crow reservation in Montana, working uneven hours as a surveyor, translator, rancher and tribal advocate.

The whites called him "lazy, dishonest, meddlesome, here today and there tomorrow, a regular coyote," as the Curtis aide Phillips remembered. They didn't like Upshaw because he spoke well, could argue the law and was a frequent witness in court cases where the Crow were fending off speculators buying big pieces of Indian land in questionable deals. Curtis and Phillips spent more than a week looking for him in that first year among the people of the northern plains, hearing stories of "Upshaw the Terrible" and "Upshaw the Renegade." When at last they found Upshaw the Available, they put him on the payroll.

As Curtis prepared for the 1907 field season, he assigned Upshaw to crack the Custer story, ordering him to get at what really happened, no matter how it might conflict with the iconic version. At about the same time, Professor Meany, who'd studied and written about Sioux history, agreed to come aboard for that part of the project. Meany's other task, hustling a subscription or two in Seattle, had not gone well. He was embarrassed to report to Curtis that his school, the University of Washington, had yet to commit itself to a full set. But not to worry, Meany assured him, his brilliance would soon be known to all. Curtis remained troubled: American appraisals always came with dollar signs. He would be a nobody if he went broke.

"It matters not how much good work I might do," Curtis replied. "If I were out of money I would be cursed for a fool and kicked from every door." Even the one family member who worked with him daily, the worshipful Phillips, had his doubts that Curtis could do twenty volumes in five years, or ten, and still cover his bills.

"You are insanely optimistic!" Phillips told his boss in a fit of voice-elevated candor.

The nation's attic, the Smithsonian, dealt another setback. Undeterred by the previous rejection, Curtis had pressed a well-connected intermediary into asking yet again for the stamp of the institution on the immense cataloguing and photographing of the country's first people. For a second time, the Smithsonian authorities said no, and now they threw water on the scope of his work. "It appears that Mr. Curtis's original idea has become very much expanded," wrote the secretary of the Smithsonian, Charles Walcott. "As you are well aware, it will not do to claim too much for such a publication; otherwise it will get the general condemnation of all interested in the subject." Curtis got the message: think small. Brown University, one of the prestige colleges that Curtis had hoped would buy a full subscription, also snubbed him, after the school's resident Indian authority opposed the library's acquisition. The expert, it seems, had never heard of Curtis. They would regret it, Curtis vowed. "By the time I get through with the Southwest country I will have so much to say that no library can refuse us," he wrote Hodge.

What lifted Curtis's spirits and gave him a tailwind of confidence that lasted many months was an endorsement from a much higher source: the president of the United States, no slouch among scholars. His foreword to *The North American Indian* had arrived months before the unofficial deadline. The words from the White House matched the image Curtis had of himself—produced without coaching or cajoling. Roosevelt *got it*. And Roosevelt got Curtis.

The president was not much of a stylist, despite having published nearly twenty books by his fortieth birthday. He repeated words and phrases, a habit used in speechmaking that often found its way into writings that called for more subtlety. And, as he frequently contributed to journals, he could be thick with the insider jargon. The foreword, a spare 350 words or so, was none of that:

> In Mr. Curtis we have both an artist and a trained observer, whose pictures are pictures, not merely photographs; whose work has far more than mere accuracy, because it is truthful. All serious students are to be congratulated because he is putting his work in permanent form; for our generation offers the last chance for doing what Mr. Curtis has done. The Indian as he has hitherto been is on the point of passing away. His life has been lived under conditions through which our own race passed so many ages ago that not a vestige of their memory remains. It would be a veritable calamity if a vivid and truthful record of these conditions were not kept. No one man alone could preserve such a record in complete form. Others have worked in the past, and are working in the present, to preserve parts of the record; but Mr. Curtis, because of the singular combination of his qualities with which he has been blest, and because of his extraordinary success in making and using his opportunities, has been able to do what no other man has ever done; what, as far as we can see, no other man could do. He is an artist who works out of doors and not in the closet. He is a close observer, whose qualities of mind and body fit him to make his observations out in the field, surrounded by the wild life he commemorates. He has lived on intimate terms with many different tribes of the mountains and the plains. He knows them as they hunt, as they travel, as they go about their various avocations on the march and in the camp. He knows their medicine

men and their sorcerers, their chiefs and warriors, their young men and maidens. He has not only seen their vigorous outward existence, but has caught glimpses, such as few white men ever catch, into that strange spiritual and mental life of theirs; from whose innermost recesses all white men are forever barred. Mr. Curtis in publishing this book is rendering a real and great service; a service not only to our own people, but to the world of scholarship everywhere.

Some would quibble with, even condemn, the cultural superiority inherent in Roosevelt's take: the poor Indians, living as whites once did during a long-ago primitive age, are passing away, and as they go, they remain unknowable, with "that strange spiritual and mental life of theirs." But for an understanding of the value of the work, the foreword could not have been better had Curtis written it himself. The president had called him an artist, an outdoorsman, a visionary; he hailed the scholarly depth — *take that, you bastards at the Smithsonian and Brown!* — and its significance to a nation that was in the habit of erasing its past.

The picture-making, just like the picture-taking, left something to chance. In his studio, working with the fast-fingered Adolph Muhr, Curtis would throw together a brew of developing chemicals in the same way that a winemaker would blend different grapes to bring out tannins and flavors. Deep in a day, he often lost track of what parts had gone into a particular blend. "I have almost forgotten that they are an essential part of photography," he told a college class. "For every negative that is a disappointment, there is one that is a joy." He refined an image, trying to bring more light or shade, to frame smaller or larger, to blur a certain face or show its every crag, to burn a halo effect behind a head or darken a background. In Seattle, they toned, printed, engraved, "night after night until the last cable car jangled its call as it slid down the hill to its terminus," said Phillips. Muhr was no rubber stamp, but he was in thrall to the work, and brought others in to make it even better. He hired a woman just out of the University of Washington, Imogen Cunningham, and she wasted no time testing the limits of this emerging art form. In college she had majored in chemistry, then traveled to Germany to study photography. Cunningham, like Curtis, loved to dare and shock; she had taken photographs of nude subjects at Mount Rainier, and explored dream states and subconscious themes in her prints. She saw in Curtis someone on par with the mighty Stieglitz, who had formed the Photo-Secession group to promote the artistic merits of photography. Stieglitz and his followers used darkroom techniques to soften a subject, or blur an image in a reach for abstraction. Curtis had been doing that since he started his studio work, and his lens was often little more than an opaque veil. Many a viewer perceived painterly metaphors and objects freighted with symbolism. "And the photographs themselves, quite apart from their historic and scientific value, show a fresh, far step in the progress of photography into the realm of fine arts," wrote a reviewer in the *Craftsman*. "Mr. Curtis has so far improved on old methods of printing and finishing as to have practically invented processes in photographic presentation. His tones, his rough surfaced papers, his color combinations are a new art, or a new science." Curtis dismissed talk from the avant-garde with his oft-stated goal: he wanted people to see human beings in the faces of Indians, and he wanted those faces to live forever.

The first pictures selected for *The North American Indian* implied that the only way Indians would find eternal life was through a Curtis lens. Of course, this would boost the value of his pictures — wishful thinking with a profit motive. In the studio, looking for the picture that was emblematic of his theme, Curtis returned to an image he had taken while wandering in Canyon de Chelly in 1904. Then, he had shot several ground-level stills of a few natives on horseback moving away from the camera — a retreat, with one person looking back, as in a last glance at a homeland. Curtis had deliberately underexposed it in the field, to give it a bit of a gauzy blur. But back in Seattle, making the print for Volume I, he wasn't satisfied with the light. He and Muhr stayed up all night experimenting with exposures and tones, using different chemical batches. One was too dark. The other too refined. One looked phony, polished. The other too removed. One had too much detail, the frame cluttered. Another was too gauzy. Curtis wanted a sprinkling of sunlight coming off the backs of people as they moved away, but not show so much that it might draw the eye away from the main image. The Indians traveled toward a mesa, or a mountain range; it was too dark to make it out, distant and blurred. By dawn's break, the heavy lifting in the studio was over: *Vanishing Race* would be the curtain raiser in the separate portfolio of photogravures that accompanied the bound text and pictures of Volume I. Curtis offered this caption: "The thought which this picture is meant to convey is that the Indians as a race, already shorn of their tribal strength and stripped of their primitive dress, are passing into the darkness of an unknown future." In a letter to a friend in Seattle, he called it "a touching melancholy poem."

The second picture chosen for the portfolio was the side-view profile of Geronimo, which countered the soft-focus valedictory of *Vanishing Race* with defiance. It was meant to be a taunting eulogy, not unlike Chief Seattle's imagined words, "Our people are ebbing away like a rapidly receding tide that will never return." And Geronimo's portrait validated the self-image of Americans who had pressed farms, villages and great iron cities into pastoral pockets of the former Indian homeland: the decline of one people was inevitable, no matter how many virtues were being discovered on the deathbed.

Within the smooth-textured leather binding of Volume I were pictures that were less gloomy, though still intended to trouble the mind. Curtis opened with *The Pool—Apache*, a visual complement to his words defining people through nature. A nearly naked man, hair falling well below his shoulders, stands barefoot on rocks at the edge of a calm river. The water is a mirror, and the countryside is lush. The Apache man appears to be deep in thought. Throughout the rest of the book, water is a repeat motif. Curtis fought with Hodge over whether to include several nudes, which he believed could best illustrate tribal myths, dreams and stories. Curtis insisted that the way to explain a part of the Indian inner world was "to make the most of the nudes." But Hodge, perhaps fearing a censorious reaction from buttoned-down colleagues, prevailed: in the end, only partial nudes were included.

The facial close-ups, with Curtis the portrait photographer at the top of his game, are less affected, and in an odd way more natural and journalistic, from the infant with bright cheeks, *An Apache Babe*, to *Escadi*, an Apache headman. His portrait of Alchise, bare-chested and leaning against a tree, shows a fifty-five-year-old man who has lived many lives. In the long shots, the land dwarfs the humans. *A Hilltop Camp—Jicarilla* provides a sense of what it's like to reside on a bluff when a mountain storm approaches. But it is with the pictures of the Navajo that the oversized rock backdrops play a starring role. *Cañon de Chelly* and *Cañon del Muerto* are mash-ups of sky, sandstone and mountain flanks, predating Ansel Adams with their shadow work and textural detail. *Sunset in Navajo-Land* is a black-and-white composition put to dramatic effect without being too precious. *Women of the Desert* makes everyday heroes of the Navajo mothers who tend flocks of sheep over stubby land that dares people to scratch a living from it. Other Navajos are fully masked, the camera catching the contrast between muscled torso and wildlife-animated facial hoods. The religious rituals that Curtis was so proud of capturing are presented like trophies: the *Apache Medicine Man* leans over what appears to be the sacred buckskin creation chart, and *Yeibichai Sweat* is the precursor to the Navajo ceremony that the men of the Smithsonian said could never be photographed.

Curtis wrote the text as if he had just returned from a visit to Homer's Greece, attempting to explain nations and their mythic stories, complete with a translation guide to languages not taught in American schools. As with the ancient Greeks and Romans, he wrote, the Indians have "a deity for every occasion and hour." He divided the book into sections on tribal history, home life, mythology and interpretations of certain ceremonies. He didn't just summarize a particular myth of, say, the origin of fire, but wrote exhaustive essays on the subjects. The story of Goshonné took up two pages. Marriage between related families was strictly prohibited, he wrote, and "it kept their blood at the very best." Men who had two wives, a common practice, made sure the women lived far apart from each other. He talked about the Apache sense of humor—pranks, practical jokes, gut-busting laugh sessions. "Surely, he who says the American Indian is morose, stolid and devoid of humor never knew him in the intimacy of his own home."

The Apache reputation for being "wild" came about largely because they had been nomadic and had developed raiding into an economic skill. He tried to counter the stereotype, again, with an appreciation of their spiritual life: "Nothing could be more logical and beautiful than many of their prayers and songs."

The various diets were explained, the food ranging from grapes and piñon nuts to deer and chipmunk. So were the Indians' sex lives and property rights, and the role of women, children and the elderly. Perhaps most astonishing, for a man who by trade was a studio photographer, was his lengthy appendix of the different Athapaskan dialects among the Southwest tribes. With considerable help from Myers, he wrote up a comparative chart showing the English, Apache, Jicarilla and Navajo pronunciations for a given word.

He labored throughout with the meaning of "savage" and "primitive," words used by even the most sympathetic of early-twentieth-century anthropologists to describe Indians. "There are two sides to the story and in these volumes such questions must be treated with impartiality," he wrote. In this struggle, Curtis went back and forth with the Crow translator in his crew, Alexander Upshaw, who clearly influenced him. Upshaw was conflicted throughout his life. In a picture at the Carlisle Indian School, he wears a dress shirt and pressed pants, with his hair cut short and parted in the middle, the very image of assimilation. He also wrote an essay for the school newspaper arguing the merits of giving up the old ways and learning to live like a white, titled "What the Indians Owe to the United States Government." But once he moved back home and went to work for Curtis, Upshaw took up the cause of tribal rights; he seemed to "return to the blanket," as Phillips described it. He posed without a shirt and in a head bonnet. He fought with the Bureau of Indian Affairs, even when he worked for it.

As Curtis went over his notes one night in Montana, not long after hiring Upshaw, the conversation moved to the idea of an "educated Indian" compared with those who refused schooling. A government agent who sat with them, as federal interlopers often did when trying to keep an eye on Curtis, asked the Crow interpreter why his people didn't show much of an American work ethic. Upshaw rose, pointing to a row of buffalo skulls lining a cabin shelf.

"They tell you why," he said. "While those buffaloes were alive we did not need to work. Only niggers and white people farmed. We were a superior people and had nothing but contempt for those who worked." The government man mumbled something about other tribal members who had successfully taken up the hoe and the merchant's life. "Do you expect us in the fraction of a lifetime, in the quarter of the age of an old man, to have changed our whole life, and even to have forgotten the days of the old freedom, when we were lords of all the great plains and mountains?" said Upshaw. "In what way does your civilization benefit us? Before you had attempted to force your so-called civilization upon us we had every desire of the heart!" Curtis took Upshaw's side of the argument, but the translator wasn't through. "What has your civilization done for us? Robbed us of our land, our strength, our dignity, our content. Even your religion has robbed us of our confidence in the hereafter."

With Upshaw's words rattling around his head, Curtis tried to find a middle ground. Privately, his thoughts were moving toward those of his Crow crew member. "As to his being a savage: if we are to take the general definition of the word, there were no savages in North America at the time Columbus landed, as they all had a religion, notwithstanding statements to the contrary by the early explorers and priests," he wrote in a note from the field for the Morgan archives. In the published book of Volume I, he editorialized in places, despite his promise not to revisit the many indignities. "With advancing civilization," Curtis wrote of the Apache, "they seem to have gathered all the evils of our life and taken little of the good." By contrast, the Navajo "have been the least affected by civilizing influences," he said in a tone that was clearly celebratory. "The Navajo is the American Bedouin, the chief human touch in the great plateau-desert region of our Southwest, acknowledging no superior, paying allegiance to no king in name of chief, a keeper of flocks and herds who asks nothing of the Government but to be unmolested in his pastoral life and the religion of his forebears."

He scorned government agents for trying to force the mountainous Apache to become farmers, an absurd proposition in a harsh land. "No tribe is more capable of living on natural products." And he did use both "primitive" and "savage," though with the first word it was almost always as a compliment, and the second was employed to describe bounty hunters paid by the Mexican government to lift Apache scalps — women's and children's included. In the end, the book was mostly practical and matter-of-fact. For instance, he gave a recipe for how to make strong beer from mescal, the Apache way.

Curtis decamped to New York, to the Hotel Belmont, just across the street from Grand Central Terminal, for the final publishing push in June of 1907. "I have the material for the first two volumes practically in shape and will be able to turn it over to the printers in the near future," he wrote Morgan. The financier was still in Europe, buying art and precious objects with his latest mistress, as a crumbling stock market prompted urgent cables for his return to New York. In Italy, he was a walking bank. Even in the shrine city of Assisi, Franciscan monks who had taken a vow of poverty tried to entice Morgan to share some of his fortune on their behalf. He bought an autograph manuscript of Beethoven's last violin sonata (No. 10 in G Major), and focused his freight-train gaze on a number of Botticelli paintings.

In Morgan's absence, young Belle da Costa Greene handled correspondence and controlled acquisitions for the library. She had moved her office to the new marble and limestone palace, and with her active social life was a frequent subject of gossip in the papers. "I've come to the conclusion that it really must be grudgingly admitted that I am the most interesting person in New York," she wrote, "for it's all they seem to talk about." Pleaders from all levels of the arts world made frequent calls. Curtis saw Greene in New York, and though he may have been as intoxicated as anyone in her presence, his correspondence with her in 1907 was all business. As per their agreement, he presented Miss Greene with the master prints and promised twenty-five copies of the first volume at year's end.

With the evanescent Belle Greene, with Harriman and his crowd in Manhattan, with Roosevelt and Pinchot in Washington, with the gentlemen of the National Geographic Society and others who put on black ties and silk gowns to look at lantern slides of Indians in buckskin, Edward Curtis was a man without a breath of doubt — the tall, reservation-trotting, horse-whispering westerner in his Abercrombie and Fitch. But to his few close friends, Curtis was a different man, still not completely free of the homesteader's shack and the humility of foraging to make a living. He distrusted scholars in particular, and it seemed as if everyone he encountered in academia knew he was a grade school dropout. The exception was Professor Meany, who shared all of Curtis's enthusiasms and none of his insecurities. At a moment just before publication, when Curtis should have been at his most confident, he told Meany he wondered if he was up to this task and expressed fear, again, of ending up in debtor's hell. The biggest educational institution in the Northwest, the University of Washington, continued to balk at buying a subscription for the work of its native son. The same was true of a handful of Seattle barons, men who had made themselves wealthy in the early-century boom of one of the fastest-growing cities in the world.

"Of late I have had little but swats from my home town and feel in a most disagreeable mood," Curtis wrote Meany in a lengthy, multi-page rant. "Most of those who say good things about the work would if I owed them two and a half and could not pay on the dot kick my ass and say, 'Get to hell out of this.' Yes, I will try to cheer up a bit, but when I think of some of the Seattle bunch I go mad. I am an unknown man trying by sheer bulldog tenacity to carry through a thing so large that no one else cared to tackle it." Meany again assured him that time would be his ally—the ages would remember him, even if the wealthy of his hometown would not. "The newly rich of Seattle," Meany wrote Curtis, "are foolish enough to neglect the chance of aiding one of the greatest literary achievements of the century." His advice was to ignore them, to get back into the field as soon as possible, to "just run along and play."

But before he could play, he had to sell at least a handful of subscriptions. In Chicago, he visited Edward Ayers, a man of means and a founder of the city's prestigious Field Museum. Ayers considered himself an expert on Indians and also was the main benefactor of the museum's library—not a good combination, in Curtis's experience. *The North American Indian* should have been a natural acquisition for him.

But Ayers turned up his nose at the photographer. He doubted that Curtis could break any new ground with the text; perhaps the pictures would be diverting. And, as Curtis had heard many a time, he'd bitten off more than he could chew. Ayers "thinks I have attempted too big a task for one man, saying, 'It looks to me as though you were trying to do 50 men's work,'" Curtis wrote Hodge. He hoped his editor could use his influence among the small circle of museum executives to nudge the Chicago man along. Ayers was unconvinced. "After 30 years in studying this question, and the mass of literature I have read on the subject, I am still in doubt about the value of the historical part of your work," he wrote.

Besides that doubt, Ayers had to be concerned about the chilling effects of the Panic of 1907. In the fall, the country appeared on the verge of collapse. Roosevelt was perplexed. The markets continued to plummet. A global credit shortage added to the deep freeze. Morgan steamed home, his latest acquisitions in steerage. He summoned the richest men in the nation, Rockefellers, Fricks and Guggenheims among them, to his library for a summit on how to save capitalism. Under the eyes of Renaissance portraits, and facing Morgan's mottled nose, the choreographers of great capital listened to his plan. In order to stop the Bankers' Panic they had to stall the run on banks. He threatened to go after brokers who short-sold stock, trying to drive down prices for later purchase. He pledged to use his own money to shore up the banking system, urging others to follow suit. When they did so, after a nervous few weeks, confidence slowly returned to the markets. Morgan, performing the role that the Federal Reserve would play later, had saved the system, for now.

In the depths of the crisis, Curtis prepared to see his benefactor and present him with a collection he hoped would rival anything Morgan dragged home from Europe. With Myers and Phillips wandering over fresh territory in the West, the business end of the Curtis project moved into the "publication office" of *The North American Indian* in New York. There, Curtis spent many a night in rumpled clothes, at times falling asleep after a long tussle over his finances and the direction of his life work. He wrote to Morgan that he'd been through quite a bit of "blood sweating" bringing the first two volumes to the finish line, "but I'm glad to say, no delay." He outlined the work ahead with the Sioux and beyond, and reiterated his gratitude. The fact that Morgan could bother with Indian pictures when the global financial system and a big part of the Morgan empire were on the verge of ruin was not lost on Curtis. "I hesitate in troubling you with even the briefest letter in hours like these when you seem to have the burden of the whole land to carry. And let me say what millions know and would like to clasp your hand and say to you: you have saved the country when no one else could." Whether Belle da Costa Greene passed the note on to Morgan is not clear. He said nothing in reply.

Curtis was used to getting good press. But when two volumes printed on handmade Dutch etching stock called Van Gelder and a thin Japanese vellum — one of 161 pages, 79 photogravure plates and a portfolio of 39 separate plates, the other of 142 pages, 75 plates and 35 of the supplemental pictures — at last came to light in late 1907 and early 1908, the acclaim was seismic. In appearance and texture, the books were among the most luxurious ever printed. The images were done in sepia tones, from acid-etched copper plates produced by John Andrew & Son in Boston and printed by Cambridge University Press. Critics hailed a genius who made publishing history. His pictures were better than fine oil paintings. His text would be used for hundreds of years to come — a literary, artistic, historical masterpiece.

"Nothing just like it has ever before been attempted for any people," said the *New York Times*. "He has made text and pictures interpret each other, and both together present a more vivid, faithful and comprehensive view of the North American Indian as he is to-day than has ever been made before or can possibly be made again . . . In artistic value the photogravures are worthy of very great praise. They are beautiful reproductions of photographs that in themselves are works of art . . . And when it all is finished it will be a monumental work, marvelous for the unstinted care and labor and pains that have gone into the making, remarkable for the beauty of its final embodiment, and highly important because of its historical and ethnographic value."

A rival paper went further. "The most gigantic undertaking since the making of the King James edition of the Bible," said the *New York Herald*. "The real, savage Indian is fast disappearing or becoming metamorphosed into a mere ordinary, uninteresting imitation of the white man. It is probably safe to say that Mr. Curtis knows more about the real Indians than any other white man." And overseas, where that Bible had been recast, came similar waves of praise. The first two volumes "are among the finest specimens of the printer's art in the world," wrote the head of the Guildhall Library in London, which had purchased set number 7. "One special reason why the photographs will be more appreciated in England perhaps than America is because *The North American Indian* is more of a novelty to us."

Curtis was put on the same pedestal as John James Audubon and George Catlin. "We do not recall any enterprise of a literary sort ever undertaken in America that can compare for splendor of typography and for historical value with that which is just now undertaken by Mr. Edward S. Curtis," wrote the *Independent*, an American paper. "For contents, the work recalls no other similar enterprise but Audubon's monumental 'Birds of America.'"

From Chicago, where Curtis had struck out with the founder of the Field Museum, more kudos rolled his way. "It is the most wonderful publishing enterprise ever undertaken in America," wrote *Unity Magazine*. "If it ever comes our turn to vacate the continent, may we have as able an interpreter and as kindly and skillful an artist to preserve us for the great future."

In this case, superlative reviews meant nothing to the average reader, since the book was not for sale. It could not be found in any store, and could be seen in only a handful of libraries, by appointment. Morgan was sitting on twenty-five copies, a plurality of the original printing, for Curtis had failed to get anywhere near the number of subscriptions he needed. Curtis made sure that Belle da Costa Greene and President Roosevelt saw the notices. And in his letter to Hodge about the raves, he

apologized that he wouldn't be able to pay him, not just yet, the money
he owed for editing. Perhaps the reviews would help with a few reluctant institutions. In any event, Curtis had had his fill of the East Coast.
His mind was in Montana, and the Battle of the Little Bighorn, there for
the Indian side, yet to be told in full, a story that might destroy the reputation of an American hero.

Vanishing Race—Navajo, 1904. Curtis chose this scene as the curtain raiser for
his twenty volumes of portfolios—"a touching, melancholy poem," he called it.
It established the theme for his work, which the *New York Herald* called "the most
gigantic undertaking since the making of the King James edition of the Bible."

Geronimo — Apache, 1905. A few days before Roosevelt was inaugurated, Curtis caught the hard glare of the seventy-six-year-old leader of the Apache, who'd been invited to the White House for the grand ceremony launching T.R.'s second term.

Cañon de Chelly, 1904. In the heart of the Navajo Nation, where stone and sky dwarf humans on horseback, the canyon is one of the most stunning places on earth.

9

THE CUSTER CONUNDRUM
1907–1908

Hot sun on brown grass in a swollen corner of Montana: Curtis walked the graveyard yet again, site of the worst military loss by American soldiers in the West. He had been over the killing ground dozens of times, had asked the Crow scouts who'd been with George Armstrong Custer the same questions repeatedly, in only slightly different ways. The Indians begged off — they were tired of talking about the Battle of the Little Bighorn, recalling men who cried for their mothers, naked white-bellied bodies floating in the river, puddles of blood and gnarled sinew staining the dirt. How many times did they have to show the place — *yes, yes, this is where Custer stood!* — and swear it was the very spot where the commander of the Seventh Cavalry had taken his last breath? How many times would they have to summon those images of slaughter in the shadeless hills? The land drained by the Little Bighorn, with its grassy rise to the horizon, its river-sculpted fresh bottomland, its clusters of lodgepole pine and cottonwood, was not hard to like. In the winter, snowdrifts piled high against granite slabs where men had fallen; in the summer, wild floral heads nodded in afternoon breezes. But after the events of June 25, 1876, the ground could never again be just another fold of western land that might boost a spirit at sunset. Too many ghosts floated around, their final casting in the here-after yet to be sorted.

An examiner of forensics and long-buried facts, Curtis was midway through a third year of working this historical autopsy. Journeys to the Zuni and Acoma, to the Hopi and Apache, to the Pima and Mojave—he had undertaken them over the same years. But throughout that period, no question troubled Curtis more than this one. What really happened on that afternoon in 1876? Some wondered why he would devote so much time to a single battle. But the stated purpose of *The North American Indian* was to "form a comprehensive and permanent record" of the "customs and traditions" of native people, and few traditions among the Sioux were more important than violent conflict. And after four centuries of Indian wars—lethal clashes over ownership of a continent —the Battle of the Little Bighorn was the beginning of the end, to be followed a year later by the pathos of the Nez Perce's flight and then the last roundup of Comanche, Cheyenne and Apache stragglers.

In the summer of 1907, Curtis noticed some things and overlooked others. "The bleached bones of troop horses and pack mules" stood out, he wrote in his notebook, and made him wonder who rode those army animals, their ribs now whitened in the July sun. How had they fallen?

Curtis had with him three eyewitnesses—Hairy Moccasins, Goes Ahead and White Man Runs Him—superb sources, courtesy of the tireless work of Alexander Upshaw. All three were Crow natives, also known as Apsaroke, of late middle age, who had been with the commander of the Seventh Cavalry up until the final hour of his life. Custer's company was annihilated, of course. The Seventh lost 258 men. The three Crow guides and another Indian scout, Curley, had fled and lived. It was White Man Runs Him who was the first to reach another army column with the breathless report that Custer's force had been "wiped out."

Well into the early twentieth century, the popular story of Custer was much the same one that went out over telegraph lines not long af-ter his mutilated body was found. The timing of Custer's death—the height of America's centennial celebration—would not allow for nuance in the national narrative. He was the commander, all of thirty-six, who stood his ground against impossible odds, a legend while alive, a hero in death. This was the story boys read in school and acted out in the summer woods, one playing Custer to the other kid's Crazy Horse. This was the Last Stand invoked by politicians on the Fourth of July. A biography—with Custer doomed and fearless, and Major Marcus Reno, the commander of a routed side detachment, drunken and cowardly—matched the press coverage. This version was popularized by the Wild West Show of the peripatetic promoter Bill Cody. He milked it in out-door performances around the world, complete with an "authentic" re-enactment of the battle: circus Indians whooping over mismatched boys in blue. The last and most influential line of the legacy's defense was Custer's wife, the formidable Libbie, who guarded her husband's name like a wizened hawk sitting on a time-frozen nest. It was Libbie who first nagged the army into moving her husband's body from Montana dirt to an honored grave at West Point, and she who used a web of influential friends to silence anyone who dared depart from the story of his death. Yes, there had been a formal military inquiry, witnesses called, field notes reviewed. The main issue—how could a commander so misjudge the size of the enemy, thus inadvertently leading his soldiers to slaughter—was kicked around but never resolved. Custer's reputation was intact.

Early evening, with the sun's sting receding at last, Curtis moved his party uphill to a perch of level ground that afforded a broad, sweeping view of the Little Bighorn. He repeated every step in the staging leading up to the battle. "When the troops traveled slow, we did the same," Curtis wrote. "When they had halted, we halted. When the scouts went ahead, I waited where Custer had for the return of the scouts." Joining Curtis and the scouts were Upshaw, translating the Indian words, and Hal Curtis, age thirteen and endlessly entertained by the work of his father. Clara had come out to the northern plains as well—another attempt to be a part of her husband's life in Indian country. She stayed back at the larger camp on the Pine Ridge reservation, the Dakota home of the Rosebud Sioux Nation. Working with the Sioux and some Cheyenne, Curtis had conducted several rounds of interviews with veterans who took part in the fight. From them, he heard that Custer's eardrums were pierced by women before the blood on his face had dried, because he refused to listen. He was told of the bravery of Crazy Horse, who'd been swimming when the battle started, then had quickly mounted a horse and made several daring charges to split Custer's men. "Let us kill them all off today," he said, "that they may not trouble us anymore." And this rare victory was given the usual cast by the Americans: when Indians won, it was always a massacre.

Curtis had also walked the battlefield with these Indian victors, these still proud Sioux of the western subtribe who called themselves Lakota. He sat where bodies were found, pressing for information about strategy and intent. He recorded many anecdotes, the violent vignettes somewhat altered by time, but he wanted the bigger picture. "They could tell vividly of their actions," Curtis wrote, "but could give no comprehensive account of the actions as a whole." Already he had taken many pictures of the participants. He was fond of Red Hawk's portrait, his eyes full of tragedy, half his face obscured by a droopy war bonnet, and wrote that his "recollection of the fight seemed particularly clear." Red Hawk appeared to be fond of Curtis too, giving him the Sioux name of Pretty Butte. It was Red Hawk who posed for Curtis atop a white horse drinking water at a stop, the picture titled *An Oasis in the Badlands*. There, the ninety-one-year-old Red Hawk is shown on his mount with a rifle protruding from a simple saddle—a pose meant to convey that the Sioux still had some fight left in them. What Curtis saw in the Sioux was what rival tribes feared in them: a fine-honed tradition of war makers and buffalo chasers, scary good at bloodletting.

Now Curtis concentrated his work on the other side of the battle, those Indians who had worked for Custer, longtime enemies of the Sioux. The Crow feared the Sioux more than they did the whites. If captured by a Lakota, a Crow knew he would be facing mutilation, burning, eye-gouging and other forms of slow torture. So when Custer and his bluecoats arrived with cannons and rapid-firing guns, the Crow saw a chance for a permanent advantage in the northern plains. If the army could do something about another Crow enemy, the Cheyenne, it would further serve their purposes. The Crow scout White Man Runs Him had led the Curtis party up the Rosebud River, one rise over from the Little Bighorn, following the path where Custer broke from his main command on the Yellowstone. The party walked the easy miles to the divide, one side falling away to the river they had just followed, the other giving way to the bumpy valley of the battle. They dropped down a bit, to a lookout known as the Crow's Nest. It was here, said the scouts who had led Custer, that they first saw the Indians camped below. Most of them were Sioux under the guidance of Sitting Bull and Crazy Horse, though they had with them a sizable contingent of Cheyenne and Arapaho.

The Cheyenne had good reason to hate the Americans. Over three hundred years of contact with whites, from their migration out of the upper Mississippi headwaters, to the northern plains, to the eastern Rocky Mountains, the tribe had warred, traded and hunted their way to upward mobility. But then came the Sand Creek Massacre, on November 29, 1864, the most brutal slaughter of Indian innocents by U.S. combatants. A camp of about five hundred Cheyenne, almost all women, children and old people, had made a peace pact and were gathered under an American flag in Colorado when they were attacked by a former Methodist minister, J. M. Chivington, leading a volunteer army of drunks and malcontents. Curtis described what happened in Volume VI:

". . . practically all were scalped, and that women as well as men were so mutilated as to render description unprintable; that in at least one instance a woman was ripped open and her unborn child thrown by her side; that defenseless women, exposing their breasts to show their sex, and begging for mercy, were shot down with revolvers placed practically against their flesh; that hours after the attack, when there was not a militant Indian within miles of the camp, children were used as targets."

The Indian scalps were later displayed, to great whistling and applause, at an opera house in Denver. Four years later, Custer wiped out a village of Cheyenne on the Washita River. Approaching the Indians in that encounter, one of Custer's officers wondered what they would do if they found themselves outnumbered. "All I am afraid of is we won't find half enough," said Custer.

There were certainly more than enough Cheyenne and Sioux camped along the Little Bighorn. Women and children, thousands of ponies and hundreds of tipis made the gathering appear a vast, almost festive tent city of smoke, dust and chatter. About 5,000 Indians were in the valley, though the numbers varied in all accounts, and the scouts could not judge the size by what they had seen. Custer's men numbered 650 soldiers.

A bit closer to the Little Bighorn, Custer broke up his forces into three battalions. The prize was in his grasp; he was not about to let the enemy slip away and bring glory to some other commander in what might be the last battle of the Indian campaigns. One flank, under Major Reno, veered left and south, downward to the river, to cut off any escape. Another remained on higher ground. Custer moved in the general direction of the camp, though he stayed above the river, roughly parallel to it. In early afternoon, Reno ordered his men to battle. They charged into a thicket of small trees and brush, confronting women and children who appeared in a panic. The gunfire roused the warriors, who quickly massed. They swarmed Reno's men and set fire to the brush, pushing them into defensive positions in the timber. Reno was a brooding man, prone to drink during the day until he passed out at night. He and Custer, a teetotaler, despised each other. As it became apparent to Reno that his men would be routed, he ordered a retreat. His words are not carved in stone at West Point: "All those who wish to make their escape follow me!" It turned into a run-for-your-lives, desperation scramble, but it ultimately saved Reno and many of his men.

That story was not disputed. The military inquiry and several books and magazine accounts had drawn out the details, although the extent of Reno's alcoholism, and his inebriation on the day of battle, was in question. It was always assumed that Custer knew nothing of Reno's debacle until it was too late, for he was out of sight. But the three Crow scouts now told Edward Curtis a different story. They stood with the photographer on a patch of ground surrounded by barking prairie dogs.

Look below, they said, arms extended—here was an open view of the site of Reno's full retreat. Curtis estimated he was close enough that it was "almost within hailing distance." From here, the Crow scouts said, Custer had watched Reno's company bleed and run. What's more, Custer dismounted and took in the carnage while sitting on the grass, as if being entertained by blood theater, the Indians claimed. White Man Runs Him said he begged Custer to intercede, scolding him for letting soldiers die. "No," the commander replied. "Let them fight. There will be plenty of fighting left for us to do."

That story was new, and potentially explosive. The conventional account had come from the Indian scout Curley, because no one under Custer's direct command had survived. Curley, then nineteen, had fled a full hour before the battle. But White Man Runs Him, Goes Ahead and Hairy Moccasins had stayed with Custer until just minutes before battle, at which point they were allowed to make a dash for safety.

Curtis had brought with him a U.S. Geological Survey map, fresh off the press. He was the first person to use this invaluable topographical aid as a way to understand the sightlines of the combatants. At the viewpoint, White Man Runs Him told how Custer was unmoved by the slaughter of his hated rival Reno. "Custer watched all of this for 45 to 60 minutes," Curtis wrote in his notes, "and the whole fight was so close to him that he could have been in the thick of it in five minutes." By this account, Reno was a victim, Custer a coward—and a calculated one at that. "Reno's effort was truly pathetic, yet to have expected him, unsupported, to successfully meet the Sioux was comparable to presuming to stop the flow of the Niagara by waving a wand," Curtis wrote in a rough draft. Had Custer charged, at a time when the Indians had yet to fully assemble, the battle might have ended in victory for the Americans, or in a draw.

Custer did eventually make his way toward the river, where, in the usual telling, he was surprised by a mass of charging Indians, and there made his Last Stand. The Little Bighorn was difficult to ford, the story had it, because of steep ground, another reason why Custer couldn't take the fight directly to the Indian camp. But Curtis found that the riverbank was actually quite level at the place where Custer had tried to cross, not a difficult ford. All of this information astounded Curtis. He told Upshaw to question the scouts hard. Upshaw went over inconsistencies and repeated his queries so many times that it brought ridicule from the Crow scouts. At one point, Curtis held a knife to the sky; he could not make a mistake, he shouted—his life work was on the line! The Indians touched the blade of the knife and looked upward, then into the photographer's eyes.

"All we have told you is the truth."

This breakthrough would never have been possible without the fluency and persistence of Upshaw, the Indian who served the Shadow Catcher longer than any other. At night, lying on the ground under the high ceiling of a Montana sky, Upshaw and Phillips would go over the day's notes, talking at the orchestration of Curtis. They set up several tents among the Indian tipis along the banks of the Little Bighorn. After having breakfast at 7:30, they started work at 8, took a half hour for lunch and an hour for supper, followed by work in the firelight until 1 a.m. —every day. Curtis considered Upshaw an invaluable member of the team, praising him in letters, offering to help with his government problems. But they fought over money. Curtis was late with payments, a pattern that held for nearly everyone who did business with him. He could be imperious. In that year, Curtis's payroll had expanded to seventeen people at one point, heavy with translators and wranglers, and including a close friend, Ed Meany, who was hired to do research and write part of the Sioux story.

By late July of 1907, Curtis believed he knew more about the Battle of the Little Bighorn than any man alive and was excited to release his findings. At around this time, Upshaw had started drinking, and would disappear during binges. For almost a decade, the Carlisle School had drilled into him the idea that it was wrong to resuscitate stories of the Indian past. The language, war cries, ceremonies, spiritual offerings to earthly elements, the face paint, the chants, the tiers of warrior prestige based on scalping—all must be forgotten, the school taught, if Indians were going to prosper. And now here was Upshaw, working for the world's foremost project dedicated to the task of preserving those same old ways. Worse, Upshaw could see the corrosive effect on his people of a disaster in federal Indian policy. Following the Dawes Act of 1887, the government tried to break up tribal holdings, giving Indians individual "allotments" of their own land. In theory, this would make them property owners, each family with a piece of ground to call its own, not unlike the philosophy behind the Homestead Act. In practice, however, after twenty years it led to the reservations losing more than half of the land they'd been promised by treaty. The new law was honey for the bears of real estate predation.

Upshaw was married to a white woman from Ohio named Emma, and had three children to support. When he went into town, in Billings, the whites mocked him for his marriage and called Emma a traitor to her race. That summer, Upshaw decided to remain on the Crow reservation and raise his family in a hybrid way. But when he tried to get his wife adopted into the Crow Nation, he ran into trouble with his own people and their government overlords. "I have concluded that it is not wise," the federal Indian inspector Z. Lewis Dalby wrote Upshaw in late July. Dalby had enormous power over the Crow; he could make arrests, prosecute people and settle land disputes. And he despised them. In his eyes, Crow women were "without virtue," promiscuous, and the men "abominably immoral." To Upshaw's earnest plea for help in bringing his white wife into the tribe, the inspector was blunt. "No white person has ever been adopted into the tribe," he wrote. "Now, Alex, as you know I have taken a deep personal interest in you and I do want to see you make good . . . You have behaved like a man, and I believe you can see the foolishness as well as the meanness of your former course, and that you now intend to straighten up and be a man. Mr. Curtis is your friend. Talk these things over with him." In essence, the educated Indian who had praised assimilation was told he shouldn't practice it.

In August, the Curtis party folded its summer camp along the Little Bighorn and trotted back to Pine Ridge, a two-week journey on horseback. Curtis had nearly wrapped up his investigation of the Custer story. He planned to check a few loose ends with the Sioux and then walk the battlefield one more time in the fall with an army commander. His time with the Sioux, in addition to the Custer story, was paying off with a rich and varied collection of pictures. His camera caught them drying meat, praying to the Great Mystery, assembling at his suggestion to reenact scenes of a war party about to strike. He documented tipi construction, embroidery patterns of deerskin wardrobes and the way young girls were taught to ride horses, lashed to the animals' backs. The portraits in particular—of Jack Red Cloud, Fast Elk, Crazy Thunder and American Horse—conveyed the kind of inside knowledge that was characteristic of his best work. The harrowing visage of Slow Bull's wife, her eyes fixed in the caverns of an eroded face, porcupine-quill earrings and necklaces flowing below, a whitewashed sky behind her, could not have been captured by a stranger. Most of the faces, though, look gaunt—and for good reason. When Curtis had first started working with the Sioux, in 1905, they often went hungry. In the old days, an average Sioux would eat about six full buffalo a year. Without these shaggy-headed beasts, they were dependent on handouts. "It is doubtful in the history of the world that any people ever were brought so suddenly to such a radical change in their manner of living," Curtis wrote in his volume that explained the tribe. "The enforced change in diet alone so undermined them physically that they became an easy prey to every ill."

When Curtis asked the Sioux if there was anything he could bring them in the future, they answered with a single word: food.

Upon his return, Curtis had found the Sioux worse off, some near starvation because government rations never appeared. Curtis arrived with a beef steer, fulfilling his promise. He had expected a party of twenty. About three hundred showed up, milling around, anxious and hollow-eyed. Negotiations were blunt and quick: the Indians would work for Curtis, explain their customs and recall the warrior traditions, but they had to be fed, and now. The Dakota plains, so full of buffalo during summer days past, were a ghost prairie in 1907—an empty pantry. And at Pine Ridge Curtis saw a stark replay of what had motivated the Sioux to go to war back in 1876. By treaty, they had been promised nearly all of modern South Dakota, and hunting access to twenty-two million acres in eastern Montana and North Dakota. But the treaty lasted no longer than any other, a story Curtis had heard many times. Custer had guarded a railroad survey into Sioux territory in 1873, a clear violation, and then led an expedition to the Black Hills in 1874, the tribe's sacred ground. When gold was discovered in 1875, Sioux land was overrun by prospectors. President Ulysses S. Grant demanded that the Indians sell the Black Hills to the United States. After they refused to let go of their homeland, the Sioux were ordered to cluster themselves at Pine Ridge and await government food. Those who refused were considered to be at war and labeled "hostiles." That set the stage for the campaign of 1876 and the Battle of the Little Bighorn. A bloody epilogue took place in 1890 at Wounded Knee, where the cold, gaunt Sioux who had started to dream of the old life through the Ghost Dance revival were gunned down by soldiers from the same Seventh Cavalry. Curtis heard that story one day in all its murderous detail while he stared at the mass grave at Wounded Knee, twenty miles from Pine Ridge.

Curtis could not find a buffalo to feed the Sioux if he used every dollar of J. P. Morgan's money. But with the help of Meany, his team rounded up at least one more beef steer and was able to host a feast late in that summer of 1907. "Their hearts were happy," Meany wrote. "Old rites were re-enacted, old battles re-fought, old stories re-told; and Mr. Curtis's pen and camera recorded it all."

Trouble now came from within the Curtis family. On the ride from Montana to Pine Ridge, Hal had slumped in the saddle and almost fell off; he was not nearly as talkative or observant as he'd been earlier in the summer. At night he appeared listless, without an appetite, his brow warm to the touch. He complained of stomach pain and headaches. Curtis picked up the pace, onward to his main camp at the Sioux reservation, dragging Hal behind a horse in a makeshift carrier. At Pine Ridge, when the party arrived, Clara was horrified at her boy's appearance. She immediately took charge, setting up a bed for Hal in a tent under the shade of a cottonwood. His fever hovered between 103 and 104.

He still could not eat. She said it was typhoid fever, a disease caused by a salmonella bacterium and often picked up from contaminated food or water; it could be fatal. Curtis had taken his boy to many camps that summer, and food or drink from a cowhand or a native helper might have spread the bacteria. Clara sent an Indian to the nearest railroad track, twenty miles away, with instructions to stop a train with an emergency request to get a prescription. After several days, medicine arrived from Chicago. But Hal showed little improvement. His mother fed him prairie chicken soup and applied wet compresses to his forehead. Curtis suspended all operations.

After several days, Curtis and Clara loaded Hal into a wagon and rode off to save the boy's life. Next to the rail tracks, Curtis flagged an eastbound train and brought it to a halt. After negotiations over the fare, a makeshift bed was assembled from two seats. Curtis stayed behind, watching the black smoke of the train shrink as it made its way over the prairie. He heard, more than a week later, that Hal had regained his health in Seattle, though he was still very thin. From then on, no child would be allowed to join the Shadow Catcher in Indian country.

In the fall, the crew of Curtis, Myers, Upshaw and a college assistant settled into a cabin on the Crow reservation. They planned to hole up through the winter, finishing the Custer story for Volume III and working on a separate book on the Crow and the Hidatsa, another northern plains tribe. A blush of gold held to the leaves, a last glimmer of warmth. Then snow flew early, in mid-October, and would last for six months. Winter on the high, lonely Montana plains would soon close in dark and deep, providing ideal conditions for a team of wordsmiths and image makers trying to rewrite history. Their cloister was a shelter of rough-hewn logs, snug against a huge rock embankment, just a half day's horse ride from the Little Bighorn battlefield. Inside was a large fireplace and kitchen table. They worked from 8 a.m. to just past midnight, as Curtis outlined in a letter to Belle da Costa Greene — "my only interruption being a single trip to the post office, six miles away." All other activity was restricted. "I permitted mail, but no newspapers were allowed. Every thought and every moment had to be given to the work."

If the first two volumes of *The North American Indian* had been pastoral and somewhat painterly, the next two books, on the Sioux and the Crow, would be darker, with more of a documentary look. Curtis felt the burden of a nation's cherished narrative and the reputation of a man considered "a light to all youth of America," in Roosevelt's words. As the Curtis team went through the story cautiously day by day, one side would play prosecutor, the other defender.

"Dear Meany: . . . Has there been anything published on the fact that Custer, from the highest viewpoint of the region, watched Reno's charge, battle and defeat?"

That was the crux of Curtis's major finding, and by midfall he felt he was on solid enough ground to start circulating the story. Curtis relied on Meany's counsel, and his writing and research, to help him through this section. "As far as I have read nothing of this nature has ever been published," Curtis continued. "It puts an entirely new light on the entire Custer fight." It did indeed. But the supportive Meany knew that his friend was playing with historical fire, and warned him of the consequences. "This is not a pipe dream on my part," wrote Curtis. "I have ridden the battlefield from end to end, back and forth from every important point on it, noting carefully the time of such rides." A month later, he wrote again, asking Meany to find transcripts of the military inquest. He also indicated that he would not be home for Christmas. In another note to the professor, seeking to counter doubts from friends in Seattle and New York, Curtis showed that his confidence had not dimmed:

"If you hear anyone say that I am not to succeed, tell [them] they don't know me."

By early January, the Curtis entourage was making great progress and showing few signs of cabin fever. "The work on the Sioux volume has gone like a whirlwind, and consequently happiness reigns among us," he wrote Meany. The next letter, after a lapse in the professor's response, was addressed to Mrs. Meany. "If that tall, good-natured husband of yours is still wandering around the face of the earth will you be good enough to drop me a word, and let me know when you expect him home?" Finally, early February: "Our work on the Sioux volume is practically complete."

Curtis took a break to travel to New York, again to grovel for subscriptions and to update Belle da Costa Greene on what he was doing with her boss's money. While there, he gave an interview to the *New York Herald*, offering a preview of his findings. After conducting his exhaustive examination, he had something extraordinary to share: when he published the next volume of *The North American Indian*, he explained, it would be there for all the world to see.

SAYS CUSTER THREW MEN'S LIVES AWAY

The headline was the least of it. The story reported that Curtis had proof that Custer "had unnecessarily sacrificed the lives of his soldiers to further his personal end," and that he could have won the battle with little loss of life. "I know it is unpopular to criticize a military commander," Curtis said, but the Indians who were with him felt that his judgment was flawed. "When the wise old Indian warriors that were in this fight are asked what they think of Custer's course in the battle, they point to their heads and say, 'He must have been wrong up here.'"

The article caused a furor. Two officers of the Seventh Cavalry said it was a slander against an American hero and the honor of their fallen comrades. Libbie Custer flew into high dudgeon; she went to work trying to prevent Curtis's version from ever being published. She leaned on her friends in high places, starting with the president. She battered Gifford Pinchot. How could he do so much to promote this Curtis man, she complained. She demanded that the forester quash the rewrite of the last day of her beloved "Auty." Though Pinchot was circumspect, he did the widow Custer's bidding. The newly named Custer National Forest would be unveiled in 1908, and he did not want a controversy hanging over it. He wrote Curtis of his concerns. The photographer promptly replied with an offer to send Pinchot all the material backing his conclusions.

Sensing that the knives of the Custer historical cabal were getting close enough to hurt him, Curtis tried to bring President Roosevelt around to his side. But first he went to the military, sending a sheaf of notes to three longtime army officers and to Charles A. Woodruff, a recently retired brigadier general who had arrived at the Little Bighorn days after the battle. Woodruff agreed to walk the battlefield with Curtis. After spending several days with him, the general urged Curtis to write a complete report and send it to the president. On the officer's advice Curtis explained his investigative foray for the highest literary critic in the land. "I have ridden with our blood all tingling with the swing of our horses as we galloped across the plains," he wrote, appealing to the adventurer-historian in Roosevelt. This was the way of the western man of letters—boots muddy, scholarship by walking around. The reply from the White House was written on April 8, 1908:

> My Dear Mr. Curtis:
>   I have read those papers through with great interest, and after reading them, I am uncertain as to what is the best course to advise. I never heard of the three Crow scouts that you mention, and did not know that they were with Custer. I need not say to you that writing over thirty years after an event it is necessary to be exceedingly cautious about relying upon the memory of any man, Indian or white. Such a space of time is a great breeder of myths. Apparently you are inclined to the theory that Custer looked on but a short distance away at the butchery of Reno's men, and let it take place, hoping to gain great glory for himself afterward. Such a theory is wildly improbable. Of course, human nature is so queer that it is hard to say that anything is impossible, but this theory makes Custer out to be both a traitor and a fool. He would have gained just as much glory by galloping down to snatch victory from defeat after Reno was thoroughly routed . . .

Curtis was crushed. It was the first time the president had let him down. And with each word from Roosevelt, the story that had taken three years to construct lost a stone or two of its foundation, until most of it lay in ruins. Roosevelt was not saying he doubted Curtis's material. He had no facts to refute what Curtis had found. But logic made it all hard to believe. *Wildly improbable.* If Curtis was defiant after reading the letter—his usual initial impulse—those two words could not be easily banished from his mind. With his meticulous reconstruction of the battle, Curtis had persuasive evidence to win over the educated cynics, those who never believed that the boy wonder with the camera was mining an untouched vein of valuable history. He felt, at once, that *The North American Indian* was deeply wounded, and the doubts about his Custer revisionism might kill it altogether. His careful nurturing of friendships, pacts and deals with the most powerful people in the country, the eastern men who had made his life quest possible, was mortgaged to particular conditions, some of them never written down. Curtis could plow ahead—Roosevelt, Pinchot and all of Libbie Custer's connections be damned—but that could mean the end of The Cause, as Curtis now called his work. *Wildly improbable? Wildly improbable!*

"I am beginning to believe that nothing is quite so uncertain as facts," Curtis wrote an army colonel who had encouraged his fresh examination of the Little Bighorn. It was three weeks after Roosevelt's note. A few months later, in a letter to Meany, Curtis indicated that the white flag was flying over the cabin in Montana. "I have been very guarded, and while giving a great deal of new and interesting information, I have said nothing that can be considered a criticism of Custer." The story of the Crow scouts, the many notes and depositions from White Man Runs Him, the many translations from Upshaw, the detailed and seemingly indisputable narrative helped along by Sioux and Cheyenne who'd participated in the battle, the measured fact-checking by Meany and Myers, the topographic maps and time-of-day placements—all were bundled up and locked away, the scholarship never to find a home between covers of *The North American Indian*. The story of Custer invading a sovereign nation, the rise and fall of the Sioux—"the limitless Plains theirs to roam"—a buffalo and warrior culture conquered by a ruthlessly superior one, came out in Volume III. Curtis wrote clear and passionate prose, and was often prescient. On Wounded Knee, the last real clash between the worlds, he said, "To the future historian if not to our own, the so-called Battle of Wounded Knee will appear to have been little less than a massacre." But that was as far as he went. A battlefield map of Little Bighorn was published, showing contour lines. A careful reader could perhaps discern what Curtis had found; almost nobody did until much later. Curtis printed only one of his revelations, though it was certainly not enough to force citizens to look twice at statues of Custer in their town squares:

"Custer made no attack," he concluded in Volume III, "the whole movement being a retreat."

On the Custer Lookout, 1908. Curtis went back several times to the site of the Battle of the Little Bighorn, trying to uncover the true story of the worst loss by the American army in the Indian wars. Here he faces the camera himself, with his native guides. Left to right: Goes Ahead, Hairy Moccasins, White Man Runs Him, Curtis and his aide Alexander Upshaw.

A Heavy Load—Sioux, 1908. Curtis tried to record scenes of the hard life of a winter on the northern plains.

The winter writing retreat in Montana, 1908. Curtis, his cowriter William Myers, Upshaw and others holed up here while putting together the Little Bighorn story. They often debated late into the night.

10

THE MOST REMARKABLE MAN
1908–1909

FOR NEARLY FOUR YEARS, Curtis saw more of Alexander Upshaw and natives of the northern plains than he did of Clara and Seattle. And what he saw in their last months together was a troubled man whose education had opened his eyes to the impossibility of straddling two worlds. Upshaw spent a typical workday helping Curtis recreate a time when the Crow had their own religion, dress and economy, when nobody called them inferior or immoral. And then he went home at night to a family on a reservation where nearly everything from that past was being scrubbed from the land. Through the seasons, Upshaw was with Curtis on horseback under a searing sun, in snowstorms that blotted out the Montana sky, and in a tent at night until the last candle burned out. The translator roamed all over Indian country with his boss, and had ideas on narrative, picture themes and the many qualities of Apsaroke women. Curtis called him "my great and loyal friend." Upshaw returned the compliment: the Shadow Catcher, he said, was "a fine man." Curtis paid him $100 a month—that is, when he paid him at all—far more than any of the hundreds of other Indians he'd employed over the years.

Upshaw was not only an interpreter without equal, but a strategist, helping to design an approach to a given tribe, and a sounding board, not afraid to argue with Curtis. When Upshaw left the winter writing cabin for a one-week translating job before a grand jury, the entire operation nearly came to a halt, Curtis noted. He continued to cut his hair short and dress in the clothes of the conquerors—the discipline of trying to "be a man." But this warrior's son seldom got much respect for his effort. The Indian inspector Dalby, who had told Upshaw he would not back his attempt to get his white wife adopted by the Crow, monitored his behavior as if he were on parole. Dalby's admonitions burned inside him.

"I have read your letter through so often that I can repeat every word of it," Upshaw wrote Dalby. "As to my future, I have given you my sincere words when I promised I will be a man."

A man? He couldn't go into Billings, a proper citizen window-shopping with his wife and three children, without somebody sneering or shouting out at him. A man? He had just helped to lead a highly successful scholarly expedition; he had been crucial to the reconstruction of the Battle of the Little Bighorn; he had annotated and explicated the story of his people; and yet he was still a red monkey in a white man's shoes. Once, he boarded a local train in Montana with Meany. The two men had just taken their seats at the end of a long day when a cattleman, sitting nearby, started in on Upshaw. He didn't like Indians, he said loudly, and he didn't like Upshaw sitting there. He wanted him off the train. It wasn't anything Upshaw hadn't heard before, but usually he got it for being with his white wife. Meany stood, towering over the cowboy, and said Upshaw wasn't going anywhere. At six foot four, with a wild thatch of red hair, the professor could intimidate when he had to. The cowboy backed away. "I don't think I got the worse of the bout," Meany wrote Curtis, "and I was glad to defend my Crow friend."

Upshaw's father, Crazy Pend d'Oreille, was known for bravery against the Sioux, and it was because of his family's status that young Upshaw was plucked from Montana and sent to the Indian boarding school in Pennsylvania for nine years. The institution's mission was to "kill the Indian, save the man." Upon graduation from Carlisle, Upshaw tried to fit the mold of a remade native. When rumors went out that Upshaw, while visiting a western exhibition in Omaha, had taken part in a staged battle and was dressed in tribal costume, he wrote a sharp rebuttal in the *Indian Helper,* the school paper. In fact, he'd been in suit and tie, his hair short, he insisted. "Alex would have his schoolmates know that he is trying to be a man, though in the midst of trials and tribulations." Upshaw also tried to be an evangelical Christian, and to organize a YMCA chapter at the Indian school where he taught in Nebraska. But he didn't last long at either effort.

With Upshaw as cultural guide, Curtis went deep into Apsaroke society. "Through him I am getting into the heart of the Northern Plains Indian in a way that gives me the greatest satisfaction," he wrote Hodge. It showed in Volume IV, which became a much-cited and consistently praised work of firsthand ethnology. Indeed, Hodge, who spoke from authority, said the Crow volume "is the best story of Plains Indian life ever written." The people were described as physically robust—a woman could fell a horse with her fist—healthy and confident. Their strength came in part from fighting other Indians; they had enemies to the north in the Blackfeet, enemies to the east in the Sioux, and enemies to the south in the Cheyenne. They roamed an area equal in size to New England. With the bounty from the plains keeping them fed, they had time to spend on decorative arts. "The nature of their life gave the Apsaroke a great deal of comparative leisure," Curtis wrote, "and they delighted in fashioning fine garments from skins and embroidering them in striking colors."

A young man trolling for women would ride on horseback nearly naked through a village, singing, "I am merely staying on earth for a time; all women look upon me!" Along with the words to that song, Curtis included the music, publishing a sheet with the notes. Sex was celebrated. So, while Dalby said in 1908 that the Crow were "devoid of any moral sense in connection with their sexual relations," Curtis came away with the opposite impression, writing at the same time. They are "certainly an unusually sensual people," he explained in Volume IV, but that did not mean they are "lax in morals." And in such digressions, a reader could almost hear Upshaw whispering in the ear of the author: consider, Curtis told his readers, that an Indian may find many customs in American society that are "highly objectionable and immoral."

What fascinated Curtis about Upshaw, friend and subject, was his duality. It also worried him. He could see the strain in a face turning harder by the day. As early as 1905, Curtis could sense that inner conflict was gnawing away at Upshaw. Curtis doubted that a "coat of educational whitewash," as he called the years at Carlisle, would be enough to cover the Indian in him. Not long after becoming Upshaw's friend, Curtis predicted that he would "die and go to the god of his fathers." Upshaw drank, though alcohol was outlawed on the reservation. He pushed back when a white man struck him, though such a reaction could bring a felony assault charge. He was not submissive. He used words that his neighbors had never heard—English words. "In some respects, he is the most remarkable man I ever saw," Curtis said in one interview. "He is perfectly educated and absolutely uncivilized." In that sense, Upshaw was the embodiment of a first-rate mind, defined later in the century by F. Scott Fitzgerald—a man who could hold two opposing ideas at the same time and still be able to function. Upshaw did it one better: he lived two opposing lives.

The pictures in Volume IV also benefited from Upshaw's access to Indian lives. The people were photographed as if they were family members, with a closeness that comes from long association. A Crow named Shot In The Hand is shown in high-relief profile, his chin and nose like a ridge worn by the wind, mouth in tight grimace. His bronzed head sits atop a mountain of dove-white quills, beading, animal skins and ornaments. The main source of the Custer revisionism, White Man Runs Him, is displayed in an unromantic close-up, with prominent facial scars. Portraits of Two Leggings, Wolf, Red Wing, Fog In The Morning and Hoop In The Forehead provide a wealth of detail on the jewelry worn by prominent men. Let Dalby and the Bureau of Indian Affairs insist that the Crow strip themselves of the ancient trappings of class and privilege; in the Curtis portfolio, that glory had one more showing. From the field came winter scenes, shot not far from the writing cabin, like a woman carrying a bundle of twigs to an ice-wrapped tipi, trudging through an expanse of snow—the photographic equivalent of a Tolstoy description of a peasant. And Curtis also included, in the plates of Volume IV, a portrait of Upshaw himself, who was thanked in the introduction. The picture, titled simply *Upshaw—Apsaroke,* displays a face that is somewhat mournful, the eyes liquid, as if he were close to tears. Upshaw leans on his right elbow, a traditional pose. Most revealing, he wears a head bonnet, fourteen rows of shell necklaces and long hooped earrings, and he's shirtless. This Upshaw is an Indian like his father, not someone else's definition of a man.

In the summer of 1908, Curtis sent Upshaw to the Dakota north country, along the high, wind-lashed banks of the Missouri River, to start building relations with the Mandan. This tribe had been instrumental in keeping the Lewis and Clark expedition alive, providing them winter quarters in their big earthen lodges, showing them how to find food and comfort in one of the coldest places on the plains. It was at the Mandan winter camp that Sacagawea, a Shoshone slave, was won in a gambling contest by an American member of the expedition. The artist George Catlin spent considerable time with the Mandan in 1833, trying to capture on canvas what Curtis was now doing with glass plates. A smallpox epidemic nearly wiped out the tribe; a count in 1837 found only 137 people. For survival, they joined forces with two other groups, the Arikara and Hidatsa. Their reservation, originally eight million acres by treaty, was being whittled down to less than a million acres when the Curtis party arrived.

As before, Upshaw was able to work his way deep into the community, and after two months he reported back to Curtis on a variety of good subjects. Curtis shot the Arikara medicine ceremony, adults with full-sized bear skins draped over themselves, the resulting pictures as animated as anything in the entire *North American Indian.* The men were trying to assume some of the strength of a bear, and the animal's spiritual power, as part of a larger prayer offering for rain and food. To the Arikara, all animals had souls, though trees and stones were inanimate. "This remarkable ceremony of the medicine fraternity of the Arikara has long been dormant," Curtis wrote, "the agency officials having suppressed it about 1885." He had arranged for "remnants of the fraternity" of bear medicine men to perform the outlawed ritual.

Curtis also took pictures of men offering buffalo skulls to the sky, and of women gathering berries, and he learned that the punishment for a man who committed adultery was to have one of his horses shot. The most memorable portrait was of Bear's Belly, who wears a full skin, with the bear's snout on his head and the arms, legs and back of the animal's thick hide covering his own. His face and the upper part of his chest are open to the camera; he looks like a northern plains version of a centaur—half bear, half man.

The real prize, Upshaw told Curtis, was something less flashy: the small, sacred turtle drum of the Mandan, "the object of greatest veneration." Upshaw befriended the priest who kept the effigies, a pair of buffalo-skin-wrapped drums in the shape of turtles. It would severely upset the Mandan, the translator said, should Curtis press for access. "The Mandans asserted that no white man had ever touched or had more than a possible glimpse of them," Curtis wrote in his notes of the visit. "Naturally this intrigued me." The guardian of the turtles was a man named Packs Wolf, who lived away from the main tribe in a log cabin. For several days, Upshaw went to see him, returning with the same news: the turtles were off-limits. Upshaw upped the payment offer. Negotiations continued. Finally, after a high fee was agreed to, permission was granted. It felt sneaky, somewhat dirty, money for spiritual access. Curtis knew such an unveiling would be "an unethical affair," as he wrote, but such were the unseemly methods of field anthropology.

On a chilly morning, Curtis and Upshaw went to Packs Wolf's cabin. "It was made clear to me this business was being done without permission of the tribe," Curtis wrote, and if others found out, "dire things could happen to all of us." Curtis and Upshaw were told to strip in preparation for a purifying ritual in the sweat lodge. They could not enter the House of the Turtles without first cleansing themselves, Packs Wolf explained. They spent the better part of a day inside a dome-shaped willow lodge with a pit of hot rocks in the middle. As sweat poured out and steam rose from their skin, Upshaw thought Curtis would pass out. Not to worry, the photographer said: he'd been through many a sweat bath and knew what to expect. The next day, they were ushered into the turtle domain, a log house dimly lit by two small windows. The priest brought out two objects, tightly wrapped in buffalo skin with an outer layer of feathers. Curtis wanted to peel away the feathers to see the turtles. A fresh round of negotiations ensued, with Upshaw again doing the bargaining for his boss. Curtis was vague in his account of what happened next. He wrote in Volume V that "unexpected permission was granted to photograph them without the feathers." He was ordered not to turn the turtles over — "if you do all people will die." Curtis, his nerves unsteady, trembled as he made several exposures. Outside the cabin, a group of Mandan on horseback approached. The turtle temple had been violated. No, no, the Indians were told, the Curtis party had only been discussing turtle lore — no pictures had been taken.

Later, Curtis felt triumphant. "I am more than happy to tell you that we actually got our hands on the sacred turtle of the Mandans and secured pictures of them," he wrote Meany from Minot, North Dakota. The finished picture, *The Sacred Turtles,* shows two small, quite ordinary objects of tightly stitched buffalo skin in afternoon light on the floor. Their power, of course, was in what they represented — spirits harnessed from all over the Dakotas. In rationalizing his actions, Curtis said, "Fortunately, taking a picture leaves no mark." But it may have left a mark on Upshaw, acting as the agent of betrayal of fellow Indians.

Throughout 1908, the first volumes of the Curtis magnum opus came under critical scrutiny from high places in Europe and the United States. Curtis had steeled himself, expecting to take a few hits. They never understood him, the culture czars. They were jealous. His work showed how lazy they had been in their thinking, how so many of their ideas were nonsense. He wrote Hodge of one snub by a "Doctor Cullen," from an institute in Brooklyn, who had declined to purchase a subscription. The learned man didn't like the photographer because of "my failing to comprehend his personal deification," Curtis explained to Hodge. "On seeing him in the lobby of a Portland hotel I stepped up to his Highness and laid my profane hand on his shoulder and spoke to him with the familiarity of an equal." But Curtis's defensiveness was unnecessary — the latest reviews were stunning.

From the Peabody Museum of Archaeology and Ethnology at Harvard came a note from Professor F. W. Putnam, rapturous in his commendation of "your great work." He had met Curtis some years before and was an early enthusiast. Now, after seeing some of the finished product, he praised the scholarship. In particular, he said the anthropology and ethnology were of the highest order, considerably advancing the work of those fields. Came another, from *Review of Reviews:* "*The North American Indian* cannot be compared with any publishing venture in the annals of American bookmaking, or indeed in those of any other nation." An old Curtis mentor, C. Hart Merriam — one of the men he'd rescued on Mount Rainier a decade earlier — wrote an unqualified endorsement: "Every American who sees the work will be proud that so handsome a piece of book-making has been produced in America; and every intelligent man will rejoice that ethnology and history have been enriched by such faithful and artistic records of the aboriginal inhabitants of our country."

FEAST FOR BIBLIOPHILE
REMARKABLE WORK ON RED MAN OF AMERICA

That was a *Washington Post* headline of a story touting "one of the most remarkable and expensive publications ever planned." From Geneva came a formal letter from Dr. Herman ten Kate, a leading European intellectual: "You are doing a magnificent thing, building not only an everlasting monument to a vanishing race, but also to yourself. I am sure that if the Indians could realize the value and purpose of your work, and perhaps a few of them do, they would be grateful to you. In fact, viewed in a certain light, your work constitutes a redemption of the many wrongs our 'superior' race has done to the Indian. Some passages you wrote are masterly."

Those "many wrongs" inflicted on small nations by the much larger one continued to trouble Upshaw. The Crow reservation, on an ownership map, now looked like a quilt made of several thousand square scraps. Not only was the tribe still losing people — in a generation's time, the population had been cut in half — but its reservation was being carved out from under them. Much of the good land, with its pasturage for cattle and its well-watered valleys for growing grain, had passed into white hands. In all respects, the modern age meant only one thing —decline.

"You are decreasing at the rate of three percent a year," Curtis lamented to Upshaw one night as he went over census numbers. "Take this pencil and figure out your own solution." Upshaw didn't have to do a calculation.

"If I live to be an old man there will be none of my people left," he said.

"There will be a few left," Curtis replied—but only those who can master the ways of the dominant culture.

When Upshaw wasn't at Curtis's side, he was in court, or in meetings with state politicians—the public face and mouthpiece of the Crow. He started to push back in his correspondence with the imperious government overseer Dalby. The lord of Indian country in Montana had mentioned that he was off to Washington, D.C., for congressional hearings. Instead of his usual lip service about trying to "be a man," Upshaw was direct. It was crucial that the Indian inspector stand up "in this trying time in order to get justice."

In the last full month of Teddy Roosevelt's presidency, Curtis was invited to Washington for an informal sit-down with the writer-politician who had done so much for an unknown man from Seattle. Curtis raised an improbable idea with Upshaw: why not go with him to the White House? There, he could argue his people's case.

In late February of 1909, Washington society opened its doors to the Shadow Catcher and his Indian friend. The president was the subject of much speculation over whether he would try to return to power in four years. Not a chance—he was off to Africa, he insisted, done with politics. The balloon figure of William Howard Taft, a walrus-mustachioed midwesterner given to long naps and multiple-course early-bird dinners, would soon be president. For Roosevelt, it was time to play again. He asked Curtis, who'd been such a kinetic companion at Teddy's Sagamore Hill home, if he wanted to come along as photographer of his upcoming African safari. Curtis was flattered, but had no time for a yearlong diversion.

Exhibitions at galleries, clubs and the homes of political elites filled the Curtis calendar for the first few days in Washington. He was honored at a reception attended by Roosevelt and Taft, by ambassadors, counts, foreign ministers and "a score of the most prominent people in Washington's social and scientific circles," the *Post* reported. In its pages, Curtis was described as "perhaps the greatest living authority on Indian lore and Indian life in general." Despite such accolades, he had yet to snag a subscription from the Smithsonian. While in the East, he did manage to get Andrew Carnegie to sign on for a single set of the books, and he used the praise from prominent figures to add an additional few to his list. The checks passed quickly through Curtis's account and into those of Hodge, Myers, Upshaw, the printers in Boston and other creditors.

Curtis and the Crow native walked into the White House on the afternoon of February 25. Roosevelt was hearty in his greeting and open to hearing Upshaw's case, at least for a few moments. That was all well and good, he said quickly, but the Indian should take up his grievances with the new man, Taft. They toured the White House, they shared a meal, they talked of mountain ranges and rivers in the West and of wild creatures on the Dakota plains. Such lovely country, all of it. And the work of Curtis — *it was bully!* Curtis thanked him again for his contribution to *The North American Indian,* and Roosevelt said it was nothing; he was humbled to be a part of something so monumental.

EXPLORER AT THE WHITE HOUSE

The *Washington Post* had numerous errors in its story on the visit, calling the grammar school dropout "Professor Curtis" and claiming he was an "explorer" of Indian lands, rather than someone who took pictures and explained cultures. The article said his work would be finished in two years. Hah! Only five of the planned twenty volumes had been published. The paper asserted there was no truth to the rumor that Curtis would accompany Roosevelt to Africa. As for the "copper-skinned" companion, Alexander B. Upshaw, at least his presence was noted. The *Post* called him "a full-blooded Crow Indian," but never gave his name. At his supreme moment of influence, this delegate from an old nation in

Montana side by side with the president, the educated, assimilated native, was not a man with a name, just an Indian — a full-blooded one at that.

Later that year, as Curtis made plans for fieldwork with his Indian aide in New Mexico and the Columbia River Plateau, came shocking news from Montana.

EDUCATED CROW DIES IN JAIL

Upshaw's body was found on the floor of an icy cell, the story in the *Billings Gazette* said, blood splattered on the bars. He died of pneumonia, the paper reported. He had been on a drinking spree, and was arrested after someone found him in a dingy hotel room in town. In jail he started vomiting blood until it killed him. "He is survived by a wife, a white woman," the paper said, "whose marriage to the young graduate of Carlisle caused quite a sensation." Members of the Crow Nation told a different story to people who'd worked for Curtis in Montana: they said Upshaw had been murdered. The details were sketchy, but this version had Upshaw in an argument with several white men. Punches flew. Upshaw was severely beaten, then dragged off to jail to die.

Curtis was heartbroken. His close friend, his best interpreter — *perfectly educated and absolutely uncivilized* — was gone, left in a frigid jail cell to gag on his own blood. They finished each other's sentences, these two, and in the writing of *The North American Indian* Upshaw often did that for Curtis as well. The life had been snuffed out of Upshaw at the age of thirty-eight. On the reservation, the death of the most remarkable man Curtis had ever met was noted only for how unremarkable it was for an Indian to die so young.

Upshaw—Apsaroke, 1905. Curtis's friend and interpreter Alexander Upshaw, "perfectly educated and absolutely uncivilized," as Curtis said of him, had trouble shuttling between two worlds. He chose to pose in the clothes of his ancestors.

Bear's Belly — Arikara, 1908. The ceremony of the bear medicine fraternity had been dormant for some time, Curtis wrote, until it was revived for his camera.

Eagle Catcher—Hidatsa, 1908. One of many remarkable scenes that might never have been recorded had Curtis not been aided by Upshaw.

11

ON THE RIVER OF THE WEST
1910

IN A YEAR, ENOUGH water pushes through the Columbia River Gorge to bury an area the size of California under eighteen inches of pure snowmelt. It runs 1,214 miles, this stream once full of giddyup, from its slow-drip birth in British Columbia's Rockies, to the steep narrowing where it breaks the backbone of the Cascade Mountains, to a final sashay at a ten-mile-wide mouth, emptying more river into the Pacific than any other in the Western Hemisphere. In midspring, when snow from the high peaks of two Canadian provinces and three American states slides downhill in a transformative rush to water, the Columbia is most engorged. And it was at this time that Curtis, Myers, a young hired hand called Edmund Schwinke, a reluctant old bar pilot and a Japanese cook who answered to the name of Noggie prepared to descend the most treacherous, spray-generating stretch of what was then the largest free-flowing river in North America.

They had built a small boat — "nondescript and flat-bottomed," in Curtis's shorthand — square at the stern, bowed in front, with a small gas engine for scoot-up power in settled water. And now they stood above Celilo Falls, where the river went into free fall, all froth and fury. Curtis had with him the notes Lewis and Clark took when the Corps of Discovery passed through this very place nearly a century earlier.

Among all the misspelled, bloodless observations of those nonemotive explorers, no sentences convey more terror than their description of the canyon that lay just below the Curtis party in 1910. They called it "an agitated gut swelling, boiling and whirling in every direction."

Curtis was there in search of the once prosperous tribes of the Columbia. For centuries, these natives had only to walk a few steps from their cedar-plank homes to have all they needed to eat. At Celilo, millions of Pacific salmon made the transition from long-haul distance swimmers to high jumpers. They had to leap up the side pools of the falls, a fight with gravity and a down-pounding current. For American Indians, there was no easier way to take protein. They used nets, gaff hooks, spears and baskets to bring home the tastiest species of salmon, the oil-rich Chinook. Some years, upward of ten million fish would pass by.

Celilo Falls hosted a trade mart as well—an open-air exchange in a desert surrounded by snow-hooded volcanoes. Inland tribes arrived with bison skins and elk hides and teeth; coastal dwellers came with jewelry made of surf-polished seashells. Curtis was in his element shooting the Columbia tribes in their element—the Walla Walla, the Umatilla, the Cayuse and various smaller Chinook bands, doing what they had done for centuries. He framed men with thick forearms spearing salmon. He captured teenage boys leaning over platforms, rickety-looking contraptions that hung above the swirling Columbia, scooping fish from white water with their long-handled dip nets. He did not have to stage these scenes, as he did when he asked the Sioux to reassemble a war party, or when he requested that an old chief put on his eagle-feathered bonnet one more time for posterity. But he knew these pictures would soon have historical value. There was talk among the merchants and boosters of the fast-growing communities of the interior Northwest of damming the Columbia, though it seemed preposterous that anything could tame such a torrent.

His task on this spring day was simply to make it down a drop of eighty feet, as the Corps of Discovery had done in 1805, without getting killed. He and his crew hauled the boat out of the water and onto a single flatcar on a rusty length of rail track parallel to the falls. This track led to a cauldron below. The plan was to lower the launch, using ropes to slow its descent, and try to make a soft enough landing in the water that the boat would not be crushed. Waist-deep in the Columbia at the head of Celilo, Curtis barked at his men through the spray.

"The roar of the falls was so great they could not hear my calls for instruction," he wrote. He waded to shore, shouting out a plan of action. Noggie would have none of it; the cook sat on a rock, head in hands, sobbing.

"What the hell's wrong with you?"

"I know you will drown," Noggie said. Tears streamed down his cheeks. "I know you will drown!"

Curtis wanted to slap him. He had no time for this crap. His crew had thinned considerably. He couldn't pay Bill Phillips, now absent. And his cousin-in-law had fallen in love, and showed less interest in The Cause. Upshaw was dead, and God, how he missed him. Bill Myers, who had taken on more of the writing duties in addition to his field-work, was still with him, of course. The new hire, Schwinke, the son of German immigrants, was getting his first tryout as a field stenographer. He was just twenty-two and willing to work cheap. Meany was back at the University of Washington, a much-loved professor in his pulpit, dazzling young minds at a school that had grown overnight into a sprawling campus. This expansion had come about because the university had been the site of the 1909 Alaska-Yukon-Pacific Exposition, Seattle's coming-out party. Holding a world's fair at a university that then had only three buildings and was surrounded by an old-growth forest was Meany's idea. The fair was a success beyond the wildest projections. The Olmsted brothers, the designer sons of the man who drew up New York's Central Park, had been hired to frame the exposition. By the time the fair ended in October, 3.7 million visitors had come to the nation's far corner for a look. Curtis had a prominent place at the exposition grounds; the five printed volumes of *The North American Indian* were given trophy display. This marked the first time that people in Curtis's hometown could see an extensive layout of what their famous resident had produced.

"You will drown!" Noggie started in again. Curtis forced his will on the crew, and with careful guidance they lowered their boat down the edge of the falls, its sides slapped by water. The skiff crash-landed at track's end, but remained intact. They were at the point where the river was pinched by high basalt cliffs, squeezing into the narrowest, most powerful hold—a doubling, at least, of hydraulic power. And they had eight more miles to go, though no other section would be as steep as Celilo Falls. Still, Curtis showed no fear, no panic. To be out in the wild again, breathing air that whistled through the Columbia Gorge, was a tonic for a tired forty-two-year-old man. Unbound, he was always in a better mood.

The year had been clouded by problems on many fronts, despite his international celebrity. All winter, Curtis had been cooped up in a new writer's cabin, across Puget Sound from Seattle, on the Olympic Peninsula, not far from the little piece of ground the Curtis family had homesteaded in 1887. The retreat was near a village called Waterman, and it was aptly named, for it rained, or threatened to rain, nearly every day. Once again the confinement—in this case, low clouds and steady squalls—was ideal.

"We are entirely shut off from the world," he wrote his editor Hodge. "Our camp is certainly as cheerful as one could wish in this weather, which is the sort well-adapted to ducks." He refused to let newspapers in, and allowed only one mail delivery a week—the same regimen he'd enforced in Montana. For breaks they took walks in the mist. With Myers fact-checking and assisting with big portions of the writing, Curtis worked that wet winter through all of Volumes VI and VII and the first part of VIII. He was trying to cover a tremendous amount of ground: the Blackfeet, Cheyenne and Arapaho in Volume VI, which closed out the northern plains; the Yakima, Klickitat, Interior Salish and Kutenai in the next volume, taking in many of Washington State's dry-side Indians; and the Nez Perce, Walla Walla, Umatilla, Cayuse and Chinook, from the Columbia region. Much of this material came from earlier Curtis forays. One of the main writing challenges was how to present the Nez Perce, Chief Joseph's people. Curtis was especially fond of them, dating to his football weekend in Seattle with the aging tribal leader. He felt bitterness at their treatment. He had pored over the events leading up to the Nez Perce War of 1877, and knew he had as much new to say on this subject as he did on Custer. But he chafed at the restraint of trying to tell a straightforward history, bound by his own published promise in the introduction not to revisit injustices. When he stared at the picture of Chief Joseph—those eyes!—he could feel a bit of the ache from the old man's heart.

His sentiment had been evident in the section on the Cheyenne, in the draft of Volume VI. Along with the Sioux and the Apache, they were the last nation to be placed on a reservation, and their holdout had clearly won over Curtis. He called the land given to the Northern Cheyenne in southeast Montana "a small and discouragingly sterile reservation" and described their treaty as "a delightful bit of satire." In that pact, the Indians were allowed to homestead on ground that had once been theirs. In his *Return of the Scouts* and *Before the Final Journey* he showed the Cheyenne mounted, at full gallop. For an additional boost of pride, his best portrait from the Cheyenne is a warrior— *Two Moons,* one of the veterans who defeated Custer. He wrote up sheet music, including "A War Song of the Dog Men," sung by a special breed of Cheyenne soldiers.

At times, Curtis slipped out of the writers' roost to work with Muhr in the Seattle studio. His many days with the Piegan and Blackfeet had paid off with a wealth of material for Volume VI. But one picture troubled him. It showed Little Plume and his son Yellow Kidney, with their high foreheads and prominent braids, sitting in a buffalo-skin tipi stuffed with everyday objects. Right between them, on the earthen floor, is a more prosaic accessory—an alarm clock. How had Curtis missed this? He agonized. It was a revealing photo, as he said in his caption later, "full of suggestions of the various Indian activities." But could those activities include a device for getting up early, perhaps for a tedious job somewhere? He had Muhr retouch the photo, removing the alarm clock—one of the most significant of his manipulations of a picture. Happy with the finished product, Curtis returned to the writing camp.

At the cabin, Curtis was closer, geographically, than he'd been to

Clara for some time, barely twenty miles across the sound. But the two were more emotionally distant than ever before. Their only son had recovered from the typhoid fever that nearly killed him, but the family was shattered. Hal went east, to a boarding school in Connecticut, courtesy of a wealthy Curtis benefactor. "I never came home because there wasn't really a home after that," he said later. Clara had started to withdraw from the family, perhaps as protection for her own pain, and spent more and more of her free time with Nellie, her sister and confidante. At the age of thirty-five, Clara had given birth to a daughter — their fourth child, Katherine — on July 28, 1909. The baby was the last trace of intimacy between Edward and Clara. By 1910, their marriage was a sham, irrevocably broken, though no divorce proceedings were started. Clara kept the house, with sole parenting duties over the three children at home, and still managed the studio.

Curtis moved into the Rainier Club, in its fancy new downtown digs on Fourth Avenue — a Kirtland Cutter design inspired by Jacobean manor houses of England. Thereafter, he listed the club as his home address. It was the finest dining and gentlemen's parlor in the city, but it was not free. Curtis was broke, as usual. So the club made a deal: he could stay there, in a small room upstairs, with full privileges, but would have to work for his keep. How so? Pictures, what else? And so the most famous portrait photographer in America entered a long period of indentured servitude to the Rainier Club, taking customary Curtis portraits of the members — with the soft lighting, the finished photogravure touches, the fishhook signature that was his brand but often did not come from his actual hand — in return for room and board. He also gave the club Indian pictures to pay the rent, including many of his masterpieces. With every prolonged stay, the Rainier Club added to its collection, becoming in time a museum of sorts to a destitute member.

While he was no longer seeing Clara except for stiff and restrained discussions of family and business, Curtis kept up his correspondence with the guardian of J. P. Morgan's library, Belle da Costa Greene. She was his lifeline; should she turn against Curtis, Morgan might well cut him off. From the Puget Sound winter cabin, he sent her pictures and letters.

My Dear Miss Greene:

Just to let you know that I am alive and at work, and should be able to close up this camp by the middle of May. This has proved to be a very satisfactory and comfortable working camp. I am taking the liberty of sending you a small picture of the cabin, so that you can see what wintertime looks like in this region.

He dropped pictures from many western locales into Miss Greene's mailbox, a form of showmanship that other artists in Morgan's circle could not rival. There he was on a white horse among the Spokane, with a tip of his hat, and there on a mesa in Arizona, and this one shows him fording a river in the Rockies, and just look at the privation of these writing cabins. In every picture he was a man of action in the middle of the scene. But these shots masked a person who had lost his infinite sources of energy. Heavy cigarette smoking in confined, damp spaces and lack of sleep exacted a toll. By the end of that winter in Waterman, Curtis was exhausted. He took to bed for ten days, trying to edit while lying on his back — the most painful convalescence he'd suffered in two decades. Back then, he had Clara to care for him, and she adored him. This time, he had the faithful Myers at hand, but his talents were limited to sprightly shorthand and lucid prose of the type that took final shape in the volume on Joseph's tribe.

"The Nez Perce, a mentally superior people, were friendly from their first contact with white men, and as a tribe they always desired to be so," he wrote, drafting Volume VIII. "Their history since 1855, and particularly in the war of 1877, tells how they were repaid for their loyalty to the white brother." It was an opinion. But also a fact. The Nez Perce had been betrayed — *kicked in the ass,* as Curtis put it to Meany once — perhaps more so, without cause or reason, than any tribe. They had not raped and scalped and raided and plundered. They had done nothing but cooperate with whites, without pandering to them. Curtis had pulled his punches with Custer, and kept his views to himself about the brutal mistreatment of the Navajo at the hands of that well-regarded American hero Kit Carson. Even in his description of the Cheyenne, aside from the account of the Sand Creek massacre, he'd shown restraint. But—*damn all!*—he would not hold back on the Nez Perce. If a reader could look into the face of Chief Joseph, could hear the story of the long retreat, the broken promises, the imprisonment in Oklahoma, the decimation of a superior band of human beings, and not feel some anger, then Curtis would have trouble living with himself. His *North American Indian* was a record, after all, and the record on this band of people was horrid. Look what they'd started with: fine, timber-framed houses, a horse-breeding culture that Lewis and Clark said was better than that developed on Virginia plantations, music and language behind stories that explained the mysteries of the world, and a diet and way of life that promoted longevity. Look what they'd ended up with: early death, jail, treaties ignored, the noble descendants of a line of intelligent, resourceful leaders staring at winter snows in exile on the Columbia Plateau.

"Their unfortunate effort to retain what was rightly their own makes an unparalleled story in the annals of the Indian resistance to the greed of whites."

And once Curtis had started down this narrative road, he could not stop, and did not want to. Myers and Hodge might second-guess him, but these words would stand, because the Nez Perce were subject to "dishonest and relentless subjection." So, for the first time, a gust of outrage made it into *The North American Indian.* Even after surrendering their land, after living as prisoners of war in arid country far from the Northwest, after the tribe had been broken up along religious and treaty factions, they faced new indignities. That, in the view Curtis now held, was the way the United States did business with nations that were recognized as sovereign. All of this, Curtis concluded, "is nothing more than we might have expected, for we as a nation have rarely kept, unmodified, any compact with the Indians." There was no turning back; from then on, *The North American Indian* was not just a showcase of the best of the native world, but a bullhorn for a man who had seen the worst of it.

After the near-calamitous drop down Celilo Falls, the Curtis party scooted through several more stretches of violent white water, arriving at a place known as Bridge of the Gods. It was no bridge but the crumbled foundations of an arch that indicated an ancient basalt piece of the mountain had once straddled the river. It was here that Lewis and Clark had used ropes to lower their canoes down. Myers laughed as Noggie continued to cry.

"Take *his* picture," said Myers, pointing to the cloudy-eyed cook. For anyone who thought the Curtis Indian work was all glamour and exploration, the tears of Noggie would tell another story. At Bridge of the Gods, Curtis could use the one major mechanical manipulation of the river to date, a section of primitive but effective government locks. It was little more than a side channel of the main river, an escalator, both ways, of water that allowed passage. After clearing the locks, the group faced a fresh section of swollen and enraged river. The lock keeper said he could not recall when the river had been so high. But the old bar pilot, who had hired on with Curtis for one last ride down the Columbia, thought otherwise — wasn't anything he hadn't done before. Sure, the lock keeper said, but not in a boat as small and fragile-looking as the one owned by *The North American Indian.*

"No man alive could make it with that . . . tub," said the lock keeper. "The currents have changed since your day." Curtis fired up the gas engine. He was determined to go ahead; the tiny propeller would give them just enough oomph to get through. He ordered everyone aboard.

"Well, Captain," the lock keeper told the pilot, "it's your funeral." Curtis moved to the bow while the pilot guided the tiller. But as they started, the sea-weathered skipper seemed to lose his nerve.

"This ain't navigation," he shouted above the percussive claps of the Columbia, "this is a boxing match . . . Ride 'em high. Don't let a whirlpool get us." As they plunged through the first series of breakers, icy water crashed over them. Then, bobbing through another round, the boat pitched headfirst, bucked up and shot sideways. The lurch nearly threw Curtis into the river. They struggled to stay atop the crests, waves on either side of them. They wrestled with the currents of several eddies, where the water encircled and gripped whatever came its way, and there the engine proved a lifesaver. In one of the whirlpools was a large tree, stripped of its branches, vertical in the water. They had no sooner evaded that trap than a ridge of water collapsed over them. The boat was buried, but popped up and drifted to a side where it was calmer. Soaked and badly shaken, the men pulled their craft ashore. Noggie looked catatonic with fear. The captain was white-faced, lips purple, body trembling. The worst was over. But the price proved high for Curtis's team. Both cook and river pilot said they'd had enough. They quit and departed immediately for Portland. Now it was left to Curtis, Myers and Schwinke. "I became both captain and cook," wrote Curtis. That was just as well, for Curtis had complained about the lousy food made by all of his cooks.

And that night, he showed a skill that he'd first developed as a boy braising muskrat for his family in Wisconsin. He bought an enormous salmon from a fisherman, a spring Chinook, filleted it and cooked it next to a fire, Indian style, on cedar sticks, searing the outside, keeping the inside tender and moist. "It was the fattest, juiciest salmon I've ever tasted," Curtis wrote in one of his culinary digressions. "We ate until there was nothing left but the bones."

Afterward, the picture-taking and story-gathering took on a mournful tone. Where the Corps of Discovery had written of long-settled communities, Curtis struggled to meet a soul. The native people were spent by time and disease. At the site of a formerly large village "we found only two descendants." In other places, the tribes were gone completely, their only trace a bit of rock art scraped onto basalt columns. Just the "old friends" of Curtis, the Wishham, still had a somewhat active village, on the north shore of the river, down from the falls. In talking to Wishham elders, Curtis heard stories of creation, and of how a good spirit had vanquished an evildoer who tied people to a log at the Columbia's mouth and left them to die. The river's bounty, he was told, was a result of a god who had opened a pen where all the salmon had been kept and let them run free forever. He also heard stories of death and decay, the later myths conforming to the loss of the societies.

Both women and men were tattooed. They used canoes in the way inland tribes used horses. They were sexually open, had large, permanent villages and held slaves. The collapse arrived slowly at first and then all at once. The first wave hit after initial white contact, when the diseases for which the Indians had no immunity—cholera, measles, smallpox—killed indiscriminately. Alcohol was next, overwhelming people during the late nineteenth century. This pattern was familiar in its mortal precision, and no part of it surprised Curtis. What stood out in this case was the river. Indians would cross the Columbia in their dugouts to trade salmon and furs for whiskey. They returned drunk, and "whole families were thus wiped out in a moment," Curtis wrote.

The problems for the natives now came from trying to find their way in the twentieth century with greatly diminished numbers. The national census of 1910 had begun, and if counters found anything like what Curtis had seen up close over the last decade—with the Crow, the Sioux and the Indians of the Columbia River—the tribes were even more endangered than he believed. That year, in doing advance work, Myers had found only two surviving members of another tribe, whose name was associated with a famous Pacific Coast oyster, the Willapa. As a conservative guess, Curtis estimated that 95 percent of the original population along the lower river was gone. With the exception of the Wishham, "the Chinook tribes on the river . . . were practically extinct."

For all their troubles, Curtis presented the Wishham in their best light, from a beautiful woman pounding salmon to a sinewy man netting fish. He shot pictures of petroglyphs, fishing platforms and heroic people in the face of a river's power—in line with his original desire to have "nature tell the story." Some years in the future, these images would be hanging in a gallery, a museum, a home, a tribal headquarters or on the wall of a prestigious private club, and people would see what life had been like before all the river was flaccid, clipped by more than a dozen big dams, a "slackwater empire," as the writer Blaine Harden later called it.

To the ocean, the Curtis party of three pushed on, the rapids behind them, the Columbia bar, that collision of high surf and emptying water, ahead of them. The river was so wide it looked like a slow-moving lake, littered with the flotsam of forests. The most productive American fishing fleet was in full frenzy along the shore, with the canneries at Astoria packing salmon to feed the world. Curtis knew he should not risk passage over the bar at river's end. The biggest danger on the Columbia was known as the Graveyard of the Pacific, where more boats had been lost than any other place on the West Coast. In the best of times— calm, windless—it was a tussle between tidal might and river current. Even long-experienced bar pilots guiding sea-tested vessels found the crossing a white-knuckle drama. Sailors would tie themselves to their ship masts to keep from being tossed overboard. Just upriver from this battleground, Curtis anchored his tiny craft and went ashore. He picked oysters at low tide, a kind known for its sweet, somewhat briny taste. He started a beach fire of driftwood, and stoked it until there was a bed of hot coals. Then, with the tide rising, he unleashed his boat and let it go—into the arms of the River of the West, away to violent swells of the bar, "our worthy but nondescript craft adrift that it might float out to meet the ocean breakers and be battered to fragments." At sunset, Curtis cooked the oysters; just a few moments on the coals and the hard shells popped open with a hiss. The men sat on the sand at land's end and ate their fill, Curtis, Myers, and Schwinke, all that was left of the field team, slurping bivalves in the fading light of early summer, wondering if the continent itself had run out of Indians.

The Fisherman—Wishham, 1910. Curtis took a wild ride down the undammed Columbia River in 1910. To his dismay, the once thriving tribes that had lived for millennia off the river's salmon had dwindled to a handful of natives.

12

NEW ART FORMS
1910–1913

BACKSTAGE AT CARNEGIE HALL, Curtis waited for the lights to dim and the orchestra to finish tuning up. When the hum of chatter died down, he peeked out at a house packed with pink-jowled swells in stiff-collared tuxedos and women with jewels glittering atop perfumed décolletage. The New York social set had paid top dollar to listen to the Shadow Catcher talk about *savages*. And more than talk: he was presenting "The Story of a Vanishing Race," a picture opera. But tonight's offering was not purely opera. Nor was it all static picture show. This touring spectacle was a uniquely Curtis hybrid. The visuals were slides from the photographer's work over a fifteen-year span. He had painstakingly hand-colored the slides, so that rock walls at sunset in Canyon de Chelly had an apricot glow, and the faces shot at the magic hour in New Mexico gave off a rugged blush. Montana's alto-cumulus-clouded ceiling could never be the true robin's-egg blue, but it was close. Using a stereopticon projector, or magic lantern as it was called, Curtis could dissolve two colored-tinted pictures, creating narrative motion. He supplemented the stills with film, some of it sandpaper-grainy and herky-jerky, but still—action! And all of these images buttressed a story, narrated by Curtis himself, about an epic tragedy: the slow fade of a people who had lived fascinating lives long before the grandparents of those in Carnegie box seats sailed from Old Europe to seize their homeland. What made the entire experience memorable was the music, from an orchestra playing a score conducted by the renowned Henry F. Gilbert and inspired by the recordings of Indian songs and chants that Curtis had brought home on his wax cylinders. Gilbert had been among the first popular composers to use black gospel music and ragtime. He now took on the challenge of translating Indian music through conventional instruments. The whole of it was a visual-aural feast of the aboriginal, as the critics called it, created by a most American artist at the height of his fame.

Curtis was pleased to see that "The Story of a Vanishing Race" was a sellout, especially in Manhattan. There was no more prestigious interior space in the land than Carnegie's Main Hall, two blocks from Central Park, a venue then twenty years old and home to the New York Philharmonic. But when he looked from behind the curtain one last time, his heart sank at the absence of a single person—Belle da Costa Greene. Curtis had written her from the road, from Boston, with updates of the reviews and crowds as the production rolled through Concord, Providence, Manchester and New Haven on the way to New York. The show was a hit. Capacity crowds! Standing ovations! Rave reviews! He enclosed tickets—front row, of course—for J. P. Morgan, Miss Greene and any number in their entourage. On November 15, 1911, the day of the Carnegie show, came a reply from the librarian: Morgan would be spending the evening with his daughter. "As you know, it is very difficult to get him to go anywhere," Greene wrote Curtis at his hotel.

Yes, of course he knew. Since obtaining the initial financing in 1906, Curtis had seen very little of Morgan, despite long stays in Manhattan. "He spends his time lunching with kings or kaisers or buying Raphaels," said a British patron. The cigar, the top hat, the cane, the hideous purple nose—Curtis experienced very little of the Morgan persona after signing his initial deal. The face of the titan, if not the hand that wrote the checks, was in the person of the enchanting gray-eyed Miss Greene. So, while Curtis didn't expect the aging Morgan to trundle uptown on a November night, he held out hope that the public representative of his patron would be in attendance on the evening of his highest honor. Earlier that year, he had taken his son Harold to visit Belle Greene at the Morgan Library. Hal was impressed at the setting and people in the rich man's circle who knew and praised his father.

In her reply to Curtis's invitation, Greene was cryptic about her plans for the night, sending "our best wishes for your success in your lecture this evening." It wasn't a lecture, damnit! This was something new, groundbreaking, a picture opera. Here was a chance for Belle to see Curtis in another light. Not the desperate man of those lengthy letters from some distant outpost, answering accounting questions, begging for more time, another check in advance, please, please, Miss Greene. Not the harried, deadline-driven artist whose latest installments always carried a note of apology for the tardiness of the publication schedule. Yes, he knew he'd promised Morgan to deliver twenty volumes in five years, and with the time almost expired on their agreement, he was just bringing out the eighth volume. He was reminded regularly that he was woefully short of the five hundred subscriptions he'd promised to sell as a way to keep himself from going back to the well of the tycoon. So be it, Curtis told himself: doing something world class meant deadlines and dollars were never going to fall in line.

Belle Greene did not lack for a social schedule, most of it on behalf of Morgan. At night, she liked to be seen, and was known to drink and flirt with people ranging from the archbishop to the artist yet to sell a first painting. By day, though, she was all business. "If a person is a worm," she once said, "you step on him." She wrote many of Morgan's letters. She bought gifts that he presented to others as his own thoughtful touch. She gossiped, in private parlors and in letter form, about the mistresses of Mr. Morgan. She posed for the painter Paul César Helleu, who presented her in a regal side profile. And, most importantly, her influence over what artifacts of artistic or literary merit would find their way into Morgan's library had expanded as the rich man grew befuddled and sluggish in his eighth decade. The secret of her past was intact, though still subject to much speculation. Her father was far out of sight, living at the world's edge in a diplomatic post in Siberia. Belle had not spoken to him in at least ten years. And she kept lying about her age: was she twenty-five or thirty? "She moved her birth date around like a potted plant," the Morgan biographer Jean Strouse wrote. At the time that Curtis was hoping to impress her at Carnegie Hall, Belle was twenty-seven years old and in an open love affair with a married man, Bernard Berenson, a Renaissance art historian whose principal home was a hillside villa outside Florence. How could Curtis compete with that?

For adulation, he had to settle on the man who introduced him that night in New York, Henry Fairfield Osborn, director of the American Museum of Natural History. A nephew of J. P. Morgan, Osborn was wealthy by birth, hugely influential in some circles, and largely in the Curtis camp. He was also a kook who believed, like other educated men of his age, in the inferiority of some races and their inherent criminality, which could be determined by the size of a person's skull. He had even written President Roosevelt, going on at length about the head size of people from Sicily, implying that the great wave of Italian immigration sweeping over the United States was not a good thing, and raising concern about "the blending of long-skulled and short-skulled types." In other writings, he said the "Negroid race" was in a "state of arrested brain development" because blacks had come from hot equatorial climes that did not foster intellectual advancement. (How might he explain the intelligence and charm of Miss Greene, his uncle's keeper, had he known she was from a black family?) Nordic whites came in for much praise, defined as "broad-headed, gray-eyed Alpines or Celts, short of stature, very Irish in appearance, but without the excitable Irish temperament."

Though such nonsense passed for science in the highest New York circles, Curtis would have none of it. His theme, consistent from the beginning, was that Indians were spiritual, adaptive people with complex societies. They had been massively misunderstood from the start of their encounters with European settlers, and were passing away before the eyes of a generation, mostly through no fault of their own. For them, the present was all of decline, the future practically nonexistent, the past glorious.

"The average conception of the Indian is as a cruel, blood-reeking warrior, a vigorous huntsman, a magnificent paint-and-feather-bedecked specimen of primitive man," said Curtis in a full-page profile in the *New York Times*, reading from his talking points for the picture opera. "Of such we have no end of mental pictures, but to the wonderful inner and devotional life we are largely strangers." The *Times* praised Curtis for the work he had done to preserve tribal languages — twenty-nine vocabularies, recorded and transcribed, thus far. The paper was one of the few institutions to notice this remarkable feat. "Five hundred years from now the value of this work will be beyond all calculation," the *Times* said. "And it is chiefly for posterity that he and Mr. Morgan are working." But for the first time, in print, Curtis revealed the bare truth about his schedule. He was far, far behind, he acknowledged: it would take at least eight more years, until 1919, to finish all twenty volumes.

Osborn appeared nervous as he introduced the man now heralded as the world's foremost expert on American Indians; his voice was weak, tinny, and he failed to rouse the audience. But as the house lights dimmed and the orchestra burst into sound, as images filled the screen and Curtis walked to the side of the stage to read his words, Carnegie Hall was transformed. Gilbert conducted the musicians with one hand and guided the projectionist with the other, synchronizing pictures with music. The screen jumped to life with terraced houses reaching into a desert sky and deep gorges where the first Americans still lived, followed by pictures of slender canoes in the crashing Pacific surf, whirling rapids of the Columbia River, the wind-raked high plains east of Glacier National Park, the red earthen pueblos of New Mexico.

"My greatest desire tonight is that each and every person here enter into the spirit of our evening with the Indians. We cannot weigh, measure or judge their culture with our philosophy. From our analytical and materialistic viewpoint, theirs is a strange world. Deity . . . is everywhere present." And off Curtis went on his oratorical flight, explaining the Great Mystery, the logic behind fasting and sweat lodges, the offerings to the sun, to snakes and to cedar. But it was wrong to see nothing more than primitive animism in these rituals. "It is often said of certain tribes that they are sun-worshippers," Curtis told the audience. "To call them sun-worshippers is, I believe, in most instances about as nearly right as it would be to call all Christian people cross-worshippers. In other words, the sun is but the symbol of the power."

The music swelled as the painted slides passed by, featuring faces to match the surroundings: deeply lined elders on a bluff and smooth-cheeked maidens nearly naked by a waterway, idyllic in their settings but also, especially in the portraits, steely and recalcitrant. Just look at Joseph, and Geronimo, and Red Hawk. Men who never sold out their people, hauled off to prisons far from the lands of their birth, then sent to their graves in humiliation. He let these dead warriors glare at the Carnegie crowd, a bit of psychic revenge. The cinematic portion of the night included the Yeibichai Dance of the Navajo and the Hopi Snake Dance that Curtis had participated in.

The audience loved it. They were "lifted out of the prosaic into the wild, romantic life of the redman," the *New York Evening World* wrote. A few days later, Curtis was given an equally rapturous reception in Washington, at the Belasco Theater, where he entertained a sold-out crowd that included foreign ambassadors, judges, senators and President Taft. "A pictorial and musical gem," the *Washington Times* called it. Roosevelt was not in town, having vacated the White House more than two years earlier, but he sent Curtis a note praising him for doing "a good thing for the whole American people." Curtis was hailed by one paper as "a rare interpretive artist," and by another as "at once a national institution and a national benefit." And lo, shortly thereafter, he finally cracked the thick sandstone walls of the Smithsonian Castle: the board agreed to buy a full subscription of *The North American Indian*. Writing to Meany, Curtis was euphoric at the reaction. In New York, Osborn had turned to him and said Curtis had just won over an audience "that few men in their lifetime have the privilege of facing." One night, a show at the Brooklyn Institute got off to a rough start with a host, the scientist Franklin Hooper, who was skeptical of Curtis's contributions to native scholarship. By curtain's close, Hooper told Curtis he was the first man to give "the real Indian" to an American audience.

"Dear Brother Meany," Curtis reported on his New York appearances, "the enthusiasm was quite out of the ordinary." As usual, this triumph had come with no small amount of sweat and pain. "I passed through 17 kinds of hell in getting this thing underway." In a rare breach of modesty, Curtis confided that he might allow himself to revel in his reviews—if only for a moment. Go ahead and gloat, Meany advised. "You are too sensible to let your head swell too much, but the temptation would certainly entrap an ordinary mortal." The swelling could never last anyway, Curtis indicated. In a letter to his editor Hodge, after recounting all the standing ovations, all the over-the-top reviews, the record crowds, the grueling pace (five shows a week), Curtis once again found himself in a familiar redoubt. "Just at the present moment we are somewhat broke."

The picture opera was supposed to solve the money woes that had shadowed Curtis ever since he abandoned a prosperous life of studio photography to hitch his years to Indian pictures. A fresh infusion of cash from Morgan, $60,000 in late 1909, went straight to Curtis's creditors. As a condition of that new money, Morgan had Curtis incorporate *The North American Indian* and put the operation in the hands of a board of directors in New York. The decision would haunt Curtis, but he was out of options. The 1910 fieldwork—on the Columbia, along the Pacific Coast of Washington and among tribes of Vancouver Island —had been conducted on a shoestring, without money for interpreters or an aide to handle logistics. And since Curtis had also moved out of his house—"address me at the Rainier Club, as usual," he told Hodge beginning in 1910—he had to set aside a certain number of hours to earn his room and board. By the summer of 1911, Curtis was faced with putting the Indian project on indefinite hold. It would be the first summer in more than a decade when he didn't spend all his time on tribal land. He was embarrassed, humbled, his confidence rattled, as he finally told his editor the truth about his impoverishment. "Outside of some absolute miracle there is no chance whatever for my getting funds for field work this year," he wrote Hodge.

It was while stuck in this eddy of despair that Curtis had come up with the idea of the traveling picture opera. The Curtis name was enough to quickly attract backers, who set up an itinerary stretching over two years. A business agent booked halls, found musicians and arranged screen setups, hotels and other work. Curtis hoped that the tour would generate enough money to get his team back into Indian country, the only place where he now felt at home. But by early fall, just as Curtis was about to launch the road show, he was already physically spent. Simultaneously, he had tried to finish the fieldwork with Columbia River tribes, initiate photographic forays among Northwest Coast Indians and handle the myriad tasks of putting together a traveling picture opera production. It was no exaggeration when Curtis was told he was trying to do the work of fifty men. For the second time in two years, he was confined to his bed at the Rainier Club. He collapsed in exhaustion.

After rousing himself for fresh touring in 1912, he took a break of sorts in the summer to work with the tribes that lived along the Pacific shore, from the Strait of Juan de Fuca north. He also managed a quick trip to the Southwest, an opposite climate. After spending time with the Hopi in 1900, 1902, 1904, 1906 and 1911, this latest visit was both jarring and familiar. No tribe had been more welcoming, save perhaps some members of the Crow. He knew enough of the language to greet old friends, and he knew enough of the religion to take umbrage at the creeping vines of missionaries moving over Hopi land. He was startled by how much things had changed. Automobiles rambled along ancient sheep paths. Packaged and powdered food from the government was taking the dietary place of traditional dried meat or cornmeal. The children, back from boarding school, had short hair. Curtis felt fortunate that he had taken so many pictures early on, for there was little of original Hopi life left to be seen, he complained. The habits and routines of daily existence, refined over centuries, had been swapped for those of mainstream America. For the anthropologist, whether a self-educated one with a camera or a pedigreed one backed by a federal grant, there is nothing more disappointing than the banality of modern life.

His views of God had expanded considerably since his days as a boy in a canoe with the colicky preacher and his Bible verses. Early on, Curtis came to believe that the key to getting deep inside the Indian world was to try to understand — and experience, if possible — its religion. He rarely proclaimed the superiority of a Christian deity over one that was alive in the rocks or a small creature. In his enlarged tolerance for the native spiritual world, Curtis grew increasingly impatient with those who tried to impose a dominant religious orthodoxy on these people. And, no doubt, self-interest was at stake: his life's toil, after all, was devoted to Indians "still retaining their primitive ways." Could his camera ever find anything in a church pew, the men in clipped and combed hair, the women with dowdy shawls, to match a naked priest in glorious body paint at dawn?

Curtis had been questioned while on tour about his picture opera's title and the theme that ran through every volume of his work: vanishing race. To the surprise of some authorities, the census of 1910 counted 276,000 Indians in the United States—a gain of 39,000 over 1900. Yet Indians made up less than a single percent of the nation's 92 million people. But vanishing? How could that be if the overall numbers were going in a positive direction? Several scholars, quoted in Curtis profiles in the newspapers, started to take issue with him. "We have as many Indians now as ever existed in the United States," said one authority in the *New York Times.*

Curtis called that "an absolutely ridiculous statement." He said the census had been too broad, counting those with just a strand of Indian heritage. Curtis estimated only about 100,000 "purebloods" were left from shore to shore. He explained what he had witnessed over the past ten years. Along the Columbia River, where Lewis and Clark had seen thousands of people in numerous communities, Curtis found only two small villages with a combined population of less than 200. Around the greater Puget Sound area, where the government had estimated 75,000 natives at treaty time, "today there are scarcely 2,000," said Curtis. The Crow had gone from a population of 9,000 in the nineteenth century to 1,787 in the twentieth. The Atsina numbered barely 500, down by 75 percent. The Piegan, who once counted 12,000 members, now had barely a tenth of that. All the evidence—again, as he saw among the Hopi—was of diminishment and loss. Curtis cited Geronimo's own words, from his ghostwritten autobiography of 1906, in which he said,

"We are vanishing from the earth." Geronimo himself had recently left the planet, after he got drunk one night and fell off a horse-drawn wagon.

Beyond that, raw population figures were not the crux of the issue. Religion, lifestyle, language—fast disappearing. "Whether the American aborigines are a vanishing race or not, the vital question is one of culture rather than of numbers," he said in defense of his work. In his public appearances Curtis was often asked: in a generation's time, would anything be left of the real Indian? And on occasion would come a rejoinder, though not from him: it's not up to a white photographer to define authenticity.

In the fall of 1912, he was back on the road with the picture opera, the same routine as earlier, till the end of the year. The tour was a runaway success, judging by the reviews and the crowds, but it did not make Curtis financially whole. In business matters he was a consistent failure, and his hard-luck streak continued with this production. Like a lot of artists, Curtis had a reverse Midas touch: the creative dream, stoked by audacity, always trumped pragmatic concerns. A more earthbound man would have made a radical change in plans when troubling signs appeared at the first stagings of the musical. Ticket sales were strong, but after paying for everything Curtis came up short—$300 to $500 per show, even after sellouts. Road expenses were much higher than he had anticipated. "Cheer up," he wrote Hodge, a bit of springy sarcasm creeping into his voice, "the worst is yet to come."

Indeed, a few months later he was staring at bankruptcy. "My losses during the winter have been very heavy," he confided to one friend, halfway into the tour. He took out loans from J. P. Morgan, though he tried to keep it secret, for these were not the kind of patron-and-artist deals of earlier days that had been sent to the newspapers for favorable headlines; this was survival money, at 6 percent interest. Two promissory notes in the Morgan archive, one for $12,500, another for $5,000, show Curtis going deeper into his benefactor's keep. No matter: he would never give up, he explained to the House of Morgan. His written list of subscribers included the following names:

His Majesty, George, King of England
His Majesty, Albert, King of the Belgians
Andrew Carnegie
Mrs. E. H. Harriman
James J. Hill
Alexander Graham Bell
Mrs. Frederick Vanderbilt
H. E. Huntington
S. R. Guggenheim
Col. Alden Blethen
Gifford Pinchot
Theodore Roosevelt

He was hustling the Vatican, the publisher of the *Los Angeles Times*, Harrison Gray Otis, and more than three dozen institutions, ranging from the National Library of Wales to the Spokane Public Library. More than ever, he was two people: the public Curtis, celebrated onstage, fussed over by some of the most famous names in the Western world, and the private Curtis, a lonely man without a permanent home, who couldn't display two nickels that he hadn't borrowed from someone else. Curtis had obtained a $3,000 loan from Pinchot, who was ginning up Teddy Roosevelt's independent run for the presidency on the Bull Moose ticket in 1912. The prickly forester was quite the nag on the repayment schedule, and the money may have been more bother than it was worth. In a long explanation for Morgan's staff on how he had come up so short, Curtis blamed his youth and naïveté at the time when the titan first agreed to fund him. The terms of the contract, in which Curtis worked for free and had to rely on advance payments of $3,000 per subscription just to bring the books out, were fatally flawed. Expenses far exceeded income. His team never rested, having traveled enough "to encircle the globe twenty times." He accepted the blame, and faulted himself for letting early flattery overwhelm common sense. "Frankly, being young then, I did not properly discount the enthusiastic commendation and gush," he wrote. To Belle Greene he was more candid, confiding his deepest fear: that the great project was not just stalled, but was over — dead well before its finish.

"It is with considerable hesitation that I speak in this way," he wrote Greene, "but it is only fair that you have knowledge of the situation." With her, he said, he felt "a sympathetic interest" in the work. He explained how he had given his life to creating a lasting record of the continent's first people, and in so doing, "I have made about every sacrifice a human being can for the sake of the work, and the work is worth it." Long gone from the pages of that letter was any trace of the cocksure Shadow Catcher who strode into Morgan's den in 1906 and walked out a King of the World. Now he spoke of posterity and the greater good, like his preacher father appealing for funds to do the Lord's work. His Indian volumes would belong to the ages, and for that "the people of the American continent will look upon it as one of Mr. Morgan's greatest gifts to man." The stunning news in this letter, buried deep, was that even if he could get back on his feet financially, Curtis would need many more years than he'd envisioned to complete all twenty volumes. Originally, of course, he told Morgan he could finish in five years. Then, to the *New York Times,* he had stretched that deadline to thirteen years. Now he told Belle Greene, "field research is a matter of twenty-three to twenty-five years." Yes, a generation's time, and maybe then some, was needed. By that calculation, Curtis might not be done until 1931 — an eternity.

At the same time, Curtis no longer held back in press interviews when asked about government treatment of Indians. Once he'd crossed his own line with Volume VIII, on the Nez Perce, he didn't hesitate to express open contempt. Clipped of his confidence and much of his sense of self-worth, Curtis was more empathetic toward the beaten subjects he photographed. "We have wronged the Indian from the beginning," he said in a lengthy magazine profile. "The white man's sins against him did not cease with the explosion of the final cartridge in the wars which subjugated him in his own country. Our sins of peace . . . have been far greater than our sins of war . . . In peace, we changed the nature of our weapons, that was all; we stopped killing Indians in more or less a fair fight, debauching them, instead, thus slaughtering them by methods which gave them not the slightest chance of retaliation."

When the show landed in Seattle in the fall of 1912, Curtis was greeted by a fawning crowd at the city's opera house. Onstage were fake rocks and real totem poles. In the orchestra pit was a twenty-two-piece ensemble. Meany introduced his friend to the audience, was lavish in praise and then beamed throughout the production. Curtis's daughters applauded wildly; their phantom father was home, and everyone loved him. The city embraced its most famous citizen. He retired late at night to his bunk at the Rainier Club, the huzzahs still ringing in his ears.

Curtis sized up his years: he was almost midway through a masterpiece, hailed as such from coast to coast. Eight volumes had been published. If one of the streetcars clanking up and down the hills of Seattle ran over Curtis, his place in history would be assured. "Such a big dream," as he originally told Bird Grinnell, could actually be realized, though perhaps not in the span of a single man's lifetime. Nonetheless, an epic achievement. His personal life was a disaster — facing bankruptcy and a failed marriage. His mother was ill, his estranged wife could not stand the sight of him, and he was not on speaking terms with his brother Asahel. Curtis's debts were in excess of $50,000, and he had less than $150 in the bank. He had told Hodge that "if I had an earthly thing that was not mortgaged, I should immediately start out to find some one to loan me a few dollars on it." The larger problem, should he ever crawl out of this financial sinkhole, was that by the end of 1912, J. P. Morgan owned Curtis.

Now to the positive side. His children loved him, and he talked of bringing them into the business. Beth, as a teenager, showed an adult's understanding of what was required to make a great picture in the studio, and she had infinite energy, just like her father. The two standout talents on his staff, Bill Myers on the book project and Adolph Muhr in the studio, were still with him, as was Ella McBride. Their work had never been better. Money came mainly from selling Indian prints to tourists from the Curtis studio. At the age of forty-four, though he had suffered two physical breakdowns, Curtis still had the fire in his belly. At times he felt like the fearless and peripatetic twenty-five-year-old who ran up and down Mount Rainier, a cigarette clenched between his lips, heavy glass plates on his back.

And Curtis had two more things going for him at year's end: a boat and a fresh plan. The vessel was the *Elsie Allen*, forty feet long, more than ten feet at the beam, with both a gas engine and sails, a sleek craft built by Skokomish Indians for salmon fishing. Curtis had purchased the boat, cheap, at the end of the Columbia River expedition in 1910, not long after he let his tiny craft go to a watery grave off the Pacific shore. The new boat had proved tough and seaworthy plying the high surf off the Washington coast in that year, where Curtis got to know the continent's western whaling people, the Makah. And it was just the right size for sailing in and out of the fjords of British Columbia. Curtis was developing an obsession—not unlike his love of the Crow and Hopi—for the coastal tribe up north known as Kwakiutl. The new plan had to do with sailing away on the *Elsie Allen*, up the Strait of Georgia, to put together a feature-length film. Curtis had traveled with a motion-picture camera since 1906. By 1912, thanks to advances in technology, this fledgling entertainment form had taken off; every American town of any size now had a picture theater. For Curtis, film was a logical next step. When he ducked into a nickelodeon to watch a half-dozen short films, he found himself in a familiar setting—live music and a projection onstage, just like his touring show. Some of the early silent films even had painted negatives, giving a number of their scenes color, though the process was costly and labor intensive. The problem with these silent cinematic bites was length. *The Great Train Robbery*, produced in 1903, made use of pioneering techniques like cross-cutting and close-ups, but it was only twelve minutes long. The popular films of the first years of the century were mostly primitive westerns—a cowboy aiming his pistol at the camera, causing many in the audience to shriek and duck—or chase films, a thief pursued by cops, or stagy theatrical numbers. By the time Curtis was mulling over his film, multireel picture shows were starting to hit theaters. Using several projectors, the way Curtis had employed a pair of stereopticon portals to put his still images onscreen, filmmakers could show a continuous story lasting almost an hour.

Curtis wanted to film a mythic tale of native people in the days before European contact. He thought the Kwakiutl, with their ornamented war canoes, their striking totem poles and house posts, their large-timbered communal lodges, their hunting prowess off the dangerous Pacific shore, and a history that gave some credence to those who said they once dabbled in headhunting and ritual cannibalism, would be the perfect subject to fill a movie screen. There would be action, drama, love, war, mystery and history, all of it from a world about which Americans knew little. No tribe on the continent had developed more elaborate, artistically detailed masks and costumes of salmon, wolves, turtles, frogs, bears, eagles and ravens. "Their ceremonies are developed to a point which fully justifies the word dramatic," Curtis wrote.

He would seek to re-create a story of maritime magical realism. Yet it would not be fiction, as he imagined it, but rather "a documentary picture of the Kwakiutl tribes." This was a novel idea. The newsreel era was still some years away. What passed for reality cinema — called actuality films — were travelogues or boring clips of ships arriving in port or trains pulling out of a station. Curtis would use an all-Indian cast, all Kwakiutl, not a single Italian in face paint on a Hollywood back lot. He would shoot on location. He would make sure that every prop used, every costume worn, was authentic. The artwork, the houses, the totems, the dugout canoes, the masks, the weapons — all would be made by Kwakiutl hands. He would record native music and get musicians to play it. In essence, the film was a grand expansion of his still pictures and written narratives. Most people who heard his outline thought it was brilliant. Curtis had no doubt he could pull it off, though it would involve a new round of begging from fresh donors. But this film business, he insisted, would be a moneymaking proposition, unlike the picture books. Film was the future. Going over the numbers, he thought he would have little trouble making enough on this movie, and several others, to win freedom from debt and get his great work back on track. He organized the Continental Film Company and sent out a prospectus to investors. "The profits to be had from such pictures are quite large," he wrote, "and exceptionally substantial dividends can be depended upon." With success, he estimated, the company could make a profit of

$100,000 on his first film. And so, with this venture into the new world of motion-picture storytelling, Edward Curtis doubled down: the way to save *The North American Indian* was to create the world's first feature-length documentary film.

In British Columbia, Curtis hired a man who lived in both the native and the white realms to be his guide to the Kwakiutl. George Hunt was a chap-faced, sunken-cheeked, foul-tempered son of a Tlingit woman and a Scottish Hudson's Bay Company drunk. As a boy, he learned to read by copying labels at the trading post. His father beat him for his efforts at literacy, which sent young Hunt to a hideaway in the woods to continue his self-education. When he signed on with Curtis, Hunt was just short of his sixtieth birthday, with a droopy, frost-colored mustache, a freckled bald head and ever-present suspenders holding up his trousers. At first he helped primarily with Volume X. Unlike the previous books, this one would be devoted to a single tribe. Hunt found subjects and settings, and smoothed over disagreements. He was Curtis's ticket to participate in sea lion hunts and forbidden ceremonies. "Inherently curious and acquisitive, and possessed of an excellent memory," Curtis said of Hunt. "Our best authority of the Kwakiutl Indians is this man who, without a single day's schooling, minutely records Indian customs in the native language and translates it word by word into intelligible English." For the film, he designed sets, contracted actors at 50 cents a day and worked on story lines. Hunt was well qualified for his tasks: he'd married into the Kwakiutl, spoke the language of course, but also understood the needs of outside researchers. For nearly two decades, he had worked for Franz Boas, the German-born Jew considered the father of American anthropology. Their most significant season was a winter with the Kwakiutl—brooding and dark, with ceaseless rain outside, but full of theater and bright storytelling inside—that informed two expansive works Boas published on these people. In addition, Hunt helped to bring a Kwakiutl village to Chicago's world's fair in 1893, which gave him a taste of the staging and stereotypes that played best for a big urban audience. In Hunt, Curtis saw traits of Upshaw, his beloved Crow interpreter. He liked Hunt's feistiness, his ambidextrous qualities on land and sea, his rough edges; in Hunt's hard-scrabble background there also was something of Curtis.

Building on what Boas and Hunt had assembled—and the original information collected on an earlier field trip of Myers's—Curtis had plenty of written material for his account of Kwakiutl life. The problem was that what most interested him for his film had been outlawed by the Canadian government. Religious ceremonies, masked theater, exchanges of food and goods for the betterment of clan relationships—all were forbidden in Canada by decree in 1884. It was as if British authorities, during the long rule over the Irish in their homeland, had outlawed the Roman Catholic mass or dances built around Celtic songs. At one time, Hunt had been jailed for his role in resuscitating native rituals; he was released only after convincing the government that his actions were anthropological study—science.

At night, over a smoky fire of hissing wet wood, Curtis and Hunt would exchange rants against the government in distant Ottawa. They were particularly upset that it had outlawed the potlatch. Curtis had participated in this great giveaway, practiced by Northwest tribes from the Columbia River to Alaska, after the reburial of Chief Joseph. He knew it well, and he tried to set the record straight in *The North American Indian*, even correcting the much-respected Boas. The potlatch, said Curtis, was a source of great pride for the giver, rather than an act of greed for the recipient, as some missionaries had portrayed it. The government thought it would bankrupt families. But after participating in the Nez Perce giveaway following Joseph's death, Curtis believed the potlatch was a way to ensure that riches were always passed around, that tribal wealth never stayed in one clan. In this belief he echoed the sentiments of Maquinna, the powerful Nootka chief, who compared the potlatch to a white man's bank, saying, "When we have plenty of money or blankets, we give them away to other chiefs and people, and by and by they return them with interest, and our hearts feel good."

At the risk of imprisonment, Hunt went to work organizing a potlatch and other banned ceremonies for the film. Curtis also ordered him to collect skulls, angering some elders, in order to re-create what the ancient Kwakiutl did with the heads of rivals. This gave Curtis his movie's title, with more than a nod at the popular market: *In the Land of the Head-Hunters*. To make film history, he would have to break the law.

With the picture opera tour at an end, and Hunt's advance work under way in the north, Curtis returned to settle his personal affairs in Seattle. He rested, sleep coming much easier in the long night of the Northwest's early winter. He renewed his work at the studio, catching up with some of the latest techniques in luminescent black-and-white printing being developed by Muhr, his wizard of the darkroom. Raising money for the new medium of film, he found, was not going to be nearly as difficult as selling subscriptions for the books. And then word came on December 11, 1912, of a personal loss: his mother, Ellen Sherriff Curtis, died at the home of her other Seattle son, Asahel. It was not unexpected; she was sixty-eight and had been ill. Young Ed Curtis had been the breadwinner for his mother in Wisconsin starting at the age of fourteen, and later at the Puget Sound homestead. After his studio became a success, he had moved her into his own crowded home in Seattle. But over the past decade, the famous son was never around, and she grew closer to Asahel. At the funeral, in the chapel at Butterworth & Sons in downtown Seattle, and at the burial at Mount Pleasant Cemetery, the two brothers did not speak to each other.

Curtis moved to New York for the winter of 1913 to manage what had become a much more complicated enterprise under a board of directors. While fund-raising for the film, he'd stopped soliciting subscriptions for *The North American Indian*, much to the dismay of his overseers. They were in the midst of deciding how to resolve his debts when, on the last day of March, a Marconi wireless carried news of global impact from overseas: J. P. Morgan had died in Rome, at the age of seventy-five. After traveling to Egypt with his daughter and son-in-law, Morgan had suffered a series of small strokes, and then a much larger one. In Rome he took an eight-room suite at the Grand Hotel and tried to recover. Morgan turned the heat up in his quarters and refused to eat, though he sucked on a lit cigar. As word had leaked about his condition, the financial markets turned shaky. There was little the doctors could do but sedate him with morphine. On the day of his death, his temperature shot up to 104.5 degrees, and he faded in and out of consciousness. The titan's body was taken by train to Paris, and then by ship to New York. Select mourners were allowed to view his casket at the Morgan Library. On the day of his funeral, the New York Stock Exchange was closed until noon in his honor, and a parade of prominent capitalists walked past five thousand roses at the service in St. George's Church.

"My heart and life are broken," said Belle da Costa Greene.

She would be even more devastated after Morgan's will was read. His estate, valued at about $80 million, was not nearly as great as had been speculated. Morgan had put most of his money into art, much of it housed in his library at Thirty-sixth and Madison. His collections were worth perhaps three times as much as the liquid assets in the will. After leaving multimillion-dollar trusts for his daughters, millions more for friends, charities and causes, he designated $3 million outright and the bulk of his fortune in stocks, bonds and property to his son, Jack. That included the library. Belle Greene was given $50,000 (just under $1 million today). The will stipulated that she be kept on in her current position.

To Curtis, the death meant more than the loss of a patron who had given wings to his work, the only rich man who stuck with him. Morgan as Medici also gave him freedom: he never told Curtis what to write or how to print a portrait. He never urged him to hold back on Custer, or bite his tongue when he lashed out at the government. His name was on the checks and on the title page of every volume to date, with a gracious credit.

Within days of the old man's funeral, Jack Morgan signaled a change in direction. Art purchases that had been in the works were frozen, along with other commitments. When Curtis asked Belle Greene to lobby on his behalf, she informed him that Jack Morgan's auditors were going over the books and were concerned about expenses run up by *The North American Indian*.

Curtis wrote a long missive to Greene in his defense. The problem was not too much money spent, he said, but too little. J. P. Morgan's backing had been an excuse for other rich people to decline. He was extremely grateful, mind you, but "the attitude of letting Mr. Morgan do it has been difficult to overcome." Back in 1906, total costs were pro-jected at $1.5 million. Morgan had contributed an initial $75,000, leaving Curtis to raise more than $1.4 million from subscriptions. If he secured 100 subscriptions a year, in five years he would reach the goal. But he was averaging only 23 a year. More than the money, the work had at times strained him to the breaking point. *The North American Indian* was not "a pamphlet at six bits," he raged, but "a real piece of investigation" and "a real book." The House of Morgan was lucky to have a man of his fortitude. "Few men have been so fortunate as to possess the physi-cal strength I have put in this; and year in and year out I have given to the very maximum of my physical and mental endurance in my effort to make the work a worthy one."

He closed with a wish to see Belle in person, perhaps socially. She let him know that it was not possible just now to meet face-to-face. As for the future, everything was under review—including the library itself. They would have to wait, both of them, to see what Jack Morgan had in mind for their fate.

Shore of Shoalwater Bay, 1912. Curtis spent more time with Indians of the Northwest Coast than with any other natives. He wanted to capture the essence of daily life in a thick-forested land by the sea.

13

MOVING PICTURES

1913-1915

T HOUGH HIS EARS were bruised by the street sounds of New York City, and his quarters at the Belmont Hotel could not have been more confining, Curtis let his mind drift to the opposite edge of the country, to the seagoing people of the Northwest Coast. Writing Volume IX and sketching his film outline on the Kwakiutl, he wanted to present the wizards of the Pacific shore as some of the most artistically talented people in the world. For everything the Hopi could do weaving yucca strands into basketry, for every geometric pattern the people of Acoma could paint on clay wedding cups, for every dazzling design a Sioux or a Crow could stitch to a buffalo hide stretched around pine poles—it paled in comparison to the communities of the coastal rainforest. Cubist art by the young Pablo Picasso and others was then popular in Paris, works that forced one to see a woman's nose or an apple in a still life from multiple views. But these Indians had been doing that for centuries: haunted stares locked in cedar, faces of sharp, surreal angles, part human, part wolf, part eagle. A single totem, rising thirty feet, was a log with a life, an elaborate story embedded in the grain.

Without money for fresh field ventures, Curtis rummaged through his past work. He put together everything from his home region and packaged it in New York for the next offering of the book. He would

publish the picture of Princess Angeline, taken seventeen years earlier, and a few more from those days, including *The Clam Digger, The
Mussel Gatherer* and *Shores of Puget Sound*. For this portfolio he added
pictures from a 1912 summer sortie to the Olympic Peninsula, the far
Washington coast and Vancouver Island. He could have found Indians
on the streets of Seattle in that year; some had begun to appear on corners downtown, selling baskets. His brother Asahel took one such picture, a huddled group of Makah: they look like beggars stranded in the
urban wild. This seemed a direct slap at the brother who was lost to
him, the brother who wanted nothing to do with sad-eyed Salish squat-
ting on sidewalks, hands out.

He kept his focus on people in the half-dozen or more tribes still
close to nature in the coastal Northwest. Whereas his previous volume
was a picture story of a ferocious river and the people who defied its
twists to pull fish from the water, this book would present a more or-
derly gathering of food from the sea. Their salmon camps, their spreading of nets, the call of a tidal shift twice a day were sedate by comparison with the rock-balancing acts on the Columbia River. He would
show bare-breasted women in cedar-root skirts, and many silhouettes
against muddied skies. As before, Curtis had an eye for monumental carpentry, revealing the massive, rough-hewn timbers hoisted atop
posts in the house and lodge frames of the Cowichan.

In Seattle, Myers shared Curtis's enthusiasm for the tribes in their
backyard. As they mailed drafts back and forth across the country, the
cowriters shaped a narrative of people who had very little in common
with the Indians of the interior West. This book included songs about
a potlatch, a canoe and love. There was an alphabet, as always, and observations on appearance and accessories: "To heighten their beauty as
well as to protect the skin from wind and sun, both sexes rubbed on
the face a cosmetic compound of grease (preferably kidney fat of the
mountain goat)." And Curtis continued to lash out at the historical record of mistreatment. In explaining the Medicine Creek Treaty of 1854,
he wrote that numerous tribes had given up most of the Puget Sound
region in exchange for a couple of parcels totaling four thousand acres

— "ludicrously inadequate in area, these lands were for the greater part totally unsuited to the needs of the Indians."

J. P. Morgan died as the book was going to press. Just days after the funeral, Curtis added a tribute:

IN MEMORY OF MR. J. PIERPONT MORGAN

In the final hour of producing this volume we are saddened and borne down with the loss of the patron who made the work in its full scope possible . . . In this as in all matters with which he was associated he saw the scope; in a measure the magnitude. The fact that he was so able to comprehend this meant the rendering of a service to the world of art and literature of much value. It meant a substantial and comprehensive addition to the documentary knowledge possessed by the human race.

In closing, Curtis vowed to finish the work, essentially daring Morgan's heir without naming him, and without alluding to his own troubles.

The effort from now until the final volume is written will be for work so strong that there will be an ever-increasing regret that he could not have remained with us until that day when the last chapter is finished.

Curtis was summoned to the House of Morgan barely a week after he wrote that tribute. J. Pierpont "Jack" Morgan Jr. had shown a bit of the collector's knack of his namesake father, though he was less ostentatious about it. He was a bibliophile too, once boasting of the deal he got on a draft of Thackeray's *Vanity Fair* while on a trip to London. The Morgans had been proud enough of the work Curtis had done to date that they gave out volumes as gifts to King Edward VII, the Guildhall Library in London, the Göttingen Library in Germany and numerous museums and book palaces in the United States. But all bets were off after the elder Morgan's death, and Curtis feared the worst. Young Morgan gave him a firm handshake and asked him to be seated.

"I can well understand your anxiety as to what's to be done about *The North American Indian*," he said, and then got right to the business end of things. He'd been going over the books, and yes, as Belle Greene had indicated, there were questions about how the money was spent and why Curtis was so deep in the hole and behind on the original promise of the schedule. Morgan's advisers had conducted a lengthy debate about whether to support the project to the end or to cut their losses and call it quits now.

"As a family," Morgan told Curtis, "we have discussed the matter thoroughly and have decided to finish the undertaking father had in mind." Relief. But there would be some changes. Morgan money would continue to fund field research—on a limited basis, and only after Curtis submitted detailed proposals, dollar amounts to be decided down the road. Curtis would continue to work without salary or grant. Curtis explained that he had launched his film company, that investors were in hand and that the anticipated profits from *In the Land of the Head-Hunters* would likely be enough to cover publication of all future volumes. Very well, but there was the ongoing problem of budgeting his time. Curtis was spending far too many days soliciting subscriptions, with little to show for it. From here on out, the Morgan bank would handle more of the business, to try to limit the hours Curtis had to spend with potential donors. Curtis's job now was to get back in the field, finish his next volume and do his film.

Although this news did not guarantee financial stability, it at least meant Curtis could pack up his tripod and head out to Indian country once more. He was already thinking beyond the Kwakiutl, to California and its numerous small tribes, to new ventures among the natives of New Mexico, and finally a return to the Hopi. By committing the funds to see the fieldwork through, Jack Morgan had apparently freed Curtis of the humiliating experience of asking rich people to contribute to his life work—for now. Miss Greene would be staying on in her present job as gatekeeper and principal collector of the Morgan Library, per the patriarch's will, with a bump in salary. She was indispensable.

"Things have cheered up," Curtis wrote in a quick note to Greene before catching a train headed west.

. . .

Out of the sunless canyons of New York and into a theater of green, Curtis joined his crew in British Columbia. George Hunt had found a number of activities to photograph and was well on his way to assembling a cast and building sets for the movie. They would begin shooting in 1914, a year out. Curtis felt renewed. With a fresh bounce in his step, he walked the shore of Vancouver Island, all pulsing tides and overgrowth, more than fifty pounds on his back, and slogged through the rainforest in search of people unaffected by modern life. In one of the wettest parts of the world, the Indians spoke of two broad categories for rain: male and female. "A 'she rain' is gentle, caressing, clinging, persistent," Curtis explained in an extended note to his daughter Florence, one of the many letters to his children that picked up as he entered middle age. "A 'he rain' is quite the opposite in all ways but that of persistence."

The natives had long ago figured out how to twine cedar strands into hats, capes and skirts—water-resistant clothing spun from the forest. From the time of George Vancouver's landing more than century earlier, visitors had been intrigued by people who seemed perfectly comfortable wearing tree bark. By now, though, most of the natives had ditched traditional outerwear for coats from the Hudson's Bay Company store. When Curtis was paying for a portrait, he asked for the original garment if a family still had one.

In the fall, Curtis was called back to Seattle to confront another loss, sudden and horrid: Adolph Muhr was found dead. His contribution to The Cause could not be overstated. If a face was particularly radiant, sad, lost, lovely or revealing in a fresh way, it was due in considerable measure to Muhr's hand in the studio. He had a mortician's touch for refinishing. The nights of struggle that produced an otherworldly Canyon de Chelly came from the collaboration between the two men. A self-portrait of Curtis the young dandy was actually taken by Muhr in the studio. And he was the link between old-school Indian pictures—done for another one of his employers, Frank A. Rinehart—and those that hang in art galleries. Muhr worked for Curtis from 1904 to 1913, and passed on many of his studio tricks to Imogen Cunningham and

Ella McBride. His death was unexpected—a heart attack, apparently—and the reported circumstances were odd. Muhr had been called as a witness of a minor matter in a murder trial. He gave his testimony in the morning, describing the yard of a neighbor who'd been killed. In the afternoon, with court adjourned for the day, Muhr was strolling down the James Street hill with a prosecutor when he commented on the suddenness of his neighbor's death. "You never can tell just how near you are to eternity," he said. Half an hour later, Muhr was dead. He was fifty-five.

Curtis was beside himself. In less than a year, he'd lost his mother, his patron and his photo-finishing partner. Muhr's end came "without an instant's warning," Curtis told Hodge. In a brief tribute in Volume X, Curtis wrote: "Death has again entered the ranks of those who have labored on this publication. This time, the call came to Mr. A. F. Muhr, who for so many years gave his excellent service in the photographic laboratory." The last word was an apt description of all the creative experimentation conducted by Muhr and Curtis in the Seattle space. In Muhr's place, Curtis promoted McBride, a Curtis acolyte in many endeavors since 1898. She would run the studio. He also brought in as an assistant his daughter Beth, who was seventeen and wanted to learn her father's business. Curtis stayed in Seattle until year's end, bunking at the Rainier Club, guiding the transition and preparing to shoot his feature-length film.

By the spring of 1914, Curtis had spent parts of four seasons studying and photographing the people who would star in his movie. He was impressed by Kwakiutl women. "They retain a fairly pleasing form well past middle age," he noted. "Women who were grandmothers have unsagging breasts which would be the envy of sub-debs." The men, not so much: gloomy, like the surroundings—"they seem completely lost in dark broodings." But as he spent more time with them, Curtis picked up on their sense of humor. He particularly liked how they messed with the minds of missionaries. One day, George Hunt burst into Curtis's tent with news of a great cultural discovery made by a man of the cloth.

"What is it?" Curtis asked.

Hunt fell to the floor in laughter.

"Tell me!"

The Kwakiutl had explained to the missionary the meaning of the totem pole figures—a breakthrough for the cleric, or so he thought. "The man at the bottom, the one with the mustache, is the first Spanish explorer," said Hunt. "Above him, that naked figure, is Adam. The woman is Eve. And the bird at the top represents the Holy Ghost!"

Curtis loved the inherent drama in the tasks of a Kwakiutl day. A sea lion hunt was fraught with tension, a life-and-death pursuit of one-ton mammals in roiling seas. A funeral in that part of the world could make an Irish wake look sedate, and often lasted three days, with a potlatch as the high point. And those naval warriors in decorated canoes were just the right scene-chewing fodder for a motion-picture camera. Though Curtis wanted to show the Kwakiutl in the time before George Vancouver had sailed up the Strait of Georgia in 1792, he also intended to tell a tight, gripping story. It was mythic and indigenous, one he and Myers had recorded during earlier encounters with the Kwakiutl, but also universal: a journey of a young man in search of love and retribution. The movie would follow Motana, a chief's son, on a sojourn that could have been taken from the ancient Greeks. Motana loves Naida and intends to marry her. He upsets the spirits one night by thinking of his love during fasting. Now he must act or perish. To placate the gods, he has to kill a whale, and a sea lion, alone. His odyssey draws him into battle with a rival clan of evil headhunters, setting up a daring attack—the climax —and a victory, feasting and celebration, with a big wedding. For good measure, Curtis added a near-tragic twist at the end.

Because the Kwakiutl of 1914 dressed not unlike the average Canadian whites living in a small coastal town, Curtis and his crew outfitted the Indians in sea otter skirts and cedar bark capes, made at Hunt's direction by the natives. The movie payroll also produced fresh-carved totems, a fifty-foot war canoe and a range of masks and accessories. Clip-on nose rings and wigs were distributed. A leading man was cast —Motana was played by Hunt's son, Stanley. Three different Kwakiutl women starred as the love interest, after family members objected mid-filming and pulled one, then another, of the actresses. With Curtis directing, his young aide Schwinke running the camera and Hunt barking out orders translated from English into the native dialect, the shooting began in earnest in late May. Though it was a fictional story, Curtis described his film as a nonfiction saga, an attempt to document (or recreate) what Pacific maritime Indian life was like before white contact. They shot for three months, working every day in the long light of the north.

"Our activities are such that they should be classified as labor rather than work, but all goes fairly well," Curtis wrote Hodge on the night of the summer solstice.

The most difficult shots would be the action scenes at sea, and for that the filmmaker would need cooperative beasts. Curtis purchased a massive, fresh-killed whale from a commercial outfit up the coast, north of Prince Rupert, and had it towed to a Kwakiutl village. The whale worked for his hunt scene, and Curtis was so proud of his trophy prop that he posed in front of its maw of comblike baleen. He looks small by comparison, but the pride shows on his face.

For the sea lion shots, Curtis, Myers and Stanley Hunt took off for a distant rookery, miles from shore and sheltered harbor. There, the lions, some of them two thousand pounds and up to thirteen feet long, hauled out on a scuff of exposed land called Devil Rock. The crew clambered onto the rock, which Curtis measured at 300 by 500 feet. Curtis marveled at the clack of barking, behemoth lions, the males rounding up their harems, lords of the North Pacific, the smaller females in heat. The trio offloaded packs with cameras, dried food, notebooks, a tent and bedrolls, and Hunt paddled away, planning to pick up the men the next day. They intended to spend a night in order to film the lions at least twice at low tide. The boat had no sooner left than Curtis made a startling discovery: there was no plant life on the island. No ferns, no small shrubs of any sort, no grass, no beach mud. Instead, they found anemones, shallow tidal pools, shiny mussels clinging to wet rock.

"Do you understand the situation?" asked Myers, some panic in his voice. "There's no driftwood on this island!"

Their chart had shown Devil Rock to be forty feet above sea level. And when they landed at low tide, that looked accurate. But it was now clear that this speck of land would be completely submerged at high tide.

"Yes, Myers. I understand."

Either the chart was wrong or they had the wrong island. It was midafternoon. By midnight, in Curtis's calculation, they would be drowned. The water temperature in that part of the Queen Charlotte Islands is rarely above 40 degrees, even in the warmest months. A person could live for perhaps thirty minutes before severe hypothermia set in, and then death. Looking around, Curtis could not find a stray log from which to fashion a primitive raft or float. Still, they worked, shooting the sea lions in a boisterous ritual—magnificent footage, never seen onscreen. Then they made for the highest ground and waited. As evening set in, the edge of their temporary island disappeared. They double- and triple-wrapped their cameras. Sunset was late, well past 10 p.m., and the land slipped away faster than the light. Near midnight, the sea was calm but the water completely covered Devil Rock. From where the men stood they saw nothing but the flat gray plane of the Pacific. A light wind picked up, and sea lions flopped about. Spray lashed the men's faces. The water inched up and over their boots, to the ankles, the knees. The tide had to peak—but when? The fear was that a big breaker would come along and carry them out to sea. They shivered, trading gallows cracks. Deep in the summer night, an hour or so before the first streaks of a new day's pink appeared in the east, the sea seemed to settle, just below their waists.

Back in Prince Rupert, the Canadian authorities launched a search party. The great Edward Curtis was long overdue, and thought to be lost in the disorienting fog of the Queen Charlottes. A story went out by telegraph and was picked up by the wire services. The *New York Times* prepared a lengthy—and largely adulatory—obituary.

When Hunt arrived in his large canoe in the afternoon, he found a trembling, wet crew of filmmakers and his youngest son, the blood drained from his face. They were battered from stumbling on the slick rock, exhausted from the night and the tension, but otherwise in decent shape. The film had been saved.

Hunt started laughing. "I knew you were all dead!"

So did the *New York Times*. A writer who had interviewed Curtis earlier for a profile had been assigned the obituary. He spent several days on the piece before news came that Curtis had survived. Months later, when the writer saw Curtis in New York, he scolded him.

"The next time you drown," he told Curtis, "please stay drowned."

They shot 112 scenes in all, enough footage to edit down to six reels, about an hour. By the close of July, Curtis had his film, including the battle scenes, clashes between clans using spears and wooden clubs. At the same time, the muscle-flexing monarchies of Old Europe and the ossified rulers of the Ottoman Empire were rumbling into war. The assassination of Archduke Ferdinand of Austria, on June 29, 1914, was the first ripple. Soon, four of the world's great empires would be drawn into close-range carnage with ghastly industrial weapons, a war that would end in the collapse of two of them. For Curtis, happy to be finishing *In the Land of the Head-Hunters*, the guns of the Great War could not have been farther away. He called it a wrap and set sail for Seattle on the *Elsie Allen*.

The film opened in New York and Seattle in December of 1914. The editing had been exhausting, much more so than Curtis had expected, plus he had color-tinted scenes for added effect, a time-sucking task. Curtis missed Muhr—his judgment, his sharp eye, his work ethic. But he still had Myers, and gave him grateful credit when he applied the finishing touches to Volume X that winter, while balancing film and writing duty. "Mr. W. E. Myers, who has been so long identified with *The North American Indian*, has done his best work here, and to his valuable collaboration much of the success of this volume is due." Curtis sent a note to subscribers, with some self-congratulation at having reached the halfway point of the twenty volumes.

At the film's premiere, Curtis employed an orchestra that played a score composed by John J. Braham, who was known for his work with Gilbert and Sullivan. Braham had worked from wax cylinder recordings of Kwakiutl songs brought back by Curtis. The movie posters showed giant carved raven heads swallowing a nearly naked man; it looked like early 3D, promised "Eight thousand feet of tinted pictures by the world's master photographer!" Handbills proclaimed, "Every participant an Indian and every incident true to native life." A tag line on one poster read:

AN ABORIGINAL ROMANCE
EDWARD CURTIS'S WONDERFUL
INDIAN PHOTO DRAMA

The movie was a smash—with the critics. "A gem of the motion picture art," wrote W. Stephen Bush, a prominent early film writer. "Mr. Curtis has found the short cut of genius and he eminently succeeds where others have dismally failed." He added, "I speak advisedly when I say that this production sets a new mark in artistic handling of films in which education values mingle with dramatic interest . . . It is not a feature for the nickelodeon or the cheap house, but it ought to be welcomed by the better class of houses . . . that want to give their patrons a special treat." The poet Vachel Lindsay, writing in a book on the value of film, praised Curtis for "a supreme art achievement" and gave him credit for breaking ground on a number of fronts—location shooting, story, native cast. Even the scholars weighed in with positive notices. "The settings, costumes and the incidents themselves were also ethnologically correct and the dramatic interest of the play was well-sustained," wrote Alanson Skinner, of the American Museum of Natural History, in a note to Curtis. "I think you have succeeded in making ethnology come alive." At the initial showings at the Casino Theatre in New York—tickets 25 cents for a matinee, 50 cents for an evening show —crowds gave the film standing ovations. Audiences particularly liked the sea lion scene shot on Devil Rock. The *New York Times* praised a story told "entirely from the Indian viewpoint" and marveled at the tinted scenes, crediting Curtis with a real advance in motion-picture art by creating "new color systems." At the Moore Theatre in Seattle, reaction was equally strong. "A powerful, gripping story," wrote the critic for the *Post-Intelligencer*. "A genuine sensation." The show business trade paper *Variety* could not get over the realism, and was astonished that every actor in the film was "a genuine American Indian." (Though in fact they were Canadian Indians.)

In production, the film had gone over budget; the total cost was in excess of $75,000 — no surprise, given the maker. A weeklong run in a half-dozen cities had grossed $3,269 — not disastrous, but not promising either. But a dispute with a distributor over who would pay to get the movie into wide release put it in limbo. The film was pulled, pending litigation. Curtis could not believe it. He'd produced another masterpiece, as it was called, and nobody was going to see it. Would it rot in a basement, all that action, the world's first in a class? The investors who'd been promised sizable returns raised a caterwaul. Curtis could not sleep, could not eat. He paced his room at the Belmont and burned up phone and telegraph lines in the city. He filed suit against the distributor, claiming it had broken their agreement. But the suit was slow to get anywhere. Meanwhile, the courts held *In the Land of the Head-Hunters* hostage.

"I am sparring for my life and gasping for breath and at the same time working so hard that I am worn to more than the old time thin edge," Curtis wrote Hodge.

Eight years after *In the Land of the Head-Hunters* had opened and mysteriously vanished, a silent film titled *Nanook of the North — A Story of Love and Life in the Actual Arctic* was released in theaters around the world. Its director, Robert Flaherty, had studied the Curtis movie frame by frame and spent an afternoon with the Shadow Catcher, asking him about his methods, his location ideas, how to work with native people. Flaherty had tried to do a film on Eskimos at the same time that Curtis was finishing *Head-Hunters*, and his earlier effort was pedestrian. As a professional courtesy, Curtis explained how he built sets based on native models, hired only Indian actors and generally tried to create a lost world in an authentic way. When Flaherty set out to make *Nanook*, he followed the Curtis model. The film was shot near Hudson's Bay. Igloos were built. Costumes from the old days were made fresh for the film. Scenes showed traditional hunting, hut-making and meat-drying, and included a thrilling sequence with Nanook hunting seals by spear. The Flaherty film was a huge success, and he was credited with making the first feature-length documentary.

Two years later, in 1924, Curtis sold all rights to his film to the American Museum of Natural History for $1,500 and shipped the master print and negative to New York. The litigation had never been settled; the case had died in court. The film was bound for a vault in the museum; it was an artifact, a forgotten one at that.

Curtis with a whale carcass on the Pacific shore, date unknown. This shot was probably taken during the filming of Curtis's *In the Land of the Head-Hunters*.

Masked dancers in a canoe, a still from the movie, 1914. Recent historians have credited Curtis with a breakthrough film—shot entirely on location, using an all-native cast—that was largely forgotten for much of the twentieth century.

Wedding party, 1914. Another still from the film, in which Curtis sought to re-create a mythic story of the Kwakiutl.

14

LOST DAYS
1916–1922

I N   T H E   G O O D   Y E A R S, when she was Clara the bright, she alone shared his idea to accomplish something great and lasting, and she alone assured him he could do it. His passion was for her before it was for images on platinum. He wrote hundreds of letters to her in those days of struggle, sharing his doubts, living the Big Idea in words. Clara had saved the letters, her children explained later, because they made her feel close to him at times when she didn't know where he was or what tribe he was with, and because it reminded her of what she loved, and because—yes, *he was a genius, damnit*. Look at how he agonized. Consider the torture, on body and mind. And here and there, some sweet touches. But Clara Curtis eventually destroyed the letters, as family lore has it, leaving behind very little from the days when they were one. What lives beyond her years, the lasting words, come from a pad of court documents in Seattle, divorce case number 118324 in King County, the first filing on October 6, 1916. Here she makes the legal claims that stab at a marriage when it is down and already dead. Here she goes public with a view of a man no one would like.

"He has been guilty of inhuman treatment," refusing to communicate with her in any way, she alleges. He was an absentee mate: "The defendant has been at home but little for ten years." He gradually reduced her role in the business, pushed her out even as he brought the children in. He was "incompetent" to put their "minor daughter in charge of the studio" while leaving Clara in the dark. Everything they own in common—the studio, the Seattle house, the land across the sound—is not just mortgaged, but facing possible foreclosure. Through twenty-four years of marriage "this plaintiff has been a faithful wife to the defendant," while he "associated with other women." This last claim was news, of the screaming variety.

WIFE SUES ED S. CURTIS FOR DIVORCE
CHARGES FAMOUS MATE LIKED OTHER WOMEN'S COMPANY

The *Seattle Star* put the above two-stack headline on page one, a full eight columns across the top of the fold. It was bigger news than bootleggers paying off detectives, Mother Jones stirring up New York or speculators cornering tickets to the World Series. No names of other lovers were listed. She may simply have been trying to meet the legal threshold for divorce, charging Curtis with adultery and cruelty. In any event, "Morgan's friend," as Curtis was called by the papers, was a lout. "He made every effort to turn the children against me by false stories," Mrs. Curtis was quoted as saying. The loaded terms of broken love never make for nuanced reading in the papers. And because Curtis could not be reached for comment when Clara asked for a divorce, his side of the story went unreported.

He did respond later, in a court filing listing his assets. Clara had asked for the studio, the house and alimony payments for the one child still at home. Harold, the oldest at twenty-three, was living in New York. Beth, twenty, and Florence, seventeen, were in Seattle, though both had moved into a boarding house, and taken their father's side. "They were devastated," recalled James Graybill, the surviving grandson of Edward and Clara Curtis. "It was a real bad deal for the girls because of all the publicity," Graybill said. "My mother [Florence] was a freshman at the University of Washington, and she ended up dropping out of school because of the divorce." Only little Katherine, seven, remained with Clara.

Whatever Seattle society thought of the best-known resident of the city, they could not have imagined he was anything like the pauper who told his story in the grim detailing of his financial plight submitted to the court. For *The North American Indian* "he receives no salary" and is working without financial incentive, for he has "no contract to get returns." He is essentially living off the kindness of others: Morgans in New York, the Rainier Club in Seattle, loans from friends like Meany and Pinchot. The film, so well reviewed, so revolutionary, made no money, and in fact put him deeper into debt. Finally, he denies that he has ever been unfaithful.

Curtis was lucky to get anything fresh for *The North American Indian* in 1916. Volume X, on the Kwakiutl, published the previous year, was as impressive in narrative, illustration and breadth of information as anything he had yet done. With the new offering, Volume XI, Curtis returned to his home region for a third and final time, devoting most of it to the Haida and the Nootka, people who lived on the western side of Vancouver Island. It was almost spare, this volume, not nearly as rich in variety as prior offerings. It didn't feel quite so luxurious, and for this Curtis blamed the war. When the powers of Europe started slaughtering one another, Curtis was unable to get the handmade Dutch paper he had used in all the other books. Worse, the war froze the economy, and all subscription sales came to a halt.

Curtis made no mention of his personal troubles in writing to Jack Morgan, nor did he allude to them in Volume XI. Regardless of the turmoil, Curtis presented a handful of remarkable pictures, most of them taken in 1915. One subject was the Makah, who lived in the village of Neah Bay, Washington, a sodden place that can get nearly two hundred inches of rain a year and is as far west as a person can go on the American mainland without falling into the ocean. He found the people there a match for the weather, and wrote that "their later reputation for exceptional surliness" was deserved. They lived in unpainted plank houses, which he showed in unglamorous poses, looking slapdash and weather-worn. *Village Scene — Neah Bay* was the title of that one, with a mongrel dog foregrounding a row of low-slung, windowless shacks built around a muddy street. It was an exceptional composition for Curtis, who often went out of his way to avoid an impression of squalor, even as he tilled the theme of last days. By contrast, the houses of the snug harbor across the strait on Vancouver Island, in an image titled *Village of Nootka,* are the picture of settled native prosperity. And he certainly was more fond of the Indians on the island than those hugging the savage coast of Washington. In his history of the area, he wrote how five flags—of Spain, Russia, Great Britain, the United States and Canada—had flown over some of the coastal villages of Vancouver Island, each power prompting little more than a collective shrug from the long-time inhabitants. An odd culture was now taking shape, though Curtis hinted at its transient nature.

"The parade ground cleared of the heavy forest by Spanish soldiers is now used by Indian boys in the American game of baseball."

For all of his less-than-complimentary photos of the coastal natives in repose on the American side of the saltwater border, Curtis put his best shine on those same people when they took to the sea. His pictures of deep-water fishing, salmon-spearing and archers firing at sea otters from rocking canoes—these action sequences also capture an anthropologic moment. He found picnic-table-sized fillets of halibut, laid out on the beach for drying in the unreliable Neah Bay sun. Here was a woman cooking whale blubber over a driftwood fire, surf on the horizon. And a partially butchered humpback on the shore, eyed by two tiny women in silhouette, conveys the enormity of the creature and of the task at hand. His best work is called *The Whaler—Makah,* a full-length portrait of a barefoot, grim-faced, rat-haired man wearing what looks like a bearskin cloak. The picture was staged for Curtis, based on oral history. The man is holding a heavy wooden harpoon shaft, five inches in diameter, maybe twenty feet long, attached by rope to a pair of floatable sea lion bladders.

In his introduction, Curtis credits "the increasingly valuable assistance and collaboration" of Myers, his cowriter and chief ethnologist, and tips his hat to Edmund Schwinke for gathering the notes on Makah customs. Actually, Myers was now writing most of the text. When Hodge wanted editorial changes, the requests went straight to Myers. Meanwhile, Curtis had patched together another short-term plan for money. He contracted with *Leslie's Illustrated,* a popular weekly, to do a series of short films on the national parks, which would be shown in theaters, and pictures for the magazine. He wrote Schwinke, urging him to be ready to "leave on the shortest possible notice" to assist him with the filming. He was to meet him at the Grand Canyon, and venture from there to Yosemite, Yellowstone and other scenic wonders of the West, dividing up their work. It would be the usual Curtis dash, a pace that never slowed: "lose no time in getting everything in such shape that you can pull out for a trip of a month or six weeks."

But Schwinke had other ideas. The young, buoyant Curtis aide had not been paid for two years, since late 1914, though he didn't seem particularly upset by that. After six years of service to Curtis, working as a stenographer on the Columbia River, a cameraman on the Kwakiutl film and a field journalist among the coastal tribes, Schwinke was mulling over a career change. He was twenty-eight, unmarried, without savings. It was time to do something about his own life. One of his proposals was to have Curtis sell the studio in Seattle—the whole operation —to Schwinke and Ella McBride. It would remain the Curtis studio in name, offering Curtis Indians, but all obligations and profits would go to the pair of assistants. Curtis turned him down. No, never. The studio was his base. Without it, he had nothing. Schwinke replied with a rebuff of his own: he was through with *The North American Indian,* through with Curtis—*and please don't take it personally.* He informed Myers of his plans to quit before he told Curtis. "I notice you don't think much of photography as a vocation," Schwinke wrote Myers. "You may rest assured that mine will not be motion photography. I have had enough of that to last me at least three lifetimes." When Curtis got word, he tried to persuade Schwinke to stay on, sending a check for his *North American Indian* work, explaining that he was trying to recover money lost on the movie. "As to the Film Co: we have sued World Film for $148,000 and anything else the court might see fit to give us but like all legal matters it will be rather long and drawn out. So far we have never had one cent on the picture and I am now endeavoring to carry through other activities."

Schwinke insisted his decision was irreversible. Though the fieldwork thrilled him, beginning with those heart-stopping rides down the rapids of the Columbia River, he was tired of all the deadlines, telegrams and stress, tired of seven-day weeks, no love life, no social life, no fun. He took the summer off to hike in the mountains, sail around the islands of Puget Sound and the San Juans to the north, canoe and laze by campfires—a tonic, all of it. When he returned, he took up business with McBride, who quit the Curtis studio just as the divorce was making news. But the wartime economy was a crusher for business startups. Schwinke then moved to Ohio, married, and joined the army after the United States entered the war in 1918.

Now, Myers and Hodge were all Curtis had left on the payroll, though it was a stretch to call it that. Myers was dispatched to California to start research on the hundreds of small tribes of the state, essentially working for free, the lone pulse of *The North American Indian*. After editing Volume XI, Hodge had nothing more in the Curtis pipeline. He took a prestigious job in New York, moving to the Museum of the American Indian. He agreed to put his red pen through Curtis's work, vetting it as before, should anything new be forthcoming. Their correspondence fell away. Updates were rare, and vague. "Myers is here with me," Curtis wrote at Christmastime, 1916, from Bouse, Arizona, a mining camp in the Sonoran Desert, just the place for two lonely men. A year later, he informed Hodge that he was trying to gin up some work on the Cherokee, who'd been forcibly transplanted from the Georgia pines to the Oklahoma prairie in the nineteenth century, and now lived on an ever-shrinking reservation. He then went dark with his editor. After more than a year, Hodge did hear from Myers with news of Curtis's whereabouts. From New Mexico, the field assistant told the editor that the Shadow Catcher was "riding on work trains and carrying his luggage across arroyos."

Curtis also fell out of contact with Belle Greene. She had admonished him, just after Morgan's death, for appealing to her in such a personal way. Secure for the long term in the Morgan book palace, she became strictly businesslike with Curtis, while telling others of her fabulous love life. She continued her affair with the Renaissance art expert, yet found time to entertain marriage offers from wealthy suitors. "I sent word that all such proposals would be considered alphabetically after my 50th birthday," Greene wrote a friend.

Curtis seemed to have disappeared. Queries to the New York office were met with cryptic replies that he was "out west" and could not be reached. That was true for many months, and may have been therapeutic as much as it was an attempt to dodge Clara's lawyers in Seattle. He managed to get back on Mount Rainier, a beloved aerie, for the pictures he owed *Leslie's*, and cobbled together that work with another contract, with the U.S. Forest Service. His nights were spent on the rim of the Grand Canyon, alone, or in the welcoming embrace of the Sierra's light in Yosemite, waterfalls lulling him to sleep, or next to geysers in Yellowstone, a tired mule for company, or in a dusty train station in the Southwest, waiting for the local to carry him to the next destination. Meany received an occasional note postmarked from a national park, the divorce not mentioned, Curtis's enthusiasm focused on Indians or the love they both shared for the big volcano south of Seattle. Meany's group, the Mountaineers, was leading a number of first ascents up Rainier, and Curtis daydreamed of spending climbing days with his old friend. Several times, Curtis slipped into Seattle, sleeping at his usual bunk at the men's club, checking in with daughter Beth at work.

The studio was the crown jewel, for now, of what had been a Curtis empire. In 1916, just before the divorce papers were filed, it had moved to a new location, at Fourth and University, perhaps the most prestigious address in the city, where the University of Washington had its original campus. Across the street were the Indian terra-cotta heads of the Cobb Building, a Beaux Arts beauty completed in 1910. The Indian heads were a tribute to Curtis. A hotel that was destined to be the city's finest, the Olympic, would soon rise on another corner. The studio was a must-stop for educated tourists visiting Seattle. Inside, light flowed through large windows, illuminating the inlaid wood floor, the stunning designs of Navajo rugs and the numerous portraits in the gallery. Beth Curtis, just out of her teens, oversaw the operation. In a few short years she had gone from apprentice to boss, a source of many disputes with her mother, who had tried to keep a hand in the family's most valuable asset. Here, orotone prints were refined and rebranded as Curt-tones. This process, used only rarely by Curtis, involved printing an image directly onto glass instead of paper, then backing it with a gold-tinged spray. Curt-tones were more fragile, but could also command a much higher price; the finish jumped out of the frame.

Beth tried to keep her mother, who was full of rage, at arm's length. As Beth had risen, Clara had been marginalized. She would show up at the studio steaming, and start harassing employees. Beth was embarrassed; customers were shocked at the shouting matches, the accusations. To Beth it seemed that her mother was on a campaign of intimidation designed to drive the daughter from the business or to bring the whole enterprise down. On an April day in 1919, Clara stormed into the studio, moving with a single crutch. She had been injured, she said, and it was because of the strain of the broken marriage and family strife. When Beth approached her, Clara attacked her with the crutch. Employees were stunned—mother and daughter coming to blows, a combustion of screeching and flailing arms.

When *Curtis v. Curtis* was finally settled in June of 1919, Clara got the house and the studio. The judge ordered Curtis to pay her $100 a month in child support. She had been unrelenting in going after what she felt was rightfully hers after nearly a quarter century of marriage, and the court agreed with her. Since filing to end the marriage in 1916, she had requested preliminary financial help, but Curtis was unresponsive. In 1918, she asked that he be held in contempt for failing to pay alimony. "I am practically destitute and dependent upon friends and relatives for support," she wrote. As one example of her sorry state, she said her youngest child was in need of dental work, but there was no way to raise the $300 for it. She had also sued Beth, claiming her oldest daughter was in cahoots with Curtis to deprive her of income. In Beth's response, she said Clara had gone mad. She detailed the ugly visits in the studio when Clara tried to "harass patrons" and "greatly embarrass" Beth. It came to a head with the assault. Yes, there was plenty of vitriol, even some violence, Clara agreed—but for good reason. She said Beth had been secretly funneling money to her famous father. "He is in the habit of going from place to place all about the country, living in a manner befitting his reputation and his pretentions." In truth, Curtis was living more like a hobo, sleeping under the stars more often than he was beneath the roof of a hotel; without permanent address or paycheck, he wandered the West.

That same year, Curtis lost the most powerful and influential of all his backers, Theodore Roosevelt. The president died in his bed at Sagamore Hill at the age of sixty, a relatively young man who had lived a dozen lives in his three score years. Curtis had tried to maintain his ties to Roosevelt after the president left office in 1909. He sent him notes and pictures, always addressing him as "My Dear Colonel Roosevelt," as T.R. preferred to be called postpresidency. But starting about 1915, the notes became excuses of a sort, Curtis apologizing for being late with a promised photograph or claiming once that he had nothing to do with someone who had petitioned Roosevelt to speak on Curtis's behalf. This most energetic, athletic and prolific of presidents died of an embolism in the lung—a blood clot. Other maladies surely took their toll. He had carried a bullet in his chest since a would-be assassin shot him during a speech in the frenetic 1912 Bull Moose election campaign. The gunman's slug was deemed too deep, too close to vital organs, to remove. Roosevelt's trip to an uncharted and malarial river in the Amazon—"I had to go, it was my last chance to be a boy"—had nearly killed him, and he never had the same vigor afterward. But it was the death of his son Quentin, an aviator for the Allies who was shot down by the Germans in a war Roosevelt righteously promoted, that left him so bereft of spirit, a Shakespearean ending.

For Curtis, losing the studio was the lowest blow. His countless negatives and glass plates, the many prints he had labored over with Muhr —they were part of "the property." What would Clara, still seething and capable of assaulting her own daughter, do with these treasures? Beth, apparently, was unwilling to take that chance. Rushing to act before the keys were turned over to her mother—and moving ahead with the approval of her father—Beth and several employees worked nonstop to print up dozens of Curt-tones of some of the more iconic images and shepherd them off for safekeeping. Then, trunkloads of glass negatives were taken across the street to the basement of the Cobb Building and destroyed. It is unclear why this was done—was it to prevent Clara from going out on her own with all the Curtis property she'd won in the divorce, as some family members have said? —but what is known is that hundreds of plates were smashed to pieces.

The tired sun of Hollywood was not the ideal cast for a man who once waited days for a single instant when natural light held the world a certain way. But Curtis was now being paid by how quickly he produced a picture, and so better to move it along. Here was Tarzan in 1921, looking ridiculous in leopard-skin loincloth, fake vines in the foreground, blowing a flute. A flute! The job that kept Curtis going in 1921 found him shooting the actor Elmo Lincoln, who starred in a series of Tarzan movies at the height of the silent picture era. Lincoln had made a name for himself in *The Birth of a Nation* and *Intolerance*, two of the best-known works of D. W. Griffith, and he could be a pain.

For Curtis, Los Angeles was now home. He opened a new office at 668 South Rampart Street, a few blocks from some of the major film studios. It was just Curtis and his daughter. Beth ran the business side. Curtis labored over portraits of character actors and cowboy stars, film directors and minor starlets. He needed a fresh start, and Hollywood, with a steady payroll for pictures, seemed like the best place. It meant something, still, to have "Curtis" written across the bottom of a photograph, with the familiar fishhook signature. The jobs came at an uneven pace and did nothing to stir Curtis's blood. It was hackwork. He processed the pictures out of his home. One of the great ironies to beset his own film was that shortly after *In the Land of the Head-Hunters* was released, the commissioner of Indian affairs announced that the government would no longer allow filming of Indians in "exhibitions of their old-time customs and dances." Hollywood went back to featuring Italians and Mexicans in pulpy westerns shot on back lots not far from where Curtis now lived.

Curtis was a middle-aged, divorced man trapped by bad luck, he told a friend, without spare cash even for a train ride to Arizona. The piecemeal work paid the bills, and kept the "Home of Curtis Indians," as it said on the stationery, a going concern. What that meant was that—someday—there might be enough money to spring him from Los Angeles. At first he did only movie stills, though he certainly knew his way around any device to record an image. Tarzan was a big client. Curtis tried to bring some dignity to the work. He posed the shirtless actor straddling a stream—the familiar water motif—each leg on a rock. The studio wanted the leopard skin, and the damn flute. Who was Tarzan calling? Would creatures of the African wild respond to a summons from a white guy with a delicate instrument? These were not questions for Curtis to answer. His job was to take the publicity shots and go on his way.

In time, he found work from some of the biggest names in Hollywood, most prominently Cecil B. DeMille. For the great director, Curtis took photographs of *The Ten Commandments* in production, and also did some of the field research, such as it was. A beach in Santa Monica became the Arabian sands. Much later, DeMille gave Curtis acknowledgment as a second cameraman on the film, though he never got a screen credit. A few of the Hollywood pictures that remain reveal a dash of Edward Curtis—a high-drama chariot scene, blue-toned pictures that convey plenty of betrayal, lust and intrigue, and a handful of arty nudes.

Curtis never thought of Hollywood as anything but a sad, single-business town full of hustlers. He recognized the type. Everyone had a screenplay, of course. Even Meany inquired about getting some of his stories onto the screen. Good God. Curtis responded in blunt terms.

"The scenario schools and rewrite crooks keep leading people to think that there is a market for stories," he told Meany. "I know good writers who have from a dozen to 50 good stories on the market and have not sold one in three years."

Meany was by then a beloved figure in the Pacific Northwest; a mountain in the Olympic range would be named for him, as would Meany Crest on Rainier. He'd found it difficult to maintain his friendship with Curtis after the photographer left Seattle in 1919, because Curtis did not hold up his end. He fell out of touch, a slight. He also succumbed to depression, a fog that made him feel helpless and humiliated. In correspondence, and in the eyes of many who had considered him an American master, Curtis was a dead man.

When Meany heard in 1920 that Curtis had slipped into town, he dashed down to the Rainier Club, only to learn that Curtis had already left for the train. The professor ran the half mile to King Street station, but just missed him. Later, he heard that Curtis had suffered a complete breakdown, his depression leaving him unresponsive and unproductive through some of the Hollywood years. That would explain why he was afraid to see Meany, and would go years without writing him.

"My good friend," Meany wrote Curtis in 1921, "I certainly wish you more happiness than has been your portion of late." For all the lapses and holes in their friendship, Meany kept working on the relationship, though Curtis continued to shun him. Sam Hill, the quirky railroad millionaire, suggested to Meany that Curtis could make a bit of money touring reservations with an Indian-loving Frenchman of his acquaintance, Marshal Joseph Joffre, an Allied commander during the Great War. Hill lived in Seattle and was an early Curtis backer. He was best known for erecting an enormous castle along the treeless, windswept hills in the eastern part of the Columbia River Gorge and then stuffing it with Rodin sculptures and live peacocks. Curtis felt the suggestion demeaning. What, was he now some tourist guide for entitled toffs?

Hill's idea prompted the first letter Curtis had sent to Meany in a long time. "I fear this is not possible," he wrote in January of 1922. He was feeling low, empty and angry, and couldn't let any of it go. "Mr. Hill, always having an ample bank account at his command, is scarcely in the position to realize the situation where one has to produce something today or not eat tomorrow."

Makah Whaler, 1915. On the far western edge of the continent, Curtis loved the inherent drama of fishing and whaling. The whaler is Wilson Parker, dressed in traditional bearskin, with the spear and floats used in the hunt.

Soul mate: the towering Professor Edmond Meany shared nearly every moment of triumph and despair with his friend Edward Curtis. Here he poses with Chief Joseph and Joseph's nephew Red Thunder in a picture taken by Curtis in his studio in 1903.

15

SECOND WIND
1922–1927

T HE CALIFORNIA OF THE 1920s was perhaps the most fertile
place on earth to grow a life. In a state the size of Italy, with a
climate often compared to a soft caress, lived barely three million people—and most of them in two urban clusters, around the splendid San
Francisco Bay and in the semidesert strip of Mediterranean idyll in the
south. The natural nursery of heavy winter rains and river-delivered
black soil meant an abundance of earthly riches: cloud-busting red-
woods in the north, billowy copses of wild oak in the foothills east of
the bay, prickly pear cacti and spike-flowered yuccas in the south. It was
all elbow room and opportunity in the sunshine, unless your family had
lived there for centuries and centuries. For in the California of the 1920s
it was easier to find fake Indians in Hollywood than real ones in the land
of their ancestors. When the Spanish sent missionaries in the 1700s,
Indians numbered about 300,000 in the state. They lived in extended
clans, grouped into more than a hundred distinct tribes, none very big.
They were sustained by acorns and game in the Napa Valley, salmon
and berries around the Golden Gate, deer and roots in the Central Valley. In manner and outlook, they were as varied as the terrain. By 1848,
when the American flag replaced those of Spain, Russia, Mexico and the
Bear Flag Republic, the Indian population was about 100,000. Over the

next ten years, a tide of swift mortality wiped out 70,000 natives. What remained of the first residents of California scattered to isolated pockets of the state. The elimination—an indirect biological war—had been so systematic and complete that in 1911, newspapers around the world trumpeted a major discovery: an Indian named Ishi was found near the slopes of Mount Lassen. The last surviving member of the Yahi tribe, he was brought to the University of California at Berkeley for study and probing, a living exhibit. Ishi was short, tangle-haired and middle-aged, and spoke a language no one could understand. His name meant "man" in the Yana dialect, and he was heralded as the last "primitive" Indian in the state.

For Edward Curtis, looking to revive a life work that had been largely dormant for much of the previous eight years, California was a challenge. Even the most knowledgeable anthropologist, aided by a network of native insiders, would be hard-pressed to find remnants of the old life. How to present a culture when only a few scraps existed? Myers had been working California since the team finished with the Kwakiutl in 1914, collecting field notes, conducting interviews, checking facts with scholars. *Start in the north,* he advised Curtis: go to the mountains, the tangle of vines and old-growth trees. The Indians of California were as hidden as the Havasupai at the bottom of the Grand Canyon.

Curtis packed a tent, a cot, a bedroll, clothes, a Coleman stove, pots and pans, several cameras, a recording device, reference books and food into a Chevrolet coupe and headed upstate from Los Angeles. He drove through the Central Valley, following the San Joaquin River and then the big artery of the Sacramento before veering northwest toward the volcano of Mount Shasta and the folds of mountain ranges in the Trinity and Klamath wilderness areas. Getting out of the city and back under an open sky did wonders for his mildewed spirit. And there was an added lift: in the tiny town of Williams, just outside Mendocino National Forest, an easygoing, conversational twenty-three-year-old woman stepped off a train from Seattle and fell into the arms of her father. Florence Curtis wanted to connect with her dad as an assistant in the field. Her hair was cut short for the summer, a bob. At fifty-four,

Curtis had grayed considerably since "Flo" last saw him, and had lost most of his hair on top, which he covered with an ever-present cap. The Vandyke beard, his trademark since the 1890s, remained. He walked with a noticeable limp, and told Florence it was from an encounter with a whale while filming the Kwakiutl—the leviathan's tail had whacked Curtis, severely limiting his mobility. This tale of the tail was just that; the whale, of course, had been purchased dead and towed to the film site. But why attribute a slowing of the great man to the boring grind of age when an adventure in Indian country would add to his legend? If Curtis had begun to embellish his life, Florence did not hold it against him. She found her father a delight—"brawny and brave," she said later, but also "a gentle, sensitive man."

Clara was out of Edward's life, except for missives from her lawyers complaining about tardy alimony payments. He was kept afloat emotionally by the two daughters who worshiped him and a son who wanted to move back west. Beth was twenty-seven and married now to a portrait photographer named Manford Magnuson—a likable addition to the Curtis family. She ran the studio in Los Angeles and spoke for her father on many an occasion, in letter form or on the phone.

The studio and Hollywood work had finally generated some needed money to get Curtis out with the Indians. He'd been putting a few dollars aside in those gray years as well, from royalties of a little children's book he'd published in 1915 and continued to sell, *Indian Days of the Long Ago*. All of this gave him just enough to buy a long furlough away from Hollywood. In Seattle, he was a man from another era, and a subject of dark rumors inside the Rainier Club, where some of his best pictures—magnificently finished and framed—now covered many walls. In Los Angeles he was a minor appendage to a star-making factory. But the closer he got to Indian country, the more Curtis felt like his old self—an aging zephyr, on the move again in search of American originals. With a measure of dignity restored, Curtis felt strong enough to renew a correspondence with an old friend.

"I am certain you will be glad to know that I am in the field working with Indians," he wrote Meany in the summer of 1922, the first letter in seven months. "I am out on a three or four month trip with the Indians of northern California . . . Florence is with me. Other than that, I am alone."

Curtis had emerged from his bleak hibernation earlier that year with a characteristic burst, rousing himself for a sizable achievement in producing Volume XII. This publication was devoted entirely to the Hopi, the second time he had given over all of one work to a single tribe. Jack Morgan paid for the printing, after being nagged by testy subscribers who had not seen anything new from the Shadow Catcher since 1916. The Hopi volume was brilliant, Curtis at the top of his form, the book stuffed with some of his best images collected over a twenty-year period. He had spent seven seasons with the tribe, more than any other, though his last trip, in 1919, was a disappointment. The grim wheels of modernity, which had rolled over the mesas of central Arizona ten years earlier, had left their tracks everywhere. As a result, book twelve was a history more than a contemporary snapshot. But what a story in graphic form. His pictures had that intimacy again, devoid of subject-and-photographer awkwardness. In shots of unwed girls of the Hopi Nation, with their hair tied in those squash blossom whorls that marked their virginity and looked like giant mouse ears, you can almost hear the giggling. In a picture titled *Afternoon Chat,* some of the women cover their mouths in amusement. A crowded still life, *On the Housetop,* is a village scene that explains many facets of Hopi living—the kiva entrance, the ladder to the upper rooms, a baking area where piki bread is prepared, an outdoor oven. And perched around the village like birds on a tree limb are women with black-and-white shawls, their hair wound as tight as a lollipop. Whether in close-ups, like the picture of a child awaiting the return of the snake dancers, or in one showing a Hopi man with straight bangs and early frown lines, or in the long shots that feature architecture and building styles, Curtis offered the most detailed representation of a single tribe ever committed to film.

In the text, cowritten by Myers, it's clear how much of a hold the tribe had on Curtis. "There is a subtle charm about the Hopi and their high-perched homes that has made the work particularly delightful . . . Numerically weak, poor in worldly goods, physically small, they possess true moral courage." The setting was sublime. "The incredible blueness of the sky and brilliance of the stars take hold of the heart and call one back again and again." He detailed an ancient life on eight pueblos carved into the tops of mesas. He told how they had been able to fight off Christianity for nearly four hundred years; only in recent times had a faction of the tribe succumbed to missionaries. He lamented that "a futile decree that Hopi must wear their hair short" and the "blundering interference in harmless religious and personal customs" had resulted in "a gradual abandonment of the old order." In expressing such a sentiment, Curtis was speaking for himself as much as the Hopi. By the 1920s, Curtis concluded of this enchanted bit of high-desert ground, "There is a rather disheartening air of newness."

In California, the Curtis pair pressed the wobbly wheeled Chevy over the high passes around Mount Shasta and ducked into dark forests on the west slope, aiming for hamlets of aboriginal life along the rivers that fell away toward the coast. Most of the area was roadless, a remnant of continental America that had been largely untouched by the tide of humanity then filling other empty spaces on the map. While San Francisco County had a population of 500,000, a few hundred miles north, Trinity County numbered only 2,500 people in its two-million-acre expanse, and not a single incorporated city. Curtis named his car Nanny, for its goatlike prowess at clinging to precipitous vertical sides and leading them onward, upward, downward.

Florence was astonished at her father's pace and his skill in the outdoors. He seemed to know every bird and fish, the name of every flower and fir and deciduous tree along the way. He sensed a coming storm by cloud formations and wind, and remained strangely calm when it looked as if they were lost. In the evening, he put up camp quickly, though it did not look like a hastily thrown-together resting spot. He insisted that the tent always be placed in the finest setting, for the view. In the morning, when Florence awoke, he had coffee brewing and cheese omelets on the Coleman stove. He tried to procure fresh fish at the close of a day. For those dinners, Curtis expertly filleted the salmon and grilled it, skin side against the fire, as the Indians did, and as Curtis had done on the Columbia. He liked his vegetables barely cooked, to keep the flavor intact, and he always brought enough ingredients to toss a salad with Roquefort dressing, the recipe that had dazzled the Roosevelt family. Dessert was poached pears or other fresh fruit, slightly caramelized. All of this was camping fare, done without a kitchen. For sleeping, he weaved spruce boughs into a cushiony bed, "a work of art, and so comfortable," as Florence remembered.

Watching him assemble the set pieces of his life work, Florence was in awe of the one-man *North American Indian* project. She had seen him at work in Canyon de Chelly among the Navajo, dashing between thunderstorms, experimenting with exposures by closing and opening the flap of a tent that served as a portable studio, cutting deals in native shorthand. At the time, she was a girl of seven and could not appreciate his skills in the rugged world he inhabited outside Seattle. As an adult, Florence was amazed at how they would arrive in a strange village and, by day's close, have people posing for him. One rainy afternoon looked like it would end with nothing to show. But Curtis found a teenage girl living along the Smith River. He offered her a silver dollar if she would dress up in a cloak of her family's making and pose on a bluff against a metallic sky. The Tolowa woman was photographed in a bejeweled deerskin kilt, her face in profile. Curtis used a 6½-by-8½-inch camera for this work, the lens expanding out like an accordion, and durable for the bouncing ride of Nanny.

Another time, they camped not far from Ukiah, where Indians labored in the bean fields. The day had been hot, near 100 degrees in Flo's telling. Curtis and daughter were just settling down with the dip of the sun when an Indian girl ran into camp, breathless. She explained that her grandmother had been picking beans in the heat and now seemed dizzy, sick. Curtis must come at once. He fired up the coupe and followed the girl's directions to the Indian settlement. Inside a small lean-to he found a woman who appeared very ill. Florence urged her father to get a doctor.

"That's for them to decide."

Curtis did in fact summon a doctor, but not one with a degree. A medicine man who had been hired by Curtis as a translator arrived with herbal remedies and went to work on the old woman. Curtis and Flo returned to their own camp. The next day, the girl came back with news: her grandmother was much better. "Our medicine man knew what to do." What surprised Florence was that her father had enough faith in the Indians to heal themselves without outside help.

They crossed the coastal mountains, driving east to west, then west to east, in a dizzying zigzag, six times that summer. Nanny held up, but for one hiccup. On a mountain road carved into the red soil of the Klamath range, Curtis veered off to the side, the way narrowing without warning. His car was forced to the edge, where there was no more level ground to hold them. The coupe slipped, slouching toward a deep gorge. Curtis bit on the cigarette in his mouth and gunned the engine; it was just enough to move the car a few more feet, avoiding a free fall. But still, in the tug of gravity, the car leaned, fell on its side and started to tumble. The chasm yawned several hundred feet down. By some miracle the car came to rest on a hardy oak anchored to the mountainside. The tree saved them from certain death, they both recalled, though Curtis credited his driving skill.

"Once in a lifetime one uses good judgment in what seems to be the last moment of existence," he wrote in a long and passionate letter to Meany. "This was one of the times." After the car came to a stop against the tree, Curtis looked below. "Sitting in the seat, I could have tossed my still burning cigarette two hundred feet down to the first ledge of the gorge."

Shortly thereafter, he traded wheels for paddles. They arrived on the shore of the swift Klamath River, a gnarly old stream that drained a land where pre-glacial-age forests of northern California mingled with the newer evergreen terrain of the Pacific Northwest. Hiring two Indian guides, Curtis and daughter moved upriver, negotiating the riffles and tugs of the Klamath, great fun for Florence. Once, she caught sight of her father's face in a moment of uncluttered joy — an image that stayed with her for years.

The trip paid off with some of his most memorable work from California: Indians spearing and catching trout in weirs, harvesting water lilies in late summer light, making huts out of tule reeds. At times, Florence and her old man found a pool of water that was utterly still, providing Curtis the mirror he so loved for reflecting a subject on a rock perch. This kind of framing presented a people inseparable from an unspoiled world—just as Curtis had outlined in 1905. If, back at the government food clinic in town, an image of short-haired men in overalls lining up for powdered milk was more representative of modern Indian life, Curtis wasn't interested. Would an Irishman in a hamlet on the Dingle Peninsula prefer to be shown trailing sheep or getting a care package from America? The question answered itself. Curtis was a documentarian only of a certain kind of life.

In southern Oregon, they chugged up to the rim of Crater Lake, the ancient, lopped-off volcano that was filled with centuries of Cascade runoff, the surface holding a big sky at midday. As John Muir and Gifford Pinchot had discovered when they camped on the crater's edge, one of the deepest lakes in the world made visitors stop in their tracks. Curtis also liked the big, sweet-scented ponderosa pines with their jigsaw puzzle bark. He photographed a Klamath chief looking out at the great bowl of the lake. It was good stuff, this late-summer work, enough to make for some dramatic highlights in Volumes XIII and XIV. The first book would cover the Hupa, the Yurok, the Karok, the Wiyot, the Tolawa, the Tututni, the Shasta, the Achomawi and the Klamath. The next would include the Kato, the Wailaki, the Yuki, the Pomo, the Wintun, the Maidu, the Miwok and the Yokut. He delighted in the details he'd discovered: how the scarlet scalp of a pileated woodpecker was used as the showpiece atop the heads of Hupa dancers, or the explanation for why the Yurok people would not talk to dogs—they were afraid the dogs would talk back.

But as he gathered oral histories, building on the work of Myers and studies that had been written earlier, Curtis could not contain his disgust at the epic of torture these natives had endured—starved, sickened, raped, betrayed, run down, humiliated.

"While practically all Indians suffered seriously at the hands of the settlers and the government, the Indians of this state suffered beyond comparison," he wrote Meany from California. "The principal outdoor sport of the settlers during the 50s and 60s seemingly was the killing of

Indians. There is nothing else in the history of the United States which approaches the inhuman and brutal treatment of the California tribes. Men desiring women merely went to the village or camp, killed the men and took such women as they desired . . . Camps were raided for men to serve as laborers. Such Indian workers were worse than slaves. The food furnished them being so poor and scanty that they died of hunger." He finished with an account of treaties broken after gold was found on Indian land. "Thus the Indians became a people without even camping places which they could call their own. No story can ever be written which can overstate the inhuman treatment accorded the California tribes."

This castigation of his countrymen was not just for Meany's eyes. A very similar vent was opened in Volume XIII. As he emerged from his blue period, Curtis became ever more outspoken. Though they had fought in the Great War, and before that made up a unit of Roosevelt's Rough Riders, Indians still were not citizens in the country some had died for. Tribal holdings continued to shrink, from 138 million acres in Indian hands in 1890 to barely 50 million in the 1920s. Assimilation was the unquestioned policy. Reservations were to be sliced into pieces and sold. Tribal links were considered anachronistic, the customs and rituals barbaric. Indians would blend and fade into the carpet of twentieth-century America until they were no longer identifiable as a people apart, until they looked and talked and worked like everyone else.

In 1923, Curtis helped to found the Indian Welfare League, taking up a political cause—with artists, museum curators and lawyers, based mostly in southern California—for one of the few times in his life. The group was formed to find work and legal services for the tribes, and got heavily involved in the issue of Indian citizenship. But as a one-sided crusader, Curtis often strayed from the script, neither weak-hearted liberal nor hard-nosed realist. His campaign was a mix of tough love for Indians and scorn for Washington experts. In a speech in Santa Fe, he said Indians must stop feeling sorry for themselves. "Self-pity is absolutely fatal," he proclaimed. "It is worse than dope."

At one extreme were government censors and know-nothings, choking the life from native culture and trying to wash the Indian identity

from the people. In Curtis's view, these agents of authority should oc-
cupy a special place in hell, alongside missionaries. At the other end,
Curtis had no tolerance for people who believed Indians could do anything they wanted to so long as it was considered "traditional." He was
particularly upset that men in some of New Mexico's tribes had sex with
young girls because it was somehow tied up in ritual. Curtis knew that
people thought he cared only for "the old Indian, with no interest what-
soever in the economic welfare of the Indian, his education, his future,"
as he said in Santa Fe. In fact, his work to immortalize the Indian past
informed his campaign for the Indian future. That initiative paid off in
1924, when Congress passed the Indian Citizen Act, making native people full stakeholders in the republic. The tribes with treaties, signed by
presidents and passed by Congress, would remain sovereign — nations
within a nation, in the words that came to define the relationship.

The same year saw publication of the two latest editions of *The North
American Indian*, the volumes from work in northern California, Oregon and Nevada. In recording, translating and passing along the words
in numerous tribal tongues, Curtis noted that more languages were spoken on the West Coast of the United States than in all of Europe. In
recounting the near genocide of the first nations of the Golden State,
Curtis was blunt: "The conditions are still so acute that, after spending
many months among these scattered groups of Indians, the author finds
it difficult even to mention the subject with calmness." Reviews of the
new books were practically nonexistent. Americans, in the frothy fever of the Jazz Age, had little interest in Indian pictures. And Curtis? Is
he still with us? There was no mention of him in the papers, even after
the towering achievement of the Hopi volume. Meany tried to cheer his
friend: Curtis was six books from the finish line, and should never give
up so long as he could draw a breath.

"About the only thing my friends can do is hold a little belief in me,"
Curtis replied. "I am working hard and trying to justify such faith as
my friends may have. The problems are many, however the real work
moves on."

The real work then went into high gear, almost matching the pace of Curtis's early years. He and Myers spent the fall of 1924 in the Land of Enchantment, among the pueblos of the Rio Grande, all the way up to Taos. As the Spanish had interbred with many of these tribes, by conquest and settlement, some of the faces looked vaguely European, though Curtis found plenty of fascinating material for his camera. He took issue with some of the earlier conclusions about these people published by Matilda Coxe Stevenson, the anthropologist who spent years in New Mexico under the sponsorship of the Smithsonian. And she took issue with him. "Mr. E. S. Curtis declared to me that to reach the inner life of the Indian one must have his pocket book overflowing until the money runs out in a stream upon the ground," she once said, in reference to the days when Curtis was flush with Morgan money. Were he a credentialed scientist, she said, this would have bothered her greatly. But because he was an artist, she eventually gave him her full support. "Mr. Curtis's work is beautiful as it is." Of course, Curtis always wanted to be known for much more than beauty. Writing Hodge, he and Myers were almost breathless in reporting that, once again, they would be correcting the record; much of what was in textbooks about Acoma, Taos and other communities of New Mexico was simply wrong. This work would fill volumes XVI and XVII.

The next year, 1925, Curtis made a rare business trip to New York. Where once he had crisscrossed the country routinely, he now did so only for the most pressing concerns. Jack Morgan had agreed to see *The North American Indian* through to the end. The House of Morgan was now more than a quarter million dollars into their Indian photographer. Still, its portion covered barely a fourth of Curtis's expenses. This final investment would come with a steep price: Morgan raised the issue of transferring the Curtis copyright to him. More than a decade earlier, Curtis had lost business control over the project itself when it was turned over to Morgan's bankers. He had also given up all rights to his movie in 1924, part of a scramble for desperation cash. But he still held the copyright to the plates and negatives of *The North American Indian*. With his latest investment in Curtis, Morgan expected something in return. It was not a charity they were running. Negotiations would continue.

Curtis headed for the northern plains in the summer of 1925, meeting Myers in Montana. From there, they crossed the Canadian border into Alberta, with its lacerating winds and oceans of grass. The tribes were spread over an enormous expanse of tableland at the foot of the Rockies. Reaching them, getting their stories and taking their pictures, was akin to going into an area the size of Germany and looking for a handful of old ethnic-Polish families.

Curtis and Myers traveled to Calgary and then spread out in search of Sarsi and Cree. It helped tremendously that Curtis had so much prior knowledge from his days with Bird Grinnell among the Blackfeet and Piegan. The Alberta natives depended on caribou, as the Plains Indians to the south relied on buffalo. They were nomadic, following food sources, living most of the year in tipis. The pictures that Curtis took are stark, stripped of artifice. He framed wind-sanded faces and silhouetted men on the bare backs of ponies. He shot Cree picking blueberries and Chipewyan pitching tents in aspen groves. As usual, Myers worked the written narrative. "We were lucky to find a very good source of information for the Cree and Chipewyan, and pumped it dry," Myers wrote Hodge. This work filled Volume XVIII.

The following year, 1926, would be given over to field research for the final book on Indians in the contiguous United States—the tricky task of finding intact indigenous communities in the state of Oklahoma. Then the work would close out, in Volume XX, with people of the far north. Oklahoma was a dumping ground for tribes from all over the country, with reservation boundaries that were as erasable as letters on a crossword puzzle. To Curtis, it was the place where native ways went to die. The name itself is a combination of two Choctaw words—*okla*, which means "people," and *humma*, the word for "red." Nearly a fourth of all Indians in the United States lived there, as Curtis noted. But very few had been in Oklahoma for long, or by choice. What to do, for example, with the so-called Five Civilized Tribes that had been marched from the South and settled in Oklahoma?

Curtis would concentrate on the once fearful Comanche (known as the Lords of the Plains), the Wichita, the Southern Cheyenne and the Oto. He told Myers to be in Oklahoma on May 1, the date of an intertribal gathering. But Myers, a year shy of his fiftieth birthday, had started to drag. He was married, with a business proposition awaiting him in California, and had promised his wife a much-delayed trip to Europe. For days on end he agonized before he penned a painful letter to his boss and partner: "It is an unpleasant thing to have to write you that I shall not be able to do any field work this summer. An opportunity has presented itself to make a lot of money in the next two or three years—a real estate transaction. It is one of the kind that rarely occur, and I am getting too old to pass it up in hope that another will be at hand when the Indian work is finished."

Myers, like Hodge in New York, had been working for minimal compensation, laboring through the 1920s to help Curtis finish *The North American Indian*. But at least Hodge had a steady paycheck from his job at the museum. Myers had nothing to fall back on. The country had gone on an economic tear in the giddy years after the war, the stock market doubling, tripling, commodity prices doing the same thing, real estate that had warranted barely a glance now shingled in gold. Middle-aged, with nothing to show for giving his best years to Ed Curtis, Myers felt he had to leap at a chance to make a deal or two that would set him up for his old age. He had moved to San Francisco with his wife, and using her money, he had bought a building. The plan was to renovate it and then sell it for a large profit. But the project would be time-consuming, leaving little room for anything else. He had no choice but to quit *The North American Indian*. "As you probably know, the desire to finish the job is what has kept me at it these last few years on a salary that doesn't amount to much in these times," he concluded, "and only a very remarkable chance could have induced me to drop the plowhandle."

Having lost Muhr, his photo-finisher, Morgan, his patron, and Upshaw, his translator; having had Phillips, his field stenographer, and Schwinke, his cameraman, go off to other callings, Curtis counted on Myers as a brother in The Cause. Myers was his second self, his ghost in the writing, his chief ethnologist, journalist, editor and wordsmith combined, the only person alive who knew the work as well as Curtis, who bled the project. What's more, he and Curtis truly got along. After almost twenty years together, "we never had a word of discord," Curtis wrote. *The North American Indian,* with its exhaustive accounts of languages, customs and histories that had never been fully recorded, might never have existed without Myers. Not only was his work ethic extraordinary, matching Curtis in long hours, but his temperament was suited to the thankless task. He rarely complained. But it was all over now.

"Like a bolt of lightning out of a clear sky" was how Curtis described the news to Hodge.

He paid tribute to his partner in the introduction to Volume XVIII, the last book to which Myers contributed. "In the field research covering many years, including that of which the present volume is the result, I have had the valued assistance of Mr. W. E. Myers, and it is my misfortune that he has been compelled to withdraw from the work, owing to other demands, after so long a period of harmonious relations and with the single purpose of making these volumes worthy of the subject and of their patrons," Curtis wrote. "His service during that time has been able, faithful, and self-sacrificing, often in the face of adverse conditions, hardship, and discouragement. It is with deep regret to both of us that he has found it impossible to continue the collaboration to the end." Myers wept when he read the dedication.

The new kid was just out of the University of Pennsylvania, a native of Vermont. Did he know anything about the West? About Indians? About ethnology? Not much, as it turned out, but Stewart Eastwood had taken some anthropology classes and had come highly recommended by an authority on "Eastern Woodland Indians," as his résumé said. Eastern Woodland Indians? Who the hell were they?

Curtis had tried to lure Hodge out of the office to take up the final fieldwork with him, knowing he liked to flee the city, particularly for trips to the Southwest. But Hodge had a full schedule at the museum, so he vetted the Ivy League kid and sent him out to Oklahoma to meet the Shadow Catcher. It was a rough go. Eastwood joined Curtis at a large intertribal gathering in the flat light of Oklahoma. They spent weeks working sources, looking for faces to shoot, stories to tell. It was depressing. "The program is tentative," Eastwood reported back to Hodge, "we are up in the air since so many problems have arisen . . . The five civilized tribes are so much civilized, so white, that they will be impossible while the wealthy Osage are not only becoming civilized but wealth gives them a haughtiness difficult to overcome." It was a problem, this business of civilized tribes and tribes grown rich from oil discoveries on tribal land. Curtis noted that "idle wealth" was like a disease among the Osage; the men were chauffeured around in new cars, while the women—in an ironic twist—employed poor whites as their housekeepers.

The Wichita were another kind of problem. Mormon and Baptist missionaries had been all over them, and as a result, many tribal customs were now banned as pagan rituals. Their practice could mean a sentence to hell. "Couldn't even take a picture of one of their grass houses," Eastwood complained. (Curtis eventually managed to shoot that very image, titled *Grass House—Wichita*, for Volume XIX.) Tribe after tribe, it was the same story—no story. The past had not only been banished but wiped away, no trace of it in this new land. The urgency of his work over nearly a third of a century, always in a hurry to stay one step ahead of "civilization," was never more justified than in Oklahoma. There, Curtis saw his worst fear; it was why he'd lamented, time and again, that with each passing month "some old patriarch dies and with him goes a store of knowledge and there is nothing to take its place."

No tribe in the country had fallen so far as the Comanche. Once, as masters of an enormous swath of flatland, they had forced Texans to retreat behind settlement lines and Mexicans to run at the sight of them. Indians from other tribes would slit their own throats before allowing themselves to be taken prisoner by a Comanche. There were no better buffalo hunters, nor more efficient warriors, than this tribe. They reveled in scalping and torture of enemies, particularly fellow Indians without battle skills. Their raids for wives and horses were legendary, going after the Apache, the helpless Five Civilized Tribes and assorted natives up and down the Rio Grande and north into Kansas and Colorado. All of it was carried out with an exuberant "blood lust," as Curtis wrote. The sight of the Comanche now, forced into stoop labor, raising chickens on a reservation in Caddo County, Oklahoma, was pathetic to Curtis. "The old wrinkled men," he wrote, "sit about and tell of the days of their ancestors when life was real and full of action." The best he could do was to concentrate on portraits. Only in the faces could Curtis find some hint of the authentic. He did not care if they appeared before his camera in starched shirt and tie; what fear the Comanche still struck in the hearts of others would have to emanate from a glare that carried a sense of menace from their grandparents.

The text was a struggle from start to finish. Hodge judged it an inferior work and asked for a major rewrite. He complained to Eastwood about his spelling, accuracy, sentence structure and the paucity of new information. It was a mess. They clearly needed Myers's hand. And Myers himself was sorry that the work had suffered so much from his departure, feeling author's remorse. "I am distressed by your report on vol. 19," he wrote Hodge, "it really causes me regret that I yielded to the lure of Mammon." By early 1927, after hammering away at Eastwood, Curtis felt the kid was improving, though he was not holding up well to the withering critiques from Hodge. Eastwood threatened to quit.

"You're a good editor but a bum diplomat," Curtis wrote Hodge. "It has taken a lot of quick figuring and hard talking to keep the boy in line. To have him drop out at this last moment would wreck the ship." Hodge insisted they keep their standards high this close to the end. "There is no need of being thin-skinned in a work of this kind. The manuscript is either right or wrong, and if wrong should be righted." The writers went back to their notes, but it was hard to find water when the well was dry. As they closed out the editing, Curtis conceded that Volume XIX probably would not stand among the rest. Time had robbed him of the chance to find the pulsing heart of Indian life in the state with more Indians than any other.

"You say the Comanche material is inadequate," he wrote Hodge in a testy exchange. "I grant you that it does not make a strong showing, but one cannot make something from nothing . . . The only material we could find was countless, meaningless, fragmentary obscene stories of the camp fire type."

There remained one chance for redemption: to finish on a high note in the far north. Alaska had held a special place in Curtis's heart ever since his sea journey there with the Harriman expedition of 1899. He was thirty-one then, still on the boyish side of manhood. The gimpy-legged graybeard of 1927 who made plans for the final field trip of *The North American Indian* was broke, divorced, a year shy of his sixtieth birthday. He had a lifelong nicotine addiction and the smoker's hack to go with it, as well as assorted grumpy complaints about his bad fortune at this stage of life. And yet in one respect he moved as he always did: confident in motion itself as the animating virtue of his existence. Beth would finance the trip with money from the studio and from her husband, Manford Magnuson, whose own portrait photography business was doing well. The latest home of the Curtis studio was the Biltmore Hotel in Los Angeles, which gave it a glamorous address for the stationery and was a prime spot for tourist traffic. Visitors from the East or from Europe needed to go no further than the lobby of their downtown hotel to purchase a Curtis Indian, the kind of picture that would generate stories back home and become an heirloom in time.

The new plan was to sail from Seattle to Nome, a fogbound seaport in Alaska Territory, ice-free only a few months of the year, within easy distance of the Arctic Circle. From Nome they would branch out to the Bering Sea, to islands and cliffs, in search of Eskimo people, all the way to the Siberian shore. They could work sixteen-hour days in the midnight sun, Curtis reasoned, and stretch the season out until the first snows of September. "Good fortune being with us we may, by working under great pressure, manage to finish the task in one season," Curtis wrote. The college kid, Eastwood, signed on for a second go-round despite his difficult rookie outing in Oklahoma. The joy for Curtis was the first assistant, his daughter Beth. For much of her life she had dreamed of spending time in the wild with her father. Florence had gotten to ex-

perience him in action in California. Now it was Beth's turn. When Myers heard of the final launch of *The North American Indian*, he was sick
with regret, killing time in San Francisco, his real estate deal yet to come
together.

"Curtis writes me that he is leaving for Alaska," Myers told Hodge.
"I wish I were going."

Walpi Maidens — Hopi, 1906. The young women wore their
hair in squash blossom whorls.

On a Housetop — Hopi, 1906. Curtis returned to the Hopi Nation more than half a dozen times, until his presence was barely felt. These women lived at the summit of the stone village of Walpi, in Arizona.

A Smoky Day at the Sugar Bowl—Hupa, 1923. In northern California, after many years in which his grand project was at a standstill, Curtis was revived by a trip with his daughter Florence back into Indian country.

16

THE LONGEST DAYS
1927

T HE STEAMER VICTORIA left Seattle on June 2, 1927, bound for Nome and ports in between, a journey of 2,350 miles by sea, a bit shorter than a trip by train from Puget Sound to New York. The rail travel cross-country could be made in four days. The passage to northern Alaska was supposed to take ten. A late-spring drizzle misted over Elliott Bay as Curtis and his daughter posed on deck. He was in suit and tie, with a thick woolen overcoat, cigarette in hand. Beth wore a flapper's cap, a fur-collared jacket and a cocky smile that bore her father's DNA. "It truly seemed as though I was going to the other end of the world as the boat pulled out from the wharf and I was finally on my way for the much longed for trip with Dad." Both father and daughter kept diaries. For Curtis, it was the only time he wrote a day-by-day account of his activity, and he even gave it a title: "A Rambling Log of the Field Season of the Summer of 1927."

Curtis had last plied these northern waters twenty-eight years earlier. That ship was stocked with liquor, cigars and a canteen of costly preserved foods, as the rail baron E. H. Harriman had spared no expense for the passengers, which included some of the best-known and most learned men in the United States. By contrast, the *Victoria* carried working stiffs—fishermen, bound for seasonal jobs with the salmon fleet, and argonauts, still chasing a strike in goldfields that had been played out years earlier. The trip took almost two weeks. They glided by British Columbia, past the Queen Charlotte Islands where some of *Head-Hunters* had been filmed, into the Russian-flavored port of Sitka for provisions, north to Skagway to drop off the miners, onward to Anchorage, and from there west, out beyond the long finger of the Alaska Peninsula, a sharp right turn north, through the Bering Sea, then northeast at last to the flat, treeless, dispiriting shell of Nome, coated in the mustard light of a June night.

Nome was a dump. What had been in 1910 the largest city in Alaska Territory, with a population of nearly fifteen thousand, was now a few hundred slope-shouldered souls in a hand-me-down town. Once the easy gold that could be sifted from beach sand was gone, the prospectors disappeared as well, littering the coastal plain with their garbage. Nome was left with a boardwalk of uneven planks, shuttered saloons, scraps of long-abandoned tents and heaps of rusted tin cans on the shore. Curtis looked for a quick ticket out of town, to reach the outer islands where Eskimos lived. Frustrated that he could find no one to take him to native villages, Curtis purchased a boat of his own, the *Jewel Guard*, forty feet long, twelve at the beam, with sails and an engine for windless days. It came with a skipper, a Swede called Harry the Fish. They could trust him, Harry the Fish informed the Curtis team, because he'd sworn off alcohol, women and tobacco. The sea was his only remaining vice.

On June 28, they sailed for Nunivak Island, a distance of about three hundred miles—Curtis, Beth, Eastwood and Harry the Fish. Curtis felt unbound, restored by an open calendar in an ocean of possibility. "Anxious, yet thrilled with the joy of riding the high seas in a tiny craft," he wrote. The Bering was deceptively calm at first, though studded with ice blocks. A vigil had to be kept at all hours to avoid a collision with floating hazards. The sea turned churlish one day in afternoon winds, kicking up swells the size of beach cliffs. "The waves were ten times as great as our boat & we were shipping much water," Beth wrote. They soon found safe harbor, went ashore and slept on the beach, snoozing until late afternoon. Pulling up anchor, they navigated by compass reading south through Norton Sound. More ice, the chunks bigger and menacing, appeared. Winds kicked up again, throwing water over the deck. Temperatures were barely above freezing. *Isn't this grand?* "Ice thick, headway slow, fog closed down so cannot see two boat lengths," Curtis wrote. Fearing a collision, Harry the Fish killed the engine and dropped sails. They would drift with the ice. While the others tried to sleep below deck, Curtis kept watch.

"Gloomy night, wind howls thru rigging and there is constant sound of grinding, shifting ice," he wrote, fingers numb, slipping with the churn of the sea. "Not so good a start. From the wind and movement of the ice I know it is a bad storm but being in the ice pack there is no sea." By day five, they were still a considerable distance from Nunivak Island, and the pace was a crawl—barely a mile an hour. They anchored near a sand spit, hoping the storm would be short-lived. After another day, they headed back to sea, only to face even bigger swells. Climbing one of the waves, the ship nearly capsized, a scare that forced a hard decision: back to the sand spit to sit it out. But visibility was gone; the customary Alaskan weather made Norton Sound a dreamscape of murk. "We are headed back, running like a scared jackrabbit," Beth wrote. Near midnight, they hit a sand shoal and came to a dead halt. "Solidly aground, parked on the floor of the Bering Sea," Curtis noted dryly. They were about twenty miles from shore.

As the wind and water sneered all around them, they could do nothing but wait, the boat helpless. "One minute our craft was a joyous, free bird skimming off the sea, the next a crippled thing being pounded across the bar." Curtis did the only thing he could: he waded a few feet from the grounding, set up his tripod and took a picture of the *Jewel Guard* in the grip of Alaskan sand. At least when they found their bodies, a picture would tell a story.

They waited out a cycle of the tide, an eternity, counting on the rising water to lift them. The inbound slosh moved the boat, but not completely off the spit. They sat for another cycle, and this one brought just enough of the sea to liberate the *Jewel Guard*. "Oh, boy!" Curtis wrote. "What a relief to feel her floating." That night, they killed an eider duck and cooked it with dumplings, followed by a dessert of tapioca pudding and apples.

On July 10, the vessel came within sight of Nunivak Island; it had taken them as many days to go 300 miles as it had to sail 2,300 miles from Seattle to Nome. Spirits lifted as soon as they came into the harbor: the island was free of the clutter of modern life. Joy! People rushed up to greet them in well-crafted kayaks made of tight animal skins, chattering away, pointing and laughing. Curtis was euphoric. "The natives here are perhaps the most primitive on the North American Continent," he exulted.

Beth was happy to see her father giddy and locked into his work. They had heard, back in Seattle, of a resident of Nunivak Island named Paul Ivanoff, the son of a Russian father and an Inupiat mother. A pleasant companion, he was hired as a guide. He knew everyone on the island, and ran a reindeer herd that was marshaled around the mosquito-infested tundra like a crowd of cattle. Curtis feasted on the images. And more than any other time in the field, his pictures showed . . . smiles! Native children, native women, native elders—they grinned wind-shined jack-o'-lantern faces back at the Shadow Catcher, exuding a deep beauty. Their nose rings and chin piercings were dazzling little orbs of jewelry, sparkling in the sunlight. This was a place like no other he had seen through three decades of portrait foraging. "Think of it," he wrote. "At last, and for the first time in all my thirty years work with the natives, I have found a place where no missionary has worked."

The most memorable image he called *Woman and Child*, a baby clutching the backside of his serene-looking mother, both clad from head to toe in the soft loft of duck-skin parkas; it was just two faces in a joined bundle of avian hide. The light at Nunivak was not the best—too bright to bring out the deep topography of an Inupiat face—but good weather made for long days of exploring, story-gathering and picture-taking. Eastwood, working with Ivanoff, conducted the language and historical tasks, while Curtis floated around in a kayak taking shots of Eskimos at work and play in the halo of July. Carvers of ivory and hunters of whale, they were active people for a man who loved a purposefully peripatetic life. Curtis could not get over his good fortune.

"Should any misguided missionary start for this island," he wrote, "I trust the sea will do its duty."

They left Nunivak on July 26, hearts heavy with regret. A day later, at the village of Hooper Bay on the Yukon-Kuskokwim Delta, they found a scene of squalor and grim-faced toil among three hundred or so Yup'ik Eskimos. What struck the Curtis party was the filth. The people smelled as bad as they looked, reeking of rotten seal meat, smoked fish and sea detritus. "The Hooper Bay natives have the reputation of being the filthiest human beings on the Globe," Curtis wrote. "I have not seen all the world's dirty natives but I can say that no human can carry more filth than those here." Beth had the same reaction, though without her father's lifetime of perspective. "It is positively the most disgusting place I have ever seen & the women & children have never bathed or combed their hair." Eastwood was appalled too, though he tried to give his observation some gravitas: "Living as they do in mud and dampness, it is estimated that 75% have tuberculosis." The Curtis crew stayed offshore, choosing to sleep on their boat rather than spend a night among the unkempt denizens of Hooper Bay. One evening, desperate to clean the stench of the village from his body, young Eastwood stripped naked and dove into ice-choked waters. They anchored at Hooper Bay just long enough for Curtis to get the picture he was looking for—a beluga whale hunt—and then beat a quick retreat.

Back in Nome in early August, the long days disappearing in gulps of daylight, it was time for Beth to say goodbye. She had allotted most of the summer for the grand northern odyssey with her dad, but had to return to the studio and her husband in southern California. Curtis, Harry the Fish and Eastwood would press on, north to the Arctic Circle. Beth left town for Fairbanks on a clattering, clumsy cargo plane, expressing fear in the last words of her log that "I would never see him again."

A few days out of Nome, drifting toward the Bering Strait, Curtis was drawn to a village clinging to the rocky skin of King Island. It was a terraced, seasonal town for walrus-hunting, perched above a narrow migratory passage. Curtis counted twenty-seven houses, each built from driftwood, standing on tall, rickety stilts. Should a resident step outside for a midnight pee, he might well tumble down a cliff into the sea, a hundred feet beneath the huddle of shacks. A huff of hard wind could blow all of it down. The Curtis crew shouted for a voice; nothing echoed in return. Not only was this village free of missionaries, it was devoid of natives as well. Everyone was away, Curtis surmised, and would take up residence only during the peak of the walrus migration.

"King Island is one of the most picturesque spots in all the North," Curtis wrote in his log. "The island is but a rock pinnacle standing out to sea. The village is like no other village on the continent. These people can well be called North Sea Cliff Dwellers." He managed to find a small place to tie up his boat, and climbed up the hill to investigate the town. His hip was killing him, barking pain with every upward step, but Curtis lost track of the physical irritation and time—"almost exploding with joy at our success of getting pictures of the village." In one image, he shot the stick community from the water, with the *Jewel Guard* in the foreground. This picture reinforced his diary conclusion of King Island: "Truly humans pick strange places in which to exist."

From there, with wind and current on their side, they sailed to Cape Prince of Wales. Curtis took some quick shots of a few native hunters and promised to return when more people were around. The next anchorage was off Little Diomede Island, a dollop of gray rock, only a third of a mile from the International Date Line. The rock was within shouting distance of the Union of Soviet Socialist Republics, on Big Diomede Island. Curtis went ashore with Eastwood, walking through a village of fewer than two hundred Inupiat. A flu epidemic the previous decade had devastated these people, an elder explained. Curtis spent almost a full week on Little Diomede, rarely resting—sixty hours of work for every four hours of sleep, he estimated.

When they left the far northwest of Alaska for the town of Kotzebue, it was already the third week of August, and Harry the Fish was worried, because the natives were starting to haul their boats out for the year. Winter preparations were in full swing. Curtis wanted no hesitation, but also no shortcuts. There was still too much left to photograph. They moved through the Bering Strait, around Cape Prince of Wales, crossed the Arctic Circle and took a sharp right turn to the east, aiming for three communities around Kotzebue.

"Fought the mudflats all day," Curtis wrote of trying to tie up in Kotzebue. "Ran in every direction looking for water deep enough to keep us afloat." He planned to get a decent night's sleep and then work flat out for days on end. The morning of August 19, he went ashore. It didn't take long to see that Kotzebue would be no Nunivak. "Meeting considerable opposition from the missionaries."

The next day. "Worked ashore. Raining; storm too bad for whaling trip."

August 21. "Worked ashore. Still too stormy for whaling."

August 23. The storm abated. They started upriver, looking for pictures and stories, Curtis, Eastwood and a translator. "Camped with our old man that night and he talked until midnight. Bad weather. Rained all night and we had no tents."

August 24. "Cold night, the first real freezing night we have had. Reached the Noatak Village at midnight . . . a fine supper, mostly of salmon trout, nothing equal to them in the salmon family except the small blue salmon of a small stream on the West Coast of Washington."

August 25. "Nice morning. Up early and looking over village. Spent the day making pictures. Eastwood talking with old man. Worked with old man until midnight."

August 26. "Day stormy. Worked with old man. Made some pictures."

August 28. "We are back at Kotzebue and at work."

September 1. "Up at 3:30 and on our way. Storm, wind, rough water. Arrived at Seliwik Village at 7:30 a.m. Work started badly, too much missionary. Missionary has sent out word to all natives that they must not talk to us."

September 2. "Moved up stream three miles to be near an old informant. This man has been driven from the village by the missionaries owing to his refusal to be a Christian. The old man is a cripple and a most pathetic case. Missionary will not allow relatives to assist him in any way."

The snow started that day, falling till dusk. At dawn, the world was white, not the best canvas for the Curtis camera. They worked through the week in freezing temperatures, draining of folklore another loner who'd been shunned by missionaries — "a devil man," as he was called. After three weeks in Kotzebue, they sailed south, for a second session at Cape Wales, before an attempt to get back to Nome. The natives warned them that they were pushing their luck. Harry the Fish knew as much. He told Curtis to look at the empty seas: they were the sole fools testing the elements. Must press on, Curtis insisted.

September 20. "Reached Wales yesterday a little after 3:00 . . . Harry was so mad he was frothing at the mouth. Barometer falling rapidly and storm threatens."

In a race between men and storm, the storm won. When the *Jewel Guard* scooted around the cape and tried to make it to Nome, it was hit by a blast of hard winter. In the teeth of the blizzard, they made anchorage just offshore. The storm raged for a full day. The boat iced up, taking on such a hard coating that it looked as if it were sealed in lacquer. If they did not move, the boat would freeze in place for the next eight months. Out again in open waters, the party ran into a second full day of heavy snow — and a third, and a fourth. They chipped away, Curtis and Eastwood clearing snow, Harry the Fish fuming, as the *Jewel Guard* struggled to get through the weather. "The wind picked up sections of the sea and threw it into our faces," Curtis wrote. The hull began to leak, filling with saltwater from below and slushy snowmelt from above. They were alone, a speck of floating humanity in a cauldron of white. "One nice thing about such situations is that the suspense is short lived," Curtis wrote. "You either make it or you don't."

They made it, sputtering back to Nome on a ship listing with water, its deck encased in ice. A message sent earlier from Kotzebue indicated they had been lost at sea. It was the second time in his life that Curtis had been formally given up for dead. He was overjoyed, not so much at surviving the float through a frozen maze, but at the work produced. If he could get these many negatives, this fresh material, home, he knew he could close out *The North American Indian* with a lasting triumph. He bid goodbye to Harry the Fish and sailed for Puget Sound.

Curtis arrived in Seattle on October 9, 1927. In past years, after a successful trip to some enchanted destination in Indian country, Curtis would hold court with the press. Then, he was the swashbuckler with stories for the newspaper boys, a best westerner. His shine was Seattle's shine, Curtis and the city one and the same. But by 1927, Curtis was a name from another era. If *The North American Indian* was an active project, few people in Seattle knew as much. After his steamer tied up in Elliott Bay, Curtis headed immediately for King Street station to catch a train for Los Angeles. After purchasing his ticket and storing his gear in the train car, he was approached by two uniformed sheriff's deputies and several operatives of the Burns Detective Agency. It had been only half an hour since he'd disembarked from the steamer.

"Are you Edward S. Curtis?"

Indeed. What's this about?

"We have a warrant for your arrest." The men slapped handcuffs on Curtis and marched him off to jail. He was thrown in a cell with other unfortunates. The legal trail from jail led back to Clara Curtis. She had gotten wind of her ex-husband's pending arrival earlier in the week, after reading a news story on his near-death experience in Alaska. On Friday, she went to court and swore out an affidavit saying Curtis had not paid alimony since 1920. She was owed $4,400. She said Curtis had slipped into Seattle in June, traveling "under an assumed name," and was set to return using similar deception. At the close of business that day, a judge had signed an order for the sheriff to arrest Curtis "whenever and wherever found."

Woman and Child, 1927. On Nunivak Island, in the far north of an Alaskan summer, Curtis and his daughter Beth conducted the final field trip of *The North American Indian*. Curtis was never happier. "Should any misguided missionary start for this island," he wrote, "I trust the sea will do its duty."

King Island Village, 1927. A hamlet on stilts. "This village is like no other on the continent," Curtis wrote.

17

FIGHT TO THE FINISH
1927–1932

AFTER SPENDING TWO days in jail, the figure who stood before King County Superior Court Judge J. T. Ronald on Tuesday morning was a shambles—hair matted, clothes soiled, eyes clouded. Following more than a decade out of public view in his hometown, Curtis had made "a startling, if humiliating reappearance in Seattle," one reporter wrote. Could this wreck who limped toward the witness stand, this low-voiced, snowy-headed, reedy-armed man, be the same Edward S. Curtis who once bestrode the city, friend of presidents and tycoons, a giant in the world of photographic art, the anthropologic auteur, the man once hailed by a paper in the other Washington as "a national institution"?

In court, Clara Curtis repeated the charges in her affidavit. She identified herself as a businesswoman who ran the studio—what was left of it, still in her ex-husband's name—in Seattle. She was deep in debt, and had been sued for failure to pay numerous bills. Most of her troubles, the financial ones, could be blamed on the disheveled person brought from his windowless cell, she claimed. Curtis denied delinquency, and said the bills were news to him. The judge granted bail of $2,000 and released Curtis. He was ordered to appear the following day with Mrs. Curtis to sort their affairs.

On Wednesday, the city was exposed to a view of Edward Curtis only a handful of people knew—that is, a man who'd been living on gossamer strands. He took the stand and barely looked up. The judge started in with questions.

What are his assets?

"None."

That couldn't be true. Everyone knew he was the nation's premier portrait photographer—had been, at one time, and so much in demand that he was picked to shoot the Roosevelt family wedding, for God's sake. Then, of course, he came under the patronage of J. P. Morgan, once ranked the richest man in America, if not the world. He had produced a film of some sort, yes? And *The North American Indian*—why, a single subscription sold for $3,500. How could he be insolvent?

"I have no funds, your honor. I have no business. Only *The North American Indian*—and for that I get nothing."

Nothing?

Curtis trembled, bit his lip. He looked as if he were going to cry. The judge continued: What about this studio in Los Angeles, operating out of the Biltmore Hotel? A chimera, largely, Curtis replied—run by his daughter, it was her business, from which he received nothing. Well, how did he pay his rent, put food on the table? Same as above: his daughter. She takes care of him. A second round of questions followed on *The North American Indian*. How much money had J. P. Morgan put into it? Curtis took his time to do the math.

"The Morgan estate will have paid about $2.5 million when it's done."

The judge took that revelation as news as well. Surely Curtis had something to show for $2.5 million?

"No. It operates on a deficit." And the project was not only deeply in debt, but years behind. He explained the original deal with Morgan, how Curtis was supposed to pay his way with rich donors. Even if he sold all five hundred subscriptions—he hadn't reached half that goal—he would not get anything in return. All went into fieldwork, printing costs, translators, a skipper named Harry the Fish, a cook named Noggie, a car named Nanny, a Snake Dance priest in Arizona and on and on. The judge summarized the Curtis defense.

"Do I understand that you will receive no money for this work?"

Curtis nodded, his eyes misted. "I work for nothing."

Flabbergasted, the judge shook his head. "Then why are you doing it?"

"Your honor, it was my job. The only thing . . . the only thing I could do that was worth doing."

With that, the Shadow Catcher's eyes welled up. The crowd of reporters gasped, scribbling in haste. They were sketching paragraphs for early editions, sent outside the courtroom by runners. Extra! Extra! "Nationally known compiler of Indian lore breaks down on witness stand!" The *Seattle Post-Intelligencer* described Curtis, this "international character, friend of Theodore Roosevelt and associate of the late J. Pierpont Morgan" as a "shabby, hunched and weary figure" who was "garbed in his rough hiking clothing." The *Seattle Star* sent out this dispatch: "Curtis, overcome by the forced revelation of his life's secret, wept." The sobbing grew more pronounced. Curtis had made thousands of appearances over the course of thirty years, onstage and in the press, from Carnegie Hall to the White House. He was a man's man, in the public eye. If he had ever cried in front of anyone, it had gone unreported. Ed Meany knew of a single instance, when he had written his friend after the divorce, trying to cheer him with memories of mountain climbing and better days. Curtis wrote back: "Reading it caused me to break down and cry as a child."

The judge gave Curtis a few moments to regain his composure. The witness tried to contain himself, to fully answer the question of why he could stay with such a thing if it only put him deeper into a hole.

"I was duty bound to finish."

Still, the judge was stunned. How could someone without means work for no money? What craziness was that? And to do so with no possibility of ever being made whole? Why, why, why?

"Your honor . . . I am one of those fanatical persons who wants to finish what he starts."

After a three-day hearing, the judge slammed the proceedings to a close. The evidence was inconclusive. Neither side could produce the original alimony document, the basis of late-payment claims by Mrs. Curtis. Without that filing, the judge could not hold Curtis. Plus, he was moved by Curtis's confession, stripping himself of the veneer of dignity that came with money. "The court cannot imprison a man for not doing what he cannot do," the judge wrote. Curtis was free to go.

If ever there was a sliver of doubt that Curtis had worked for nothing in order to complete the "only worthwhile thing" in his life, the House of Morgan removed that doubt when it took from Curtis the remaining ownership of his masterwork. There had been discussions over several years about Curtis relinquishing his copyright to *The North American Indian*. The number that had been revealed in court—Morgan's $2.5 million, an amount equal to about $50 million today—provided further explanation for why Curtis let the ownership go and never publicly complained about it. A document completed in early 1928 recorded the transfer from artist to institution, even though the books did not show it on the title page. He ceded copyright to the pictures and text of *The North American Indian*—the complete work—to the Morgan Company. Included were the copper- and glass-plate negatives. What Curtis got in return is not stated on the transfer document, but it appears to be little more than an agreement to publish the end of the work.

He had two volumes to go. The book on the Indians of Oklahoma, the one Hodge had sent back as unacceptable, underwent a complete rewrite by Curtis and Eastwood, with much back and forth. Seemingly every detail was put through the editorial sifter. "You say tribes, for example, which have not been influenced by Christianity," Curtis wrote in one exchange. "In my lifetime, I have seen no group of Indians not influenced by Christianity." Eastwood had improved enough that he could get through much of the writing without whimpering every time he had his ears boxed by Hodge. The last volume, on the Alaska natives, looked to be an easier production. Curtis felt he had brought home "a tremendous mass of material" from the north, he wrote Hodge.

The problem was the man behind the creation. For long periods at the end of the 1920s, Curtis fell into the black hole that had engulfed him after his divorce. For weeks that became months, he could not bring himself to write or to make prints from the plates holding those extraordinary images of an Alaskan summer. He was ashamed of his paralysis and would hide from everyone save his children. Adding to his mental torture, he was in constant physical pain. A man who had crisscrossed the continent 125 times could no longer walk a single block without sharp stabs; on some mornings, getting out of bed was a chore, though he was not an old man by any standard. "I am still suffering with my lame hip and do not get on with matters as fast as I could like," he wrote Hodge in early 1928, the only hint of his inner demons passed off as all the fault of his gimpy leg.

He was desperate for Bill Myers, who had carried him through so many obstacles in the drama of bookmaking. They had fallen completely out of touch. All Curtis knew was that Myers was managing an apartment building in San Francisco, for a small salary. "Have you heard anything from Myers?" Curtis asked Hodge in 1929. "I have not been able to get track of him." But with help from Eastwood's pen and the incalculable skill of Hodge, Curtis assembled his last two works.

He did what he could with Volume XIX, mostly portraits, and histories that took a long view of the Indian diaspora in Oklahoma. Many of the subjects look like costume Indians, reluctantly wearing deerskin leggings and bonnets in the hot sun. In a candid photographic nod, he gives in to contemporary life. One picture in particular, *Wilbur Peebo—Comanche,* is a striking departure, and shows the long arc of the Lords of the Plains, from unassailable horse soldiers to passive residents of a listless twentieth century. Wilbur Peebo is seen in a white dress shirt and tie, his hair close-cropped, slicked and parted, a regular Rotarian. Yet even that picture is true to an emotion: a pleasant face that conveys a deep level of hurt. The close-ups—the portraits, that is—are consistent with the quality of the previous eighteen volumes.

Curtis felt he had done a fair job of "making something from nothing," as he told Hodge when the first drafts were put together. He printed alphabets, pronunciation guides, many full pages of sheet music of native songs. And he tried, once again, to correct misconceptions about spiritual life, with several pages devoted to a forceful defense of the Peyote Society. The missionaries who'd described the peyote ceremony as "devil worship" and "drug-eating debauchery" had completely missed the point. In fact, many Christian converts took peyote in a ritual that lasted from dusk till dawn, a mind-altering way to connect to the Creator. As Quanah Parker, the last chief of the wild Comanche, had said in defense of the hallucinatory experience of Indian worship: "The white man goes into his church and talks *about* Jesus, but the Indian goes into his tipi and talks *to* Jesus."

Curtis described a Cheyenne, age forty-eight, educated at the Carlisle School Upshaw had attended, who became a drunk. He deserted his family, quit his job at a hospital, was run over by a wagon. He eventually found salvation and sobriety in the spiritual disciplines of the Peyote Society. "Within a few years of joining the peyote organization he has become one of the most substantial men of the tribe." Curtis ripped into the government for harassing Indians who sought to connect with their past in this way. "Worshipers have been arrested, indicted, and tried in state courts." But since Indians were now citizens, they should be protected by the First Amendment—the peyote cult, he wrote, was the Native American church.

With the Alaska volume, Curtis was magnificent, bringing home a book as original, humane and surprising as his best work on the Hopi or the Nez Perce. The exuberance of his handwritten log fully carried over to the typeset pages and printed images of the final book. What made the Eskimos—except for those ravaged by the flu epidemic on Little Diomede Island—so different from the Indians Curtis had visited over the past thirty years was that they'd escaped the worst curse of the West, those genocidal diseases. For most of North America, the devastation was consistent, Curtis wrote, from the Southwest to the Northwest, from the California coast to the Great Plains. "A notable exception was found in the natives of Nunivak Island, whose almost total freedom from Caucasian contact has thus far been their salvation," he wrote. "In all the author's experience among Indians and Eskimos, he never knew a happier and more thoroughly honest and self-reliant people." Curtis put the number of Alaska natives at 12,405—a healthy population. He described how they made parkas from bird or fish skins, and heavier coats of caribou and bear hide. Their socks were woven grass; a rain slicker was fashioned from seal intestine. The people were tattooed and pierced and handsome—as his pictures showed—save for that dirty community of Hooper Bay. He was as harsh toward them in the book as he was in his diary. "Uncleanliness of person and possessions is the rule; the floors of dwellings are deep in filth and refuse of every description." Most of the pictures are portraits of delight: laughing children in duck-skin parkas, alluring women in the angled light of midnight, limber young men launching boats for a whale hunt. He was so intrigued by the design of kayaks that he included illustrations of how they were built. And the songs: parts of the final volume can seem like the outline of a musical.

In a brief introduction, Curtis was grateful to those who believed in him through the years, the people "who never lost faith," named and unnamed. "Mere thanks seem hollow in comparison with such loyal cooperation; but great is the satisfaction the writer enjoys when he can at last say to all those whose faith has been unbounded, 'It is finished.'"

Curtis told a friend that he still held out hope of selling a couple of subscriptions, and with that money he could start something fresh. He was interested in the history of gold, and in further travel. He was sixty-one years old when he finished Volume XX in 1929, and he thought there was another act or two ahead for himself. Hodge was happy with the polished draft. But as they put the closing touches on the last words and pictures of *The North American Indian*, the nation took a turbulent turn. On October 29, the stock market crashed, the worst single day on Wall Street to that point. And the bottom was not around the corner; over the next three weeks, the market lost 40 percent of its value. Though less than 5 percent of Americans owned stock, the crash had a downward-spiraling effect on confidence, and it gutted thousands of banks holding the life savings of average people—money bet and lost in the market in a deregulatory free fall. By year's end, unemployment had tripled. Universities, museums, the rich: nobody was immune from the crash.

When the final volume of the Indian work had been printed in 1930, Curtis faced the only thing worse than a bad review: silence. He longed for a word or two from the papers that had once given full pages to him. His own personal collapse came two years earlier than the nation's, starting on the day he was thrown in jail. That he had completed the work at all was astounding to those closest to him. After he finished the thirty-year, twenty-set book, the only comment from Curtis to his editor was cursory. "I am in bad shape again," he wrote Hodge in a hand-scrawled note on lined paper that looked like the scribbling of a child. "Going from my bed to my working table is about my limit at present."

Curtis moved to Denver and checked into a long-term-care hospital, as a charity case. He withdrew from the central figures of his life for almost two years, though he did dash off notes to his children. Then, in early 1932, he reached out to the two constants over the course of his magnum opus: Edmond Meany and Belle da Costa Greene. To Meany, stalwart companion for three decades, who was tolerant of his silent spells and his lapses in meeting the basic responsibilities of friendship, he told of the pain and pathos that had visited him, and lamented that he was already a forgotten man. Meany, writing back, relayed news of his own troubles: he'd been in a terrible car accident, tearing up his knee. He could no longer hike, and could not walk without a cane. He assured Curtis that his work would grow in stature with the years: "The last two volumes of your monumental work have caused distinct revival here of talk about you . . . I can sympathize with your last sentence about feeling 'a bit lost.' You can rest assured that you and your books will be rediscovered through centuries of time."

Meany was being kind. If there was talk in Seattle of a Curtis revival, it was limited to a very small circle. In closing, he compared Curtis to other artists who had been broke, sick and depressed: "Unfortunately, this has too often been the fate of other great achievers in the realm of music, art, books and explorations. Belated honors are vicarious compensations."

The letter to Greene was blunt and needy, Curtis confiding in her as he did in Meany. She held all the power now at the Morgan Library, where she reigned as the director with full backing of the board of trustees.

My Dear Miss Greene:

Much water has passed beneath all bridges since we last exchanged a word or letter. It is years since I have been in New York ... How many times have I wished that Mr. Morgan might have lived to see completion of the work and know something of its standing as a completed undertaking ... Following my season in the Arctic collecting final material for Volume Twenty, I suffered a complete physical breakdown. For two years, I was about a 99 percent loss. Ill health and uncertainty as to how I was to solve the problem of the future brought a period of depression which about crushed me ... I am again in a measure physically fit and have much of my old courage back. During the long months of despondency I could not write to my friends; no one wants to listen to the wail of lost souls, or to the down and outers.

He was right on the last point. Greene and the Morgan Library had lost interest in the man who had once been their most famous living beneficiary. Curtis had closed with a simple request: "I am again writing and hoping I may do something worthwhile. Do drop me a line; even a word from my old friends gives added courage." She did not bother with a reply.

Belle da Costa Greene filed the letter away with the other papers, and thousands of pictures, in the Curtis trove—darkened, covered, closed. As it turned out, the Indians that Curtis spent his adult life documenting had never faded away. It was *The North American Indian* that disappeared.

Wilbur Peebo—Comanche, 1927. In the state once designated as the official Indian Territory for displaced tribes, Curtis was hard-pressed to find natives living by the old ways. In a concession to modernity, he shot Peebo, of the once fearsome Comanche, in dress shirt and short hair.

18

TWILIGHT
1932–1952

IN THE SUMMER OF 1948, the Seattle Historical Society asked a retired librarian named Harriet Leitch to assess a set of books that had just been donated by a wealthy widow, Sophie Frye Bass. The history buffs were not sure of their value, or what to make of them. The acquisition was not a complete set, just eight volumes. Still, they were luminous, these large-format books and folios of silky vellum, the pictures bringing their Indian subjects to life.

For Leitch, it was like finding the Seven Cities of Cibola. A beloved figure, once voted Librarian of the Year by her colleagues, she had certainly heard about *The North American Indian*, though sightings were rare. There were perhaps only five of the fully bound twenty-volume sets in Seattle. One was at the city's main library, another at the University of Washington, residing at last in its logical home after Professor Meany's ceaseless work to convince the school of its merit. A third was listed as belonging to Colonel Alden Blethen, the *Seattle Times* publisher who had died more than three decades earlier. A fourth was held by the Stimson family, who'd made a fortune in timber and was now building a broadcast empire. And the eccentric railroad man Samuel Hill was a subscriber during his time in Seattle.

As Leitch ran her fingers over the fine photogravures, the handset letterpress text printed on heavy stock, the leather binding and gilt edging, and gazed into the eyes of people who looked as if they sprang from some musty American storage chest, she wondered what had become of the architect of this exquisite construction of biblio-art. The last entry in the Seattle Public Library's clipping file was from 1927, when Curtis was jailed and hauled before a judge. The family had disappeared. No one was left in the region. She found a contact for Beth, who was still running a Curtis studio on Wilshire Boulevard in Los Angeles. Leitch wrote and explained her current task, with a few basic queries:

Is Edward S. Curtis still alive?

If so, could he answer some questions by correspondence?

What had become of *The North American Indian*?

Married for more than twenty years, Beth was selling prints of Curtis Indians, supplementing her husband's work as a portrait photographer. Her father resided not far from the studio, in a small apartment on Saturn Street. The address, just a few blocks from Beverly Hills, belied his living conditions: Curtis hated the place. It was confining, in a neighborhood crawling with poseurs and choked by bad air. Whenever he stepped outside, he gasped at the yellow smog; some days it was so bad he could not see the few miles to Hollywood Hills. At eighty, his hands were bent and gnarled by arthritis, he could barely walk, and he was going blind. Despite all of that, he felt fairly spry, a late-life vigor that he attributed to herbal tea from a plant in Oregon that he'd been drinking for years. And, in an effort to hold on to his eyesight, he ate a pound of carrots every day.

"Mr. Curtis is elderly," Beth wrote Leitch in late August, "but very much alive. I know he would be delighted to give you any information you might like concerning his life."

For a librarian, accustomed to dealing with voices from a muted assemblage of filed books, this news was a jolt of discovery, on par with leafing through *The North American Indian* for the first time. She wrote Curtis immediately, and thereafter kept up a string of inquiries. In her first letter, she explained how the eight volumes had come into the hands of the historical society, and she seemed somewhat embarrassed to admit that few people knew of their significance. Though, of course, *she* was not one of them. "It seems to me that your important and valuable work should be brought to the attention of the present residents of Seattle."

In reply, Curtis wrote in jittery, jagged cursive, for which he apologized, "I can't afford a typist." He said he'd been in and out of the hospital for the past year and was now bivouacked in the Saturn Street apartment, which felt like a cell. A nurse made regular visits to assist him.

"In other words," wrote the Shadow Catcher, "I am a shut in."

He would be happy to tell about his life, but first, a request: "Should you contact any of my old friends, please tell them I'm still alive and expect to be hanging around for at least five years more." There was plenty of swagger yet in the old boy.

He had started planning a new life in 1932, after leaving the hospital in Denver. "Yes I am certainly broke," he told Meany then, a condition that matched the financial state of the country. "Other than that, I am not down and out." Harold, his only son, had moved west, and was interested in mining. So was Curtis. His long stay in the Rockies had fired a passion for gold. He thought there might be a book on the subject for him, and along the way, maybe a strike or two of the precious metal. In studying the various methods for extracting gold dust, Curtis found them wanting. This void produced an invention: the Curtis Counter Current Concentrator, which he had patented. It was a device that looked like a short conveyor belt on an angled ironing board, used to separate flour-fine particles of gold from the detritus of abandoned placer mines. With his confidence restored and his clumsy invention in hand, the sixty-something Curtis charged into the mountains of California and Colorado, as fevered for gold as the Klondike prospectors he had disparaged in his youth.

In October of that year, Clara Curtis climbed into a rowboat near her sister's home in Bremerton, on Puget Sound. In the chop of a sudden breeze, she fell overboard, into the 42-degree waters, and drowned.

That was the official story. Clara was fifty-eight years old. Her obituary in the *Seattle Times* was three paragraphs.

RITES ARRANGED FOR MRS. CURTIS, SOCIAL LEADER

There was no mention of her famous ex-husband, no mention of the years she'd toiled without notice at one of the world's best-known picture shops. Her membership in several local organizations was recounted, highlighted by her presidency of the Women's Commercial Club. And one more thing: "She operated a photographic studio here several years ago."

With the death of Clara, the last Curtis child left in Seattle, twenty-three-year-old Katherine — called Billy — moved to southern California to be closer to the family. "The three oldest children had basically disowned their mother," said Jim Graybill, the son of Florence. Katherine, not unlike her older sister Beth, had been a victim of her mother's rage and instability as the marriage fell apart and she scrimped to pay the bills. Growing up, she never knew her absentee father. Through all those years on the road, Curtis had written her. Some of the letters were fanciful, others full of Indian stories from one reservation or another. But Katherine never saw those personal notes until much later, when they were discovered in an old suitcase. Her mother had hidden them from her. With Katherine's move, Curtis now had two daughters and his son nearby, and a fourth child in Oregon.

Curtis kicked around many a goldfield, scraping high mountain ground in the Sierra Nevada until dark, the Curtis Concentrator grinding away. He wrote loving, imaginative letters to his grandson Jim, often assuming the point of view of a cat, signing those letters with an inky paw print. And he wrote ruminative, serious ones to Meany. After crawling out of the basement of his depression, Curtis dashed off a forward-looking update to Meany, gossipy and full of plans. He mentioned that his editor Hodge had moved to Los Angeles, having taken up professional residence among the Indian artifacts at the Southwest Museum, with its great hillside perch. And after much sleuthing, he had found Myers at last, living in an apartment in the Bay Area, working as a company secretary at a soft-drink factory. Curtis was writing again, he reported, though nothing an academic would appreciate. "I am tired of being formal," he told Meany. Most books, he observed as an aside, are not worth the paper they are printed on. So many writers, so many books, and yet what was the value of being published? The joy was in creation, in the act of doing, in discovery. Rejection is not such a bad thing.

Writing to Meany with his newfound breeziness, Curtis hinted that he might have taken several lovers over the course of his life, though he was discreet and named no names—simply a justification. "We all know that from the earliest days of man to today, man's natural inclination was and is to indulge in sexual wandering." This was telling, and perhaps confessional. A lifetime of correspondence ended on that note, in August 1934.

Barely six months later, while preparing for his morning class at the University of Washington, Meany fell to the ground and gasped for breath, in the grip of a titanic stroke. The professor died in his office, age seventy-two. Meany was one of the last of the early Pacific Northwest Renaissance men. He'd arrived in Seattle when it was a sodden village of tree stumps and prostitutes, mud running down the streets, oyster pirates sneaking in and out of Elliott Bay. In his time, he had been a newspaper carrier and a newspaper publisher. He'd written scholarly books and short, punchy popular essays. He was one of the first to see the value in native people living camouflaged lives in the midst of a fast-changing region—Indians with a living link to a faraway world, and a culture that the new residents couldn't begin to fathom. Along with his lectures on forestry, Indians and history, with his political work that established a new campus for the University of Washington and a world's fair for a young city, he had climbed most of the mountains in the American far corner. A campus hall, a Seattle hotel, a ski lodge and a mountain crest joined to Rainier were all named for him. It was little known until much later that he'd been the soul mate and best friend of Edward Curtis for almost forty years. From the audacity of the original Indian idea, to the college football game with the aging Chief Joseph, to days when Curtis dined at the table of a president, to the midnight blackness of late-middle-aged despair, Ed Meany kept the Shadow Catcher going, always certain of his genius.

In the trough of the Depression, Curtis was living hand to mouth. The economy showed no signs of improving—indeed, it had grown worse, after fiscal belt-tightening in Washington shrank government payrolls that had given a lift to so many towns. And so when Cecil B. DeMille called in 1936 with an offer, Curtis sold his gold concentrator and once again took up the camera. The great director was shooting a big-budget western featuring the most glamorous stars of the day, Gary Cooper and Jean Arthur. It was an Indian story, in its way, taking place in the Badlands, with cameo appearances by historical characters like George Armstrong Custer and Buffalo Bill Cody. DeMille planned to shoot it on location in Montana and the Dakotas, and could use Curtis's help with photographic stills, camera work and logistics. Had Curtis finished up with that Indian business of his?

Indeed, he was free of his life work in every respect. The Morgan Library had received an inquiry about Curtis in 1932, from a collector in Sweden. "I see that the extremely valuable and significant work of 'The North American Indian' by Edward S. Curtis has come to its close with the 20th volume," the collector wrote. But there was no offer forthcoming—just curiosity. "I fear its high price will never make it possible for any library in Sweden to purchase it." In fact, the House of Morgan was looking to dump its Curtis collection. Throughout the Depression, they ceased any attempt to sell or market the work, which remained in archival hiding. And so, when an offer from a Boston rare-book dealer named Charles E. Lauriat Jr. came along, the library liquidated most of its Curtis holdings. Morgan gave Lauriat the right to sell nineteen complete sets of *The North American Indian*, in addition to thousands of prints, gravures, the priceless glass-plate negatives and the copyright— all for a mere $1,000.

It was a huge haul of material from the book that had been compared to the King James Bible. Each set contained more than 2,200 original pictures, almost 4,000 pages of text, including transcriptions of hundreds of songs and dozens of languages, plus additional portfolios of oversized photogravures printed on plates. Lauriat also acquired the original copper photogravure plates used to make the images of the book. The library records showed that over the years, only 222 complete sets were bound and given to paid subscribers, mostly institutions, and another 50 were printed but never completely packaged. The Morgan Library held on to copy number 1. A notice in its archives recorded the divorce between patron and benefactor: "On May 15, 1935, the directors of *The North American Indian,* acting as trustees, assigned all assets to Charles E. Lauriat Company for the purpose of sale." Lauriat thereafter sold the 19 sets, and eventually assembled 50 or so others into bound volumes, and he made fresh prints as well. A few of the glass-plate negatives kept by the Morgan Library were overlooked in the sale and handover, and later disposed of as junk.

On the movie set of *The Plainsman,* in eastern Montana, Curtis was home again in the land where he had deciphered the Custer story, where he and the Crow translator Alexander Upshaw had talked well past midnight about the ways of the Apsaroke. DeMille was filming a story of craven Indians and heroic white men, just a few miles east of the Little Bighorn battlefield and within a hawk's glide of the home of the Sioux. If Cecil B. DeMille had ever asked him, Curtis could tell the story of a people who rode bareback at full sprint, more graceful and powerful than any of the hired hands on this set. He knew the original names of many a mesa, mountain and watering hole. He could pronounce the words, and tell how *The People* came from a hole in the ground long ago, animated by *The Creator.* But he was not in the Badlands to convey Indian realism or Indian mythology. He was there in service to Paramount Pictures and a fiction built around Gary Cooper as Wild Bill Hickok and Jean Arthur as Calamity Jane. The lead Indian roles were played by Paul Harvey (not the radio announcer) and Victor Marconi, with Anthony Quinn in a bit part as a surly native. Curtis's job was in the background, taking stills of the stars in action, the Italians in Indian paint, the hero Custer who rides in with the cavalry to save the day. A number of Sioux were recruited for a few shots; they were ordered to whoop, holler, grunt and fall down dead.

The movie was a rare crumb of good fortune for Curtis in his old age. He returned to southern California, back to occasional pokes in the Sierra for gold and to steady research for a new book on the oldest metal lure of all. But over time, the body would no longer do the work. He could not will muscles in his bad leg to move, nor could he clamber over rocks without risking a fall. His children told him to give it up. The occasional letter found him, with a query not unlike that of the librarian: are you still alive? A curious Mrs. Gardner from Seattle wrote in 1937, wondering what had become of *The North American Indian*. "The negatives and copyrights as a whole passed completely from my hands," Curtis informed her matter-of-factly, adding that he could not use his own work without getting into legal trouble. "I devoted thirty-three years to gathering text material and pictures for the twenty volumes. I did this as a contribution; without salary, direct or indirect financial returns. When I was through with the last volume, I did not possess enough money to buy a ham sandwich; yet the books will remain the outstanding story of the Indian." At the end of the letter he mentioned that the work was valued overseas—why, in a museum in Great Britain, patrons are not even allowed to touch the pages! "A gloved assistant does it for them," he noted.

Curtis had reached that stage in life when the social rituals are not weddings or baptisms, but funerals and burials. His younger brother Asahel died in 1941, of a heart attack, at the age of sixty-six. Over the course of his career, he probably took more pictures than did Edward. He shot everything: the first skyscraper in Seattle, the Smith Tower, which for much of the twentieth century was the tallest building in the West; the earth-moving projects that left spires of the original city around as engineers tried to make a flat metropolis; Indians on downtown streets and athletes on the field; dams, schools, office buildings, ships, trains and roads. His camera had a utilitarian eye, without any weakness for sentimentality. He was best known for his outdoor work, as a climber and a conservationist. With Meany—a friend to both Curtis brothers—he guided the Mountaineers through decades of growth, and was the first person to scale many of the iconic peaks in the Northwest, including Mount Shuksan in the North Cascades. He carried his feud with Edward to the end: the brothers had not spoken to each other in over forty years. His ashes were placed at the site of the newly named Asahel Curtis Memorial Grove in Snoqualmie National Forest, east of Seattle. When a son, Asahel Curtis Jr., was asked in 1981 about the brothers' estrangement, he said only that it was "ridiculous." And when the same question was put to Jim Graybill in 2012, the sole surviving grandchild of Edward hinted at a shameful story, saying, "I just can't discuss it."

Curtis moved to a farm near Whittier, California, owned by Beth and her husband. There, he talked to the chickens, grew avocados and oranges. He was bored and restless, in need of an adventure. He spent hours preparing large meals at family gatherings, where he took issue with anyone who did not see the greatness in his cuisine. Shortly before Harriet Leitch contacted him, Curtis moved back to the Los Angeles.

Near the end of 1948, Curtis started sending memories to the Seattle librarian. While rummaging through a trunk at his daughter's home, he'd come upon a seventy-four-page memoir he'd written decades before and never published. He spent all afternoon with this account of his adventures — twenty thousand words. "I began reading it at once and found it so interesting that I did not put it down till the final word was reached." He sent a copy to Leitch, and he also shipped her the major reviews of *The North American Indian*, from all over the world. These clippings, he wrote, should give her a sense of "the considerable importance of the work." He said he'd received more than two hundred notices, all favorable but one — a critic who disagreed with Curtis's revisionist account of the Nez Perce War. (Later historians sided with Curtis.) And he urged Leitch to spend some time with a single book from the series, to pick one at random: "Look at but one volume to see what a task it was to collect such a vast number of words of assorted dialects." Along the West Coast alone, "we recorded more root languages than exist on the rest of the globe. In several cases we collected the vocabulary from the last living man knowing the words of a language. To me, that is a dramatic statement."

Leitch was impressed. And she was "thrilled," she said, to read the autobiographical sketch. She knew his reputation as a photographer, but the anthropological work, the salvage job of languages from the scrap heap of time—that was a revelation. Countless words that had bounced around pockets of the Great Plains or dwelled in hamlets along the Pacific shore lived—still—because Curtis had taken his "magic box," the cylindrical recorder, along with him when he went to Indian country. Also, he had preserved more than ten thousand songs. And yet, for all the stories, myths, tribal narratives and languages Curtis had saved for the ages, it was curious, the librarian suggested, that the photographer had never told his own story. Why no memoir beyond the sketch he'd sent her? Surely his dashing and perilous life, the unstoppable young man in his Abercrombie and Fitch, the self-educated scholar who made significant breakthroughs in ethnology and anthropology among overlooked nations, his proximity to J. P. Morgan and Theodore Roosevelt and E. H. Harriman and Gifford Pinchot, his campfire tales from Chief Joseph and Geronimo and the last of the mighty Sioux warriors—surely there was a great, sweeping story to be told.

Curtis had indeed started to record his personal history, sitting for days with his children so that they might have something for posterity. But now he lacked the oomph; the project had been shelved. "Among the foremost why nots, I am not in physical or financial condition to attempt so large an undertaking," he wrote. Plus, he'd heard a familiar refrain from the gatekeepers of American letters in New York: "A publisher told me there is but a limited market for books dealing with Indian subjects."

He spent Christmas with Beth—a "delightful" holiday. With the dawn of the new year of 1949, Curtis started to regain some energy. The stories spilled out of him, in letters mailed up the coast to Harriet Leitch. He recalled his father, the sickly preacher and Civil War private, who died when Curtis was fourteen, leaving him to become "the main support of our family." He told about his accidental avocation, how he took up photography only after a severe back injury prevented him from making a living as a brickmaker or in the lumberyards. He described for Leitch his first Indian picture, Angeline—"I paid the Prin-

cess a dollar for each picture I made. This seemed to please her greatly."
He gloried in long accounts of Mount Rainier climbs. He talked about
his work habits. "It's safe to say that in the last fifty years I have aver-
aged sixteen hours a day, seven days a week," he wrote. "Following the
Indian form of naming men, I would be termed, The Man Who Never
Took Time To Play."

Their correspondence carried through another death, in April of
1949 — William Myers, the writing talent behind *The North American
Indian*. He had married a second time and moved to Petaluma, north of
San Francisco, where he managed a small motel. He was seventy-five
at life's end, six years younger than Curtis. A routine obituary in the
Santa Rosa Press Democrat did not bring up Edward Curtis or the fact
that Myers had spent the majority of his adult life doing first-rate field
anthropology and writing about it for the most detailed study ever done
of native people of North America. He was described as a motel manager, retired and childless.

Through the summer and into the fall, Curtis worked away at the
book he was building, tentatively titled *The Lure of Gold*. The walls of
his tiny apartment were plastered with notes in his unreadable scratch.
"I'm busy with The Lure of Gold," he wrote Leitch in October, brush-
ing off a fresh round of questions from her about his Indian work. By
the spring of 1950, Curtis was almost manic with energy, again crediting his Oregon tea. "My health is improving, and now I look forward to
celebrating my 99th birthday." He parried back dozens of answers: on
the reburial of Chief Joseph, on the good work of Professor Meany, and
how together they discovered the true story of the Nez Perce, a pattern
that followed with the Custer revision. How did he do it? "I didn't get
my information from the white man."

Near the end of 1950, Curtis turned cranky. If it wasn't "that damn
television" blaring in a neighbor's apartment, it was his arthritis, which
on many days prevented him from holding a pen, let alone set it to paper. On such occasions, he said his "pen died a sudden death." A few
days before Christmas in that year, Belle da Costa Greene passed away
in New York City, at the age of sixty-six. Her sway over the Morgan

Library had lasted forty-three years, until her retirement in 1948. She never married, and took many of her secrets with her to the grave: she had burned her personal papers shortly before her death.

Curtis limped into 1951, the late-stage burst of energy having dissipated. "I am still housebound," he wrote, "living the life of a hermit." He wished for simple things—a stroll to the store to buy his own food, a taste of fresh strawberries, an afternoon on a park bench. "It's Hell when you can't go to the market and get what you want." The apartment was suffocating him. He started calling himself Old Man Curtis, and his handwriting became illegible. In July of 1951, he was forced by finances to move to an even smaller apartment, at 8550 Burton Way, in Beverly Hills. He called it "the most discouraging place I have ever tried to live in." Through that year, Curtis deteriorated further, though he responded to Harriet Leitch's prodding in brilliant flashes here and there, with some of his sharpest recollections. He told stories of the Harriman expedition to Alaska in 1899 and of meeting J. P. Morgan for the first time. Teddy Roosevelt was fondly recalled—manly, loyal, robust, a mind as kinetic as that of Curtis himself. Leitch got an account of the Sun Dance with the Piegan and the Snake Dance with the Hopi. On February 16, his eighty-third birthday, Curtis posed for a formal portrait. He still had the Vandyke beard and wore his hat at an angle—no doddering old fool, this man.

Finally, the pace of memory-collecting slowed to a crawl and the words refused to come. Curtis complained about his "scrambled life," a blur of disconnected images and places, all at the frenzied behest of The Cause. At night, in his dreams, he revisited the Hopi and Apache, the Sky City of Acoma, the Grand Canyon cellar of the Havasupai and the sublime isolation of Nunivak Island. Had he really been to these places? While asleep, he would construct "whole paragraphs in Indian words," he recalled. These images came at random, as with any dream; it was his only real escape from the prison on Burton Way. He was desperate for a new home. "I have to get away from the smog." As it became more difficult to summon his past, he apologized.

"This is a bum letter," he wrote Leitch on July 3, 1951. "I will try to do better in the future."

"I am nearly blind," he wrote on August 4. Now, even the carrots had failed him. It was the last letter from an epic gatherer of words and pictures. He had written Leitch twenty-three times over nearly four years of correspondence.

On October 19, 1952, Curtis died of a heart attack. He was eighty-four. It was a national curse, it seemed once again, to take as a life task the challenge of trying to capture in illustrated form a significant part of the American story. The Indian painter George Catlin had died broke and forgotten. Mathew Brady, the Civil War photographer who gave up his prosperous portrait business to become a pioneer of photojournalism, spent his last days in a dingy rooming house, alone and penniless. Curtis took his final breath in a home not much larger than the tent he used to set up on the floor of Canyon de Chelly.

E. S. CURTIS, INDIAN-LIFE HISTORIAN, DIES

The *Seattle Times*, which had shared his glory days as if they were the paper's own, dismissed Curtis with a six-paragraph obituary that ran on page 33. As brief as it was, the notice in his hometown paper contained a number of inaccuracies, including a claim that Curtis was "Seattle's first commercial photographer" and that he had gone on the Harriman expedition a full seven years before he ever met Harriman. The *New York Times* had drafted a lengthy life story when it appeared that Curtis was lost at sea off the Queen Charlotte Islands back in 1914. When he actually died, the paper ran an obituary of seventy-six words, and never directly mentioned *The North American Indian*. He was called an Indian authority who also did some photography. The obituary said nothing of the languages he recorded and preserved, the biographies he wrote of Indians still alive, the groundbreaking work he did in cinema. Some years later, the *Times* arranged with the collector Christopher Cardozo to sell "limited edition" lithographs of Curtis pictures, including some of the most iconic—*At the Old Well of Acoma, An Oasis in the Badlands, Chief Joseph*—and thus began a long, lucrative business offering the Indian pictures of the Shadow Catcher to connoisseurs around the globe.

Collectors were always asking if there was anything still to surface from the Curtis estate. No, Beth insisted: her father had left this world as he'd entered it, without a single possession to his name. That is, with one exception, unknown to outsiders, perhaps even to the House of Morgan, and certainly to the creditors who had chased him from one century to the next. Curtis had held on to a single set of *The North American Indian*, the twenty volumes taking up five feet of shelf space in the tiny apartment on Burton Way. Though he was alone at death, and friendless, not a single person in those books was a stranger to him.

The Shadow Catcher in winter, 1948. Curtis, at age eighty, was living out his remaining years in southern California. He dreamed of launching another project, struggled to write a memoir and spent many days talking to chickens and tending avocado trees.

EPILOGUE: REVIVAL

Twenty years after Curtis died, a rumor spread through the circle of art-photography collectors in Santa Fe, New Mexico, that somebody in Boston was sitting on an extraordinary treasure for bibliophiles. Karl Kernberger, a photographer with eclectic taste and a love of the Southwest, traveled east to have a look. Downstairs in the venerable Lauriat's bookstore he picked his way through an enormous cache of the Indian work of Edward S. Curtis. The owner, Charles E. Lauriat Jr., had survived the sinking of the *Lusitania* by a German U-boat in 1915, an act of war that killed 1,198 people. His ongoing passion was for rare books, and he had no better find than the Curtis material he had bought for $1,000 from the Morgan Library during the Depression. Lauriat was an enthusiastic seller of this work, reassembling volumes into complete sets and retailing individual pictures, but his death in 1937 put an end to widespread dissemination. The images, the many bound books and loose plates, gathered dust until Kernberger's arrival in the early 1970s. At the same time, mainstream America was embracing Indians as never before. Some of the enthusiasm was trendy and silly, but much of the reappraisal amounted to a fresh, more nuanced and humane narrative of the first people. The times had caught up with Curtis.

What Kernberger discovered was a mother lode: more than 200,000 photogravures and the priceless copper gravure plates that Curtis had used to publish his magnum opus. Over the years, a handful of prints and gravures had trickled onto the market. Some came from among the 272 bound sets of *The North American Indian* that had been sold by subscription and Lauriat's later efforts. Many of these had been picked apart—that is, the volumes were broken up and the gravures offered piecemeal. But all of this material was nothing compared to what was in the bookstore's basement.

Back in New Mexico, Kernberger talked a few friends and investors into joining him, and together they purchased the lot from Lauriat's and moved it to Santa Fe. Their gallery shows were mobbed. The Morgan Library had a similar reception when it gave a big public exhibition of some Curtis material that it had had in storage for decades. Reprints, lithographs and gravures circulated widely in galleries, and coffee-table books for the art market appeared. Eventually Kernberger's group sold the master copper plates, which then passed through several more hands before settling in the current home of a pair of Silicon Valley entrepreneurs.

When a collector in Austin, Texas, named Lois Flury saw her first Curtis pictures in the early 1970s, it changed the course of her life. "The work was very moving," she said. "I thought it was wonderful, fabulous, original and so different from contemporary art photographs." She purchased several gravures. Flury and her husband eventually moved to Seattle, where they opened a gallery devoted to the work of Curtis, a few blocks from the studio where Princess Angeline was charmed by a dashing young man. As the new gallery opened, the last Curtis studio aide died; Imogen Cunningham was ninety-three. She had refined a style that made her one of the best-known picture artists of the day, celebrated, alongside Ansel Adams and Dorothea Lange, as a giant in her field. Another acolyte, Ella McBride, had continued to climb mountains and pursue those perfect moments of a photographer's art through much of the twentieth century. After opening her own studio in Seattle, she became internationally famous for her floral pictures, particularly in

Japan. McBride died in 1965, two months shy of her 103rd birthday. In old age Curtis had said, "She was my star."

In the forty years following the discovery in Lauriat's basement, the value of all work by Curtis has steadily risen. A single photogravure of Chief Joseph, for example, sold for $169,000 in 2010. A full set of the bound twenty volumes is exceedingly difficult to find; they rarely change hands. Most are held by institutions—universities and libraries in Europe and the United States. About every five years one will come up for auction. In 2005, a set sold at Christie's for $1.4 million, "a new record for a photographic lot," as Artnet.com reported. A partial set of sixteen volumes sold for more than $1 million at a Swann's auction in 2007. It was one of the highest prices paid for a book that year, following such items as the Magna Carta and J. K. Rowling's handwritten manuscript of a Harry Potter book. A private sale in 2009, at the time of the worst economic crisis since the Great Depression, brought the highest price yet for a single Curtis set—$1.8 million.

Flury came to know three of the surviving Curtis children, and found them full of fond memories of their father, the Shadow Catcher. She was informed of the books that Curtis had kept and then passed on to Beth. After Beth died in 1973, the family set of *The North American Indian* went to Manford Magnuson, her husband. Another child, Florence Curtis Graybill, who spent that memorable summer in California with her father in 1922 and later talked him into writing and recording bits of his life story, died in 1987, at the age of eighty-eight. The oldest, Harold Phillips Curtis, outlived all his siblings: he passed away in 1988, at the age of ninety-five. Flury was concerned, as was Magnuson, that the family set might be broken up and sold in parts after the children's generation had passed. Just before Magnuson's death in 1993, Flury found a buyer: the Rare Books Library at the University of Oregon.

"So that's where the Curtis family set is now—a good home at the University of Oregon," she told me. Hardly a week goes by when Flury doesn't run into someone at her gallery whose view of Indians was changed by looking into faces frozen by Curtis's camera. "For posterity," she said, "he has given us images of who they really were."

This view is shared by many natives. After purchasing an original edition of Volume XII, devoted entirely to the Hopi, that tribe used the book to build and solidify its teachings, traditions and language. The Hopi found the alphabet and the accompanying song lyrics crucial tools in teaching words that nearly disappeared. When I visited them in the summer of 2011, tribal leaders talked about an ongoing renaissance of the old ways: in schools, among community groups, on websites and through social networks, and said that nearly half of all members of the Hopi Nation in Arizona can now speak some of the language.

Similarly, the Cherokee Nation of Oklahoma uses smartphones and tablet computers to teach a language that is now widely known by young tribal members. In Montana, Carol Murray, director of the Tribal History Project at Blackfeet Community College, found that Curtis pictures of her people were a good way to connect students to their ancestors. Murray has a special attachment to the images: she's a descendant of several subjects. At Canyon de Chelly, now a protected monument run jointly by the National Park Service and the Navajo Nation, and staffed mostly by native people, Curtis's photograph of the valley floor is on prominent display at the visitor center. When the Makah of the far northwestern shore set out to revive whale hunting in 1999 as a bridge to their past, they had trouble finding anyone alive with memory of the practice. They relied on pictures by both Curtis brothers, and the text from Volume XI, as a guide to reconstructing the ritual of the hunt. Starting in 1988, and every summer thereafter, Coast Salish tribes from the northern tip of Vancouver Island to southern Puget Sound have taken to the water to paddle from one Indian homeland to the other. To replicate the original cedar vessels for their first summer sea journey, they relied on Curtis's photos and the war canoes in his 1914 *Head-Hunters* movie. During Washington State's centennial celebration in 1989, the *Seattle Times*'s art critic Delores Tarzan Ament said that the twenty-volume work of Edward Curtis is to photography what Wagner's Ring Cycle is to opera — a view shared by museum curators and scholars of art and native studies.

Yet modern appreciation of Curtis by critics and in Indian country, and the rise in financial value of his photography throughout the world, did prompt an inevitable backlash. Starting in the 1980s, a handful of academics and revisionists complained that Curtis's subjects were not authentic, that he had posed them and sometimes asked them to change from their everyday overalls and collared shirts into buckskin leggings and war bonnets. They said Curtis dwelled too much on the past. Where were the pictures of hunger and privation on the reservation? Why not show Indians in school or an office? Why not show them receiving handouts? Curtis had heard these objections during his lifetime, and he pled guilty to all—with a shrug. His goal was to capture native people as they were before their cultures were too diluted. For more than thirty years his main concern and competitor in this project was time itself. As he said often, every day meant the passing of some person who held knowledge that might disappear entirely. Near the end, he feared that most of the Indian world would eventually look as Oklahoma did to him in the 1920s—a people utterly remade by others.

"Many of them are not only willing but anxious to help," he told the *New York Times* in 1911. "They have grasped the idea that this is to be a permanent memorial of their race, and it appeals to their imagination. Word passes from tribe to tribe about it. A tribe that I have visited and studied lets another tribe know that after the present generation has passed away men will know from this record what they were like and what they did, and the second tribe does not want to be left out." As for the posing—yes, he never denied staging some things. Many ceremonies, from the Sun Dance of the Piegan to the Snake Dance of the Hopi, were photographed as they were, in real time, with Curtis doing nothing to influence them. Others were done for his camera. But in those cases, it took months, sometimes years, working with Indian interpreters such as Alexander Upshaw to validate a story before he would use it or photograph an illustration of it. "Indians delight in stringing people along . . . and filling them with ridiculous stories," Curtis said in that *Times* profile. One reason why his project took so long to complete, requiring visit after visit, year after year, to the same tribes, was because of Curtis's oft-stated mission to get it right. "In dealing with Indians, grandstand plays should be avoided," he said. "One must be just simple, just quiet and as unostentatious as possible. Keep your dignity and stand on it. Make friends with the dogs."

Beyond the discussion of whether the bulk of his work is documentary or art or some combination, his best illustrations defy categories and connect with the heart.

The Kiowa writer N. Scott Momaday, who won a Pulitzer Prize for his novel *House Made of Dawn*, had just finished writing a story taken from his ancestors' oral tradition when he saw a Curtis picture of Plains Indians on horseback dragging a travaux. "It struck me with such force that it brought tears to my eyes," he wrote in *Sacred Legacy*, a book of Curtis pictures published in 2000. "I felt that I was looking into a memory in my blood. Here was a moment lost in time, a moment I had known only in my imagination, suddenly verified, an image immediately translated from the mind's eye to the picture plane." He summarized the photographer's output this way: "Taken as a whole, the work of Edward Curtis is a singular achievement. Never before have we seen the Indians of North America so close to the origins of their humanity, their sense of themselves in the world, their innate dignity and self-possession."

I heard this kind of praise in much of the Indian country I visited over the course of researching this book. I traveled to nearly every tribal homeland that Curtis had gone to for *The North American Indian*. People were effusive about the pictures themselves, with good reason: Curtis took more than 40,000 of them. But he also recorded those 10,000 songs, wrote down vocabularies and pronunciation guides for 75 languages, and transcribed an incalculable number of myths, rituals and religious stories from oral histories. Only in recent years has the scope and depth of Curtis's scholarship come to be appreciated. *The North American Indian*, the monumental work of a self-educated man, "almost certainly constitutes the largest anthropological enterprise ever undertaken," noted Mick Gidley, a professor of American literature who has written extensively about Curtis.

Perhaps that is an overstatement, but not by much. Also, Curtis was the first person to conduct a thorough historical autopsy of the Battle of the Little Bighorn, from both the Indian side and that of the cavalry. His work was eyewitness history, taken from survivors of the battle. Under pressure from Custer's widow, Libbie, who lived to be ninety-one, and following the concerns expressed by President Theodore Roosevelt, Curtis had held back on his most explosive revelations. But these insights are now available in a bound volume at the Library of Congress, and have proven to be an invaluable resource for modern historians. In his 2010 book on the battle, Nathaniel Philbrick credits Curtis for seeking out so many witnesses, and generally sides with Curtis's view of the battle.

In the Land of the Head-Hunters, a source of so much heartbreak for Curtis, has undergone a similar revival. After being pulled from theaters because of legal disputes, it vanished for thirty-three years. Curtis had sold all rights, and given away the master print, for a pittance. In the late 1940s, the Field Museum in Chicago came into possession of the scratched, corroded and faded movie. When it was screened, the nitrate film caught fire, forcing an evacuation. The flames were doused, but not without further damage. In 1973, the art historian Bill Holm, an expert on Coast Salish culture, and the anthropologist George Quimby, who had worked on the film in Chicago, released a restored and restructured version, titled *In the Land of the War Canoes*. They had spent seven years putting the film back together. It was praised as a landmark, and given its due for documentary realism and for the pioneering use of an all-Indian cast. Curtis "took considerable artistic license," a University of British Columbia scholar told film critic William Arnold in 2008, but he "got most things right." In particular, he lauded Curtis for filming ceremonies that were outlawed by the potlatch prohibition laws, which were not repealed until 1951. On a spring evening in 2008, a restored version of the film made a second debut, and proved to be a highlight of the Seattle International Film Festival. It was shown at the Moore Theatre, where Curtis had copremiered it back in 1914. The cleaned-up film was presented with a live performance of its original orchestral score and a dance recital by Indian descendants of the cast. Today the movie is held by the Library of Congress, part of its National Film Registry, where it is recognized for its "cultural, historic and aesthetic" value.

The most significant revival, and one that would probably have surprised Curtis, has been among Indians themselves. The 2010 census counted 2.7 million Native Americans, just under 1 percent of the population and up 18 percent in a decade. This figure includes only those who listed themselves as "Indian alone," not of mixed blood. What stopped the downward slide in population was better health and vaccinations; eventually the white man's diseases that had wiped out so many Indians had run their course.

The Tulalip, north of Seattle, where Curtis took some of his first Indian pictures, have 2,500 members living, as before, on the shores of the inland sea. With its casino just off Interstate 5, the tribe has grown very wealthy. They just opened a $19 million, 23,000-square-foot cultural center. Inside, one of the first things to greet visitors is an enormous hanging of a picture Curtis took in 1913, called *Evening on Puget Sound*.

Some of the smallest tribes have not fared so well. The Duwamish, Princess Angeline's people, were declared to be extinct by the United States government in 1916. Some surviving Duwamish have long taken issue with that judgment and have tried for decades to gain official recognition. In 2008, members of the tribe—including Cecile Hansen, the great-great-grandniece of Chief Seattle—opened a cedar longhouse near their traditional home by the Duwamish River. At the other end of the population spectrum, the Navajo now number more than a quarter-million people on a reservation that is larger than all but ten of the states. With passage of the American Indian Religious Freedom Act of 1978, which extended First Amendment protection of faith to native rites, people are free to worship the gods of their ancestors in the canyons and mesas where Curtis found them a century ago, diminished but unbowed.

Though Edward Curtis never made a dime producing what was arguably the most expansive and comprehensive publication undertaken by a single citizen of the United States, though he went to his death without the acknowledgment he so wanted in life, and though he paid for his obsession with the loss of friends, a marriage and the irreplaceable hours of watching a family bloom, he always believed his words and pictures would come to life long after he'd passed — the artist's lasting reward of immortality. A young man with an unlived-in face found his calling in the faces of a continent's forgotten people, and in so doing, he not only saw history, but made it.

ACKNOWLEDGMENTS

Anybody who thinks writing is entirely a solitary endeavor has never tried to bring a book along from its formative idea to pixels and pages. The village of helpers, healers and mentors is large. I've been lucky, as was my fellow Seattleite Edward Curtis, to live in a city that nurtures writers. I could not write in a good climate. In gratitude, I start at the top from Seattle: thanks to my wife, Joni Balter, who always gets the first look at my ragged prose. This time around I benefited enormously from sharp critiques by some very good reader-editors—Sam Howe Verhovek, Barbara Winslow Boardman and Sophie Egan. Despite my pestering, they remain good friends, and in the last case a daughter who isn't afraid to tell her dad when his stuff needs help. The Allen Library at the University of Washington is home to thousands of Curtis documents, letters and photos; thanks to the staff for their diligence in keeping these archives in great condition, and for their help in tracking down the relevant material. It's a great treasure, especially the papers of Edmond S. Meany, Curtis's pal and university pioneer. And I found wonderful material in the Seattle Room, a comprehensive collection of all things related to the city's story, on a top floor of the glass masterpiece of the Seattle Public Library.

Also in Seattle, the Rainier Club opened its doors to me in many ways, providing access not just to their Curtis pictures, which appear in every nook and cranny, but to the many portraits Curtis took of members. The club has been enthusiastic and helpful in this project from the beginning. My guide there was Russell Johanson, a rare books collector. And Marie McCaffrey, a Rainier member whose late husband, Walt Crowley, wrote a history of the club, opened the way there, and was an early and passionate supporter of the project. In addition, she is the co-founder and executive director of HistoryLink.org, an invaluable digital service for lovers of the Pacific Northwest past. The longtime keeper of the Curtis flame in Seattle is Lois Flury. For more than thirty years, her Flury and Company gallery in Pioneer Square has given display space to many of the Shadow Catcher's masterpieces. Lois helped on many fronts. John Forsen, filmmaker and winemaker, was key in leading me back to the Seattle world's fair of 1909, where Curtis was on display for the world. Three other Seattleites deserve thanks: Dr. John Gayman, for many a ruminative run (and free medical advice) during the book's long winter; Casey Egan, for issuing a challenge to make it at least as interesting as an iPhone app; and Mike Heinrich, winner of the Steve Martin look-alike contest in our extended family, and the funniest writer in my circle.

For the mountaineering material, and pictures and insights into Curtis's days as a climbing guide, I am indebted to Jeff Thomas at the Mazamas in Portland. The club does a superb job of housing all things relating to the rich mountaineering history of the Pacific Northwest, and Jeff was kind enough to allow me to use a seldom-seen Indian picture taken by Curtis on Mount Hood.

I tried to visit every Indian reservation and tribal homeland covered in the Curtis magnum opus. Some of these lands I saw earlier, while not in pursuit of the Shadow Catcher. All of the people at these places were welcoming, and warmed to the topic. In particular, the staff at Canyon de Chelly National Monument, in the Navajo Nation, was terrific. I urge any reader wishing to find perhaps the most enchanting—and overlooked—place on the continent to pay a visit. Hopi elders, memorably at the stone outpost of Walpi, and tribal officials in Acoma, the Sky City, also gave up much of their time in response to my queries. I climbed up the path to Acoma three times—each more mesmerizing.

At the Little Bighorn Battlefield National Monument, which I visited many times in the heart of the Crow Nation, it helped that my initial reappraisal of the battle was courtesy of a man who was then superintendent of the monument, Gerard Baker, a full-blood Mandan-Hidatsa.

In Los Angeles, where Curtis spent his final years, two outposts of western and Native American history proved most useful. Thanks to the Braun Research Library at the Southwest Museum of the American Indian for giving me access to hundreds of Curtis letters, even though the museum itself was closed for construction. Thanks also to the Seaver Center for Western History Research at the Los Angeles County Museum of Natural History, keeper of edited first editions of Curtis volumes.

On the other coast, in the other Washington, thanks once again to Jeffrey M. Flannery, head of the Reference and Reader Service Section of the Library of Congress. It was there that I found the complete write-up that Curtis did of the Little Bighorn (and never published). Also, it was there that I trolled the correspondence of President Theodore Roosevelt, and his aide Gifford Pinchot, with Curtis.

In New York, kudos to the entire staff at the Pierpont Morgan Library, sitting on a nest of Curtis memorabilia. My publisher, Houghton Mifflin Harcourt, has been wonderful on this project. Special thanks to Andrea Schulz, editor in chief at HMH, for showing such a deft hand (unusual in that trade!) and for all the suggestions that improved the manuscript. I failed her on a few things, but it would have required interviews beyond the grave. Larry Cooper, once again, caught many things in the copyediting that my untrained eyes had missed. Also at Houghton, my gratitude to Christina Morgan, for immense help in finding and sorting all the pictures, and to Lori Glazer, Carla Gray and Megan Wilson for the kind of work that brings readers to writers. And praise, as always, to Carol Mann, my longtime agent—a terrific literary matchmaker.

Finally, thanks to Michael Kinsley and Patty Stonesifer for allowing me into their winter refuge in the Sonoran Desert, where I edited parts of the manuscript in blissful disregard of all digital interferences. Patty is an author's best friend, at any phase of a book.

SOURCES

I. FIRST PICTURE

Description of Angeline's cabin and her surroundings, from *Seattle Post-Intelligencer*, May 31, 1896, and from wire service story printed in *Wheeling Register*, December 9, 1894, and from sketch in *Annals of Old Angeline*, by Betha Piper Venen, Denny-Coryell Company, 1903.

"Ragged remnant of royalty," from *Sealth: The City by the Inland Sea*, by Elizabeth H. Calvert, Washington State Historical Society, 1897.

City population, from "A Chronicle of the History of Seattle, 1850–1897," by Thomas Prosch, typescript, 1900, on file at Seattle Public Library (hereafter cited as SPL).

President Harrison visit, from *Seattle Times*, January 21, 1873, and from HistoryLink.org essay 5067.

Angeline's age, from a recollection of A. A. Denny in *Seattle Post-Intelligencer*, May 31, 1896.

Joe Foster Jr., hanging, from *Seattle Times*, June 28, 1870.

Reverend Blaine's comments, from *Skid Road*, by Murray Morgan, Viking, 1951.

Treaty terms, from Prosch, "A Chronology of the History of Seattle."

Denny conversation, from *Pig-Tail Days in Old Seattle*, by Sophie Frye Bass, Metropolitan Press, 1937.

Verse, from Venen, *Annals of Old Angeline*.

Catherine Blaine recollection, from HistoryLink.org essay, posted July 30, 2001.

Duwamish, known as Inside the Bay People, from *A Guide to the Indian Tribes of the Pacific Northwest,* by Robert H. Ruby and John A. Brown, University of Oklahoma Press, 1992.

Chief Seattle speech, from HistoryLink.org, undated, and from *Northwest Gateway,* by Archie Binns, Doubleday, 1945.

Description of Puget Sound, from *Atlantic Monthly,* February 1883.

Eva Curtis on brother's curiosity, from *Curtis's Western Indians,* by Ralph W. Edwards, Bonanza Books, 1962.

Curtis as the premier photographer, from *Argus,* July 18, 1896.

"perseverance," from *Argus,* December 14, 1896.

Description of Curtis as blue-eyed, etc., from lengthy profile in *Seattle Times,* November 15, 1903.

Curtis bedridden, "limp, thin and bleached," from an unpublished memoir by William Phillips, circa 1911, quoted, in part, in *Edward S. Curtis and the North American Indian, Incorporated,* by Mick Gidley, Cambridge University Press, 1998.

Curtis's early years, from correspondence between retired Seattle librarian Harriet Leitch and Edward S. Curtis, 1948–1952, bound, copied, handwritten letters on file in SPL, Seattle Room.

Regrades and building boom, from *Remembering Seattle,* by Walt Crowley, Trade Papers Press, Turner Publishing, 2010.

Largest dredging contract, from Prosch, "A Chronology of the History of Seattle."

Buildings like New York, from wire service story in *Wheeling Register,* 1894.

Early success of Curtis, from *Argus,* July 18, 1896.

Curtis in the progress edition, from *Seattle Mail and Herald,* December 19, 1903.

Curtis and Angeline, first picture, from Leitch-Curtis correspondence, SPL.

Superior beings and savages, early history, from *Reminiscences of Seattle, Washington Territory,* by Thomas Phelps, Ye Galleon Press, 1970.

Curtis's first memory of Indians, from "As It Was," unpublished memoir on file at University of Washington (hereafter, UW) Library, Special Collections.

Record of the hanging, largest mass execution in U.S. history, from *New York Times* story on calls for pardon, December 14, 2010.

Curtis convalescence, from Leitch-Curtis correspondence, SPL.

Curtis on paying Angeline and the Tulalip, from Leitch-Curtis correspondence, SPL.

Angeline's slaves, *Seattle Times,* November 7, 1957.

The big idea: Curtis writes that "the task" had its inception in 1898, *The North American Indian,* Vol. I. Hereafter, references cited as *NAI.*

Angeline obituaries, from *Seattle Post-Intelligencer,* May 31, 1896, and *Aberdeen Daily News,* June 1, 1896.

2. ENCOUNTER ON A VOLCANO

Account of 1897 climb, from *Portland Oregonian*, August 26, 1897.

Curtis's account of Rainier in 1897 and 1898, and mention of Ella McBride, from his correspondence with Leitch, SPL. Also from Curtis's own account in his unpublished memoir, "As It Was," UW Library, Special Collections.

Mazama account of the 1897 Rainier climb, from the journal *Mazama: A Record of Mountaineering in the Pacific Northwest*, Vol. 2, October 1900.

Curtis mountain pictures advertised, from his brochure "Scenic Washington," on file at Mazama Library in Portland.

Picture of two Indians in forest of Mount St. Helens, 1898, from Mazama Library files. This is one of Curtis's first Indian pictures, and rarely seen.

Curtis as heroic, his rescue and leadership on Rainier, from *Seattle Times*, August 14, 1897, and *Detroit Free Press*, September 12, 1897.

Other Rainier descriptions, from Curtis's typescript notes, "Mount Rainier, the Great Peak of the Pacific Forest Reserve," undated, on file at UW Library, Special Collections.

Questions to Curtis from Mazamas on day of summit climb of 1897, and other details of climb, from Curtis's unpublished memoir, "As It Was."

The first death on Rainier, from *Harper's Weekly*, August 28, 1897, and from *Mount Rainier: A Record of Exploration*, by Edmond S. Meany, Macmillan, 1916.

The record for most climbers, and account of the 1897 climb, from Dee Molenaar, *The Challenge of Rainier*, Mountaineers, 1971.

Statistics on climbs, from *Climbing Mount Rainier: The Essential Guide*, by Fred Beckey and Alex Van Steen, Alpen Books, 1999, and *Mount Rainier: A Climbing Guide*, by Mike Gauthier, Mountaineer Books, 2005.

Summit, and aspects of the climb from Camp Muir to top, from the author's climbs of Rainier, retracing Curtis's route to the top.

Curtis meeting distinguished men on Rainier, his rescue, from his own account, as told in letter to Leitch, identifying the famous men he rescued on Rainier by directing her to a picture, from the Harriman expedition of Grinnell and Merriam, cited above.

Grinnell background, from *Last Stand: George Bird Grinnell, the Battle to Save the Buffalo, and the Birth of the New West*, by Michael Punke, Smithsonian Books, 2007.

Merriam background, from *The Last of the Naturalists: The Career of C. Hart Merriam*, by Keir B. Sterling, Arno Press, 1974.

Curtis's methods, and description of his personality at that age, from William Phillips recollection in his unpublished memoir, in Gidley, *Edward S. Curtis and the North American Indian, Incorporated*, and Curtis explanation in *Western Trail* magazine, January 1900.

Alaska, letter, and story, from *Century Magazine*, October 14, 1897. Story behind the approach Curtis took to getting the assignment, from "Edward S. Curtis Goes to the Mountain," by Mick Gidley, *Pacific Northwest Quarterly*, October 1984.

Fallout between the Curtis brothers over Alaska, from HistoryLink.org essay 8780.

Harriman expedition details, from "North to Alaska," *Smithsonian*, June 2003.

Description of Curtis as contagious, from Phillips unpublished memoir, in Gidley, *Edward S. Curtis and the North American Indian, Incorporated*.

Grinnell invitation to Curtis, from Curtis, "As It Was."

3 · THE BIG IDEA

Trip to Browning, Montana, from Burlington Northern online history of the railroad, and from the author's trip to Browning, and to the Blackfeet reservation.

Descriptions of buildings in Browning, from *Among the Blackfeet Indians of Montana*, by A. C. Haddon, as recorded in *Edward Curtis and the North American Indian Project in the Field*, by Mick Gidley, University of Nebraska Press, 2003.

Grinnell on Curtis's method, from "Portraits of Indian Types," by George Bird Grinnell, *Scribner's*, March 1905.

Holy Family Mission, from Browning, Montana, website: www.browning montana.com/mission.html.

American Indian policy, assimilation, role of agents and missionaries, from *Now That the Buffalo's Gone*, by Alvin Josephy, University of Oklahoma Press, 1982.

Details of Sun Dance, including recordings, from *NAI*, Vol. VI, and from Curtis's letters to Leitch, SPL.

How to talk to Indians, from Grinnell, "Portraits of Indian Types," and from Curtis's unpublished memoir, "As It Was," UW Library, Special Collections.

Sweat bath, hearing music and birds, from Curtis letter to Mrs. Gardner, circa 1937, on file at UW Library, Special Collections.

Curtis with Grinnell, from UW Library, Special Collections. Random writings of Curtis, from draft of "As It Was."

Blackfeet as likeable people, and their rituals explained, from *NAI*, Vol. VI.

White Calf and wig must be "ethnologically accurate," from Curtis, "As It Was."

San Francisco interview, from *San Francisco Sunday Call*, October 14, 1900.

Curtis on the Hopi and Snake Dance, from Curtis, "As It Was."

Grinnell on Curtis the artist, from *Century*, October 14, 1897.

Descriptions of Hopi country, land and people, *NAI*, Vol. XII.

Other descriptions of Hopi country, from the author's visits to the Hopi Nation in Arizona.

Curtis's advice on subjective pictures, from *Western Trail,* January 1900.

Such a big dream, as quoted by family members, in *Curtis' Western Indians,* by Ralph W. Andrews, Bonanza Books, 1962. Same words also used by Florence Curtis Graybill in her memoir of her father, *Edward S. Curtis: Photographer of the North American Indian,* by Victor Boesen and Florence Curtis Graybill, Dodd, Mead, 1977. Earlier quote in this chapter on Curtis being single-minded, from his sister Eva Curtis, also came from this memoir.

Curtis "spending all his time" on Indian project, his letter to Hodge, September 15, 1903, in Frederick Webb Hodge Collection, Braun Research Library, Southwest Museum of the American Indian, Los Angeles. Hereafter referred to as Hodge papers, Southwest Museum.

Indian population, from census of 1900, and speculation on vanishing, from *American Indian Holocaust and Survival: A Population History Since 1492,* by Russell Thornton, University of Oklahoma Press, 1987.

4. INDIAN NAPOLEON

Description of football game, from *Seattle Post-Intelligencer,* November 21, 1903.

Roosevelt visit, largest crowd in history of state, from *Seattle Times,* May 25, 1903.

Population of Seattle, cars and streetcars, from *Seattle Mail and Herald,* December 19, 1903, progress issue.

Joseph's activity in last four years of his life, from *Chief Joseph,* by Chester Anders Fee, Wilson-Erickson Press, 1936.

More on Joseph, from *Chief Joseph and the Flight of the Nez Perce,* by Kent Nerburn, HarperCollins, 2005, and *Chief Joseph, Yellow Wolf and the Creation of Nez Perce History in the Pacific Northwest,* by Robert Ross McCoy, Routledge, 2004.

Edmond Meany background, and his quotes and letters between Curtis and Meany (extensive correspondence), from The Papers of Edmond Meany, UW Library, Special Collections, hereafter cited as Meany papers.

"Old Chief Likes City," from *Seattle Post-Intelligencer,* November 22, 1903.

Significance of the game, *Seattle Times,* November 21, 1903, and more details of the game from *One Hundred Years of Husky Football,* edited by Karen Chave and Steve Rudman, Professional Sports Publications, 1990.

Curtis writing on Joseph, from *NAI,* Vol. VIII.

Joseph's speech in Seattle, from Nerburn, *Chief Joseph and the Flight of the Nez Perce.*

Joseph's death, and Curtis letter to Meany on the death, from Meany papers, letter, October 13, 1904.

Buffalo Bill quote on Joseph, from Nerburn, *Chief Joseph and the Flight of the Nez Perce.*

Havasupai, from the author's visit to the village of Supai, near the Grand Canyon, and from Curtis's writings on the tribe, *NAI*, Vol. II.

"Strangest dwelling place," from *NAI*, Vol. II.

Description of Walpi and Hopi reservation, from the author's visit to Walpi.

Apache, from Curtis, "As It Was," and from the author's visit to the White Mountain Apache reservation, Arizona.

Apache dialogue, bribe attempt, from Curtis writings on file at the Seaver Center, Los Angeles County Museum of History, box 1.

Seattle Times profile of Curtis, from November 15, 1903.

Prettiest children contest, from *Ladies' Home Journal*, September 1904.

Alden Blethen background, from HistoryLink.org, essay 1681.

Account of Chief Joseph reburial, from Curtis, "Vanishing Indian Types," *Scribner's*, June 1906. Quotes about the digging, from Curtis's letters to Leitch, SPL.

Description of marble memorial at Joseph burial site, from the author's visit to Chief Joseph's grave on the Colville Indian reservation, Nespelem, Washington.

Account of potlatch, from "Vanishing Indian Types," and from *NAI*, Vol. VIII.

Cardozo, from *Sacred Legacy*, edited by Christopher Cardozo, Simon & Schuster, 2000.

5. WITH THE PRESIDENT

Curtis at Roosevelt home, from Curtis's unpublished memoir, "As It Was," UW Library, Special Collections.

Sagamore Hill descriptions, from Sagamore Hill National Historic Site, www.nps.gov.

Curtis on Roosevelt, on Roquefort dressing, on feeling at home in Oyster Bay, from "As It Was."

T.R. quote on Alice, from *Hail to the Chiefs: My Life and Times with Six Presidents*, by Ruth Shick Montgomery, Coward, McCann & Geoghegan, 1970.

How Curtis won contest, from "Curtis Goes to Oyster Bay — Seattle Man Will Make Photographs of President Roosevelt's Boys," *Seattle Daily Mail*, undated clipping on file at UW Library, Special Collections.

Smithsonian rebuke, Doubleday meeting, from "A Seattle Man's Triumph," *Seattle Times*, May 22, 1904.

T.R.'s view on Indians in general, from *The Winning of the West*, originally published in 1894, reprint, University of Nebraska Press, 1995.

T.R. comment on "dead Indians," from *Theodore Roosevelt Cyclopedia*, Roosevelt Memorial Association, 1941.

Curtis's orotone finishing process, from promotional brochure, Curtis studio, on file at UW Library, Special Collections.

Curtis's work habits, from his letters to Leitch, SPL.

Mathew Brady and his life quest, from *Mathew Brady and the Image of History*, by Mary Panzer, Smithsonian Books, 2004.

Acoma description, from two visits by the author. Spanish battle detail at Acoma from *The Last Conquistador: Juan de Oñate and the Settling of the Far Southwest*, by Marc Simmons, University of Oklahoma Press, 1991.

Acoma, quote on two religions, "Indians of the Stone House," by E. S. Curtis, *Scribner's*, February 1909.

Hopi Snake Dance and camera, from *Seattle Times*, May 22, 1904.

Curtis spirituality, from letter to Hodge, October 28, 1904, Hodge papers, Southwest Museum.

Curtis on the Navajo, from *NAI*, Vol. I.

Canyon de Chelly description, from the author's visit.

Canyon de Chelly history, from National Park Service, www.nps.gov.

Curtis letter to Meany, October 13, 1904, from Meany papers.

Curtis letter to Hodge, October 28, 1904, from Hodge papers, Southwest Museum.

Curtis and incident with expert at the Cosmos Club, as told by Curtis in *Seattle Mail and Herald*, May 13, 1905.

Geronimo biography, from *Geronimo: His Own Story*, by Stephen Melvil Barrett and Frederick W. Turner III, originally published in 1906, reprint, Penguin, 1996.

Bird Grinnell on Curtis, from Grinnell, "Portraits of Indian Types," *Scribner's*, March 1905.

Grosvener letter, February 18, 1905, quoted in Gidley, *Edward S. Curtis and the North American Indian, Incorporated*.

Curtis letter to Roosevelt, December 15, 1905, and reply, December 16, 1905, from Letters of Theodore Roosevelt, Library of Congress.

6. IN THE DEN OF THE TITAN

Morgan letters, contracts, from Edward S. Curtis papers, Morgan Library archives.

Morgan Library, plan and details, from Morgan Library, www.themorgan.org., and from "Let There Be Light and Elegance," *New York Times*, October 29, 2010.

The Curtis plan, outline, from Curtis papers, Morgan Library archives.

Morgan background, from *Morgan: American Financier*, by Jean Strouse, Harper Perennial, 2000.

Railroads, and how they changed the lives of Indians, from *They Built the West: An Epic of Rails and Cities*, by Glenn Chesney Quiett, Appleton-Century, 1934.

Belle da Costa Greene, from *An Illuminated Life: Belle da Costa Greene's Journey from Prejudice to Privilege*, by Heidi Ardizzone, Norton, 2007, and from Strouse, *Morgan: American Financier*.

Rave at Waldorf-Astoria, from *Craftsman*, March 1906.

Curtis-Morgan encounter, from Curtis-Leitch correspondence, SPL. Additional details from UW archives, and notes of Florence Curtis Graybill in the Curtis family files.

Headline, Morgan money, from *New York Press*, March 26, 1906.

Roosevelt letter to Curtis, February 6, 1906, from *Letters of Theodore Roosevelt*, Harvard University Press, 1952. Curtis letter to Roosevelt asking him to write introduction, August 17, 1906. Roosevelt's reply, August 28, 1906.

7. ANGLOS IN INDIAN COUNTRY

Curtis desire to get Apache secrets, from his unpublished memoir, "As It Was."

Curtis description of Myers, from Curtis-Leitch correspondence, SPL.

How Curtis gets to Apache country, from his "Vanishing Indian Types," *Scribner's*, May 1906.

Harold Curtis quotes, on being in the field with his father for the first time, from Gidley, *Edward S. Curtis and the North American Indian Project in the Field*.

Description of White Mountain Apache reservation and surrounding area, from the author's visit.

Curtis letter to Hodge, June 9, 1906, Hodge papers, Southwest Museum.

Curtis on being rejected, from "As It Was."

Descriptions of Goshonné in Apache country, from Curtis's account in "As It Was" and from another personal account on file at UW, undated, apparently written much later. Also from Phillips account in Gidley, *Edward S. Curtis and the North American Indian Project in the Field*.

Curtis's domestic strife, details from divorce papers, *Curtis v. Curtis*, on file at King County courthouse, Seattle.

Traveling party load, and how he works, "conditions cannot be changed," from Curtis undated typescript in Meany papers.

Children's point of view in Canyon de Chelly, from Boesen and Graybill, *Edward S. Curtis: Photographer of the North American Indian*, and recollections in UW Library, Special Collections.

More descriptions of Canyon de Chelly, from the author's visit, and author's visits to Chinle and nearby Old Oraibi.

Curtis quotes, "on the move," from UW lecture recollections.

Storms, weather, from untitled and undated Curtis speech on how he works, in Meany papers.

Snake Dance, from Meany papers, undated. Snake around his neck, from Curtis's written program for the picture opera.

Snake Dance, additional information, from *NAI*, Vol. XII.

Snake Dance, letter from Curtis to Hodge, September 27, 1906, Hodge papers, Southwest Museum.

8. THE ARTIST AND HIS AUDIENCE

How to write, from Curtis class lecture at UW.

Curtis letter to Morgan, August 17, 1906, from Morgan Library.

Curtis on writing Vol. I of *NAI*, from letter to Morgan, November 17, 1906.

Morgan and early panic, from Strouse, *Morgan: American Financier.*

Curtis introduction, from *NAI*, Vol. I.

Curtis to Meany, November 5, 1907, Meany papers.

Curtis to Meany, November 11, 1907, Meany papers.

Vanishing race, Curtis description, from Curtis letter to Burke, January 26, 1906, UW Library, Special Collections, various letters in Curtis file.

Phillips quote, "insanely optimistic," as told by Curtis in a letter to Meany, September 4, 1907.

Smithsonian rejection, from Charles Walcott letter to Curtis, April 16, 1907, Smithsonian archives.

Brown University rejection, from Curtis letter to Hodge on "so much to say," December 1, 1907, Hodge papers, Southwest Museum.

T.R. introduction, from *NAI*, Vol. I.

Curtis on Navajo, "American Bedouins," from *NAI*, Vol. I.

Losing track of chemicals, framing a picture a certain way, from class lecture at UW.

Imogen Cunningham, from article on Seattle Art Museum show of Cunningham's work, *Seattle Times*, August 30, 2009.

Working till last cable car, from Phillips's unpublished notes on Curtis in Gidley, *Edward S. Curtis and the North American Indian Project in the Field.*

Review of Waldorf-Astoria show, from *Craftsman*, March 1906.

Apache and Navajo details, from *NAI*, Vol. I.

The Upshaw conversation from Curtis, "Vanishing Indian Types," *Scribner's,* June 1906.

Curtis on nature of "savages," from field notes, 1906, Morgan Library archives.

Curtis on wanting to keep nudes in *NAI*, from his letter to Hodge, June 26, 1907.

Greene on "most interesting person in New York," from Strouse, *Morgan: American Financier.*

Morgan quote on Wall Street, from *The American Past*, by Roger Butterfield, Simon & Schuster, 1966.

Curtis letter to Meany, August 20, 1907, on Seattle gang not appreciating him, from Meany papers.

Meany letter to Curtis, August 25, 1907, on "greatest literary achievement," from Meany papers.

Ayers comments, fifty men, from Curtis letter to Hodge, December 17, 1907, Hodge papers, Southwest Museum.

Morgan saves capitalism, from Strouse, *Morgan: American Financier,* and from *The Panic of 1907,* by Robert F. Bruner and Sean D. Carr, John Wiley and Sons, 2007.

Morgan letter, November 7, 1907, Morgan Library archives.

Review of first two volumes of *NAI,* from *New York Times,* June 6, 1908.

Comparison of Curtis's work to King James Bible, *New York Herald,* June 16, 1907.

Curtis compared to Audubon, *Independent,* August 20, 1908.

Curtis hailed further, from *Chicago Unity,* July 30, 1908.

9. THE CUSTER CONUNDRUM

Curtis on Little Bighorn battlefield, from his own notes, on file at UW Library, Special Collections, where he discusses retracing battlefield with Sioux, with Two Moons of the Cheyenne, with Crow and with General Charles A. Woodruff.

Physical descriptions of the battlefield, from the author's two trips to the site.

Alexander Upshaw, from *Between Indian and White Worlds: The Cultural Broker,* by Margaret Connell Szasz, University of Oklahoma Press, 2001, and from "Native Agency and the Making of the North American Indian: Alexander Upshaw and Edward S. Curtis," by Shamoon Zamir, *American Indian Quarterly,* Fall 2007.

Custer account, from *The Last Stand: Custer, Sitting Bull, and the Battle of the Little Bighorn,* by Nathaniel Philbrick, Viking, 2010.

Crazy Horse, from *NAI,* Vol. III, and from *The Killing of Crazy Horse,* by Thomas Powers, Knopf, 2010.

Cheyenne, and Sand Creek massacre description, from *NAI,* Vol. VI.

Later Curtis account, all his findings on the battle that were not included in *NAI,* from *The Papers of Edward S. Curtis Relating to Custer's Last Battle,* edited by James S. Hutchins, Upton and Sons, 2000, on file at the Library of Congress.

Other Custer and Curtis comments, from *NAI,* Vol. III.

Upshaw's temptations, from the Carlisle School's website: www.home.epix .net/~landis/history.html.

Upshaw on his white wife and his work with Curtis, from Hearings Before the Committee on Indian Affairs in the Senate, U.S. Government Printing Office, 1908.

Upshaw and Carlisle School philosophy, from Carlisle School's website.

Patronizing letter from Indian agent Z. Lewis Dalby to Upshaw, July 13, 1907, from records at Hearings Before the Committee on Indian Affairs in the Senate, U.S. Government Printing Office, 1908.

Dalby's view of Crow, from Senate hearings transcript, ibid., 1908.

Curtis predicting Upshaw would go to the "god of his fathers," from class lecture at UW.

Hal's typhoid fever, from his sister's account in Boesen and Graybill, *Edward S. Curtis: Photographer of the North American Indian*, and from Curtis's letters of that summer.

The starving Sioux, from Meany, *Seattle Times*, August 11, 1907.

Curtis's work schedule, summary of the work to date, from letter to Belle da Costa Greene, 1913, Morgan Library archives.

Curtis letter to Meany, "anything published" on Custer, October 22, 1907, and all subsequent letters of that fall and winter, from UW Library, Special Collections. Letters from Curtis to Meany, from Meany papers.

Interview of Custer, *New York Herald*, November 10, 1907.

Curtis and Pinchot's back and forth on Custer, quoted in Gidley, *Edward S. Curtis and the North American Indian, Incorporated*.

Roosevelt letter, April 8, 1908, from *Letters of Theodore Roosevelt*.

Curtis letter to army colonel re "facts," from Curtis's Library of Congress file.

Curtis letter to Meany, "very guarded," August 28, 1908, Meany papers.

Custer, final words and final form of the chapter on the battle, from *NAI*, Vol III.

10. THE MOST REMARKABLE MAN

"Great and loyal friend," from *NAI*, Vol. IV.

Letters, and "fine man," from Dalby letter, September 15, 1907, in government transcript of Senate hearings in 1908.

Meany and Upshaw on a train, Meany letter to Curtis, August 11, 1907, Meany papers.

Upshaw's value, letter from Curtis to Hodge, December 26, 1907, Hodge papers, Southwest Museum.

Scholarly value of the Crow volume, from Zamir, "Native Agency and the Making of the North American Indian: Alexander Upshaw and Edward S. Curtis."

Descriptions of Crow, from *NAI*, Vol. IV.

Description of Crow reservation, from the author's visit to Crow Agency, Montana.

Description of Mandan land, from the author's visit to Fort Berthold Indian reservation and New Town, North Dakota.

Description of bear ceremony and its meaning, from *NAI*, Vol. V.

Quote by Curtis on Upshaw "educated," from newspaper clipping of 1905, in Gidley, *Edward S. Curtis and the North American Indian Project in the Field*.

Descriptions of getting the turtles, from Curtis's field notes in "As It Was," on file at UW Library, Special Collections.

Further descriptions of turtles, from *NAI*, Vol. V.

Curtis letter to Meany from North Dakota on turtles, July 31, 1908, Meany papers.

Slight from Cullen, Curtis letter to Hodge, January 14, 1908, Hodge papers, Southwest Museum.

Rave from Peabody, Professor Putnam letter to Curtis, January 22, 1908, from Morgan Library archives.

Review of Reviews, February 1909.

Dr. ten Kate letter, undated, from Curtis files at Southwest Museum.

Washington Post headline and rave, February 25, 1909.

Upshaw conversation with Curtis on nobody left, from Curtis, "Vanishing Indian Types," *Scribner's,* June 1906.

Upshaw letter to Dalby on "justice," March 29, 1908, from Senate hearings, 1908.

Washington Post, on Curtis's background, February 23, 1909, and on diplomats and the actual visit, February 26, 1909.

Death of Upshaw, from *NAI*, Vol. VIII.

Details of death of Upshaw in jail, from *Billings Gazette,* October 20, 1909, and from Yellowstone County death certificate, both courtesy of the Yellowstone Genealogy Forum.

11. ON THE RIVER OF THE WEST

Descriptions of the Columbia River, from Curtis's unpublished memoir, "As It Was."

Further descriptions of the Columbia, from the author's visit along the length of the river and the path that Curtis took (though a number of dams have changed the river).

Columbia River's power, from *A River Lost*, by Blaine Harden, Norton, 1996, and *River of the West*, by Robert Clark, HarperCollinsWest, 1995.

Curtis on Alaska-Yukon Pacific Exposition, from letter to Meany, June 1, 1909, Meany papers.

Hal Curtis's "I never came home" reminiscence, for his sister Florence's manuscript, found in random files in Curtis collection at UW Library, Special Collections.

Rainier Club information and history, from *The Rainier Club*, by Walt Crowley, 1988, published for club members, and from the author's interview with club officials, in particular Russell Johanson, historian and archivist at the club. The author is an honorary member of the club.

Curtis's writing about the Cheyenne, and picture selection, from *NAI*, Vol. VI.

Retouching the alarm clock: the caption is from *NAI*, Vol. VI. Photo showing the clock is in Library and Congress collection of Curtis photos; photo without the clock is a finished plate as it appeared in *NAI*, Vol. VI.

Writings on the Nez Perce, from *NAI*, Vol. VIII.

The rapids of the Columbia, Noggie crying, and other incidents, from Curtis writings on file at UW Library, Special Collections.

Descriptions of the Wishham, from *NAI*, Vol. VIII, and from Curtis's field notes.

Graveyard of the Pacific, description of the mouth of the Columbia, from the author's trip and boat ride over the Columbia River Bar.

12. NEW ART FORMS

Andrew Carnegie, from Curtis letter to Meany, November 19, 1911, Meany papers.

Belle Greene letter to Curtis, November 15, 1911, from Morgan Library archives.

Belle Greene's affair, from Strouse, *Morgan: American Financier.*

Morgan schedule, from Strouse, *Morgan: American Financier.*

Quotes about Greene, and by her, from Ardizzone, *An Illuminated Life: Belle da Costa Greene's Journey from Prejudice to Privilege.*

Osborn's background, his writings cited in "Rocky Road: Henry Fairfield Osborn," www.strangesience.net/osborn.htm.

Exchange of letters between Osborn and Roosevelt, December 21, 1908, from *Letters of Theodore Roosevelt*, Vol. VI.

Curtis praised in long profile in *New York Times*, April 16, 1911.

Curtis reading script for his show, from a typescript of the musical in Gidley, in *Edward S. Curtis and the North American Indian Project in the Field.*

New York Evening World, November 16, 1911.

Roosevelt praise on musicale, letters, T.R. to Curtis, November 21, 1911, Roosevelt letters at Library of Congress.

Curtis letter to Meany, November 19, 1911, Meany papers.

Curtis, "broke," letter to Hodge, November 19, 1911, Hodge papers, Southwest Museum.

Curtis letter to Hodge, "address me at Rainier Club," August 15, 1910, Hodge papers, Southwest Museum.

Curtis letter to Hodge, "Cheer up," January 11, 1912, Hodge papers, Southwest Museum.

Possible bankruptcy, letter to Dr. Kelsey (no first name given), January 11, 1912, Hodge papers, Southwest Museum.

Experts question "vanishing," and Curtis response, in Gidley, *Edward S. Curtis and the North American Indian, Incorporated.*

Curtis's "gush" explanation to Morgan board, from a long summary of work to date at end of 1912, Morgan library archives.

Curtis on treatment of Indians in profile, from *Hampton Magazine*, May 1912, reprinted in Gidley, *Edward S. Curtis and the North American Indian Project in the Field.*

"no earthly thing" without mortgage, Curtis letter to Hodge, September 18, 1908, Hodge papers, Southwest Museum.

Film history, from *Encyclopedia of the Documentary Film*, edited by Ian Aitken, Routledge, 2005.

Description of Kwakiutl, from *NAI*, Vol. X.

Film company prospectus, and Curtis on documentary, in *Edward S. Curtis in the Land of the War Canoes*, by Bill Holm and George Irving Quimby, University of Washington Press, 1980.

Hunt background, from Curtis recollections in "As It Was," and his description of Hunt in *NAI*, Vol. X.

Details of Morgan's death and funeral, from Strouse, *Morgan: American Financier*.

Curtis's future, and apprehension, from various Curtis letters to Leitch, SPL.

Curtis letter to Greene, April 6, 1913, Morgan Library archives.

13. MOVING PICTURES

Writings and descriptions of Coast Salish Indians, from *NAI*, Vol. IX.

Morgan tribute from Curtis, from *NAI*, Vol. X.

New agreement with Jack Morgan, from various Curtis letters to Leitch, SPL, and from Strouse, *Morgan: American Financier*.

Hopi, back in Arizona, from Curtis letter to Meany, undated, Meany papers.

Hopi, on how they'd changed, from *NAI*, Vol. XII.

Curtis on religion, from random writings, UW Library, Special Collections.

Curtis arguing his point on vanishing race, from lecture notes in Gidley, *Edward S. Curtis and the North American Indian Project in the Field*.

Curtis citing Geronimo, from his autobiography, first published in 1906 as *Geronimo's Story of His Life*, revised edition, Plume, 1996.

Curtis on Muhr, from his *NAI* tribute, Vol. X.

Muhr's death, and comment on eternity, from *Seattle Times*, November 3, 1913.

Curtis on Kwakiutl women, from "As It Was."

Curtis on gloomy Kwakiutl men, from *NAI*, Vol. X.

Hunt and missionaries anecdote, Curtis lecture in Gidley, *Edward S. Curtis and the North American Indian Project in the Field*.

Curtis letter to Hodge, June 20, 1914, Hodge papers, Southwest Museum.

Description of North Vancouver Island, from several of the author's visits to the island.

Film crew on Devil Rock at high tide, from a story Curtis told in "As It Was."

Film's run time, reels, tinting, posters, etc., from movie memorabilia on file at Seattle Public Library.

Reviews, first two, in Holm and Quimby, *Edward S. Curtis in the Land of the War Canoes*.

New York Times appraisal of film's merits, March 28, 1915.

New York Times review of opening, praising use of color, December 2, 1914.

Variety review, December 25, 1914.

Mr. Skinner note to Curtis, December 14, 1914, from Hodge papers, Southwest Museum.

Seattle Post-Intelligencer review, December 6, 1914, written after a screening, before the opening.

Film gross, from later assessment in *Seattle Post-Intelligencer,* July 9, 2008.

Curtis letter to Hodge, December 10, 1914, Hodge papers, Southwest Museum.

"Nanook," from Holm and Quimby, *Edward S. Curtis in the Land of the War Canoes.* This was based on Flaherty's diary.

Nanook, from Flaherty's own account, www.cinemaweb.com/silentfilm /bookshelf/23_rf1_2.htm, and "Nanook," Wikipedia.org.

Curtis sold rights for $1,500, from Gidley, *Edward S. Curtis and the North American Indian, Incorporated.* In *Post-Intelligencer* article, July 9, 2008, the figure given is $1,000.

14. LOST DAYS

Divorce details, from *Curtis v. Curtis,* on file at King County courthouse, Seattle.

Destroyed letters, from *Edward S. Curtis — the Life and Times of a Shadow Catcher,* by Barbara A. Davis, Chronicle Books, 1985.

Divorce, headline and main news information, *Seattle Star,* October 6, 1916.

Quotes from Curtis's grandson, James Graybill, on how divorce affected the children, from author interview with Graybill, February 15, 2012.

Great War hurting sales, Curtis letter to Jack Morgan, August 2, 1915, Morgan Library archives.

Descriptions of Makah, from *NAI,* Vol. XI.

Curtis quotes on history, baseball, from *NAI,* Vol. XI.

Letters between Curtis and Schwinke quoted in Holm and Quimby, *Edward S. Curtis in the Land of the War Canoes;* alas, the complete correspondence is now lost, according to the Burke Museum in Seattle.

Leslie's work, from Curtis letter to Meany, April 22, 1915, detailing the coming year, Meany papers.

Myers letter to Hodge on Curtis and work trains in New Mexico, August 5, 1919, Hodge papers, Southwest Museum.

Greene quote, from *The Incredible Pierpont Morgan: Financier and Art Collector,* by Cass Canfield, Harper & Row, 1974.

Cobb Building, from HistoryLink.org essay 7872.

Beth Curtis in charge of studio, details of fights between Clara and family, from *Curtis v. Curtis,* on file at King County courthouse, Seattle.

Smashed plates, as noted in later court papers on the divorce and legal proceedings filed by Curtis's creditors.

Death of T.R., from *Colonel Roosevelt*, by Edmund Morris, Random House, 2010.

Curtis letter to T.R., February 12, 1915, Roosevelt letters at Library of Congress.

Curtis in Hollywood, letter to Meany, January 25, 1922, Meany papers.

More Curtis in Hollywood, from "As It Was," and Curtis's account in letters to Leitch, SPL.

Meany and his achievements, from a short biography of Meany at the start of the Meany papers.

Meany letter to Curtis on Hill suggestion, December 11, 1921, Meany papers.

Curtis letter to Meany on Hill and Frenchman, January 25, 1922, Meany papers.

15. SECOND WIND

Population of California in 1920s, from census of 1920.

Indian population of California, over time, from *The Indian Heritage of America*, by Alvin Josephy, revised edition, Houghton Mifflin, 1991.

Hopi, all from *NAI*, Vol. XII.

Population of San Francisco County and Trinity County, census of 1920.

Curtis and the whale. He told this story to his children, as Florence recorded in her book, *Edward S. Curtis: Photographer of the North American Indian*, but there was no evidence of this. He never mentioned it in descriptions of his fieldwork with the Kwakiutl.

Florence Curtis Graybill on "gentle sensitive father," from the recollection in her book. Also, being with her father, what he cooked, how he worked, from her remembrances in the Graybill papers at UW, and in Boesen and Graybill, *Edward S. Curtis: Photographer of the North American Indian*.

Adventures and pictures taken in northern California, from Florence, and from long Curtis letter to Meany summarizing summer, October 8, 1922, Meany papers.

Curtis on treatment of Indians, letter to Meany, October 8, 1922, and in *NAI*, Vol. XIII.

Descriptions of Klamath, Crater Lake, northern California, from several visits to the region by the author.

Tribal holdings shrinking, from Josephy, *The Indian Heritage of America*.

Curtis speech on behalf of Indian Welfare League, from Gidley, *Edward S. Curtis and the North American Indian, Incorporated*.

Curtis letter to Meany, "hold a little faith," February 22, 1924, Meany papers.

Curtis and Myers in New Mexico, based on Myers correspondence to Hodge in that year, Hodge papers, Southwest Museum.

Matilda Coxe Stevenson takes issue with Curtis's methods, detailed in excerpts of letters in Gidley, *Edward S. Curtis and the North American Indian, Incorporated*.

Myers letter to Hodge, "pumped it dry," November 1, 1925, Hodge papers, Southwest Museum.

Descriptions of Alberta plains, from the author's visit to the province.

Myers quits, letter from Myers to Curtis, no date, but quoted in an April 9, 1926, letter from Curtis to Hodge, Hodge papers, Southwest Museum.

Curtis on Myers, his work habits, from "As It Was."

Curtis on relationship with Myers, "never had a word of discord," from unpublished Curtis memoir, "As It Was."

Curtis letter to Hodge, "bolt of lightning," April 9, 1926, Hodge papers, Southwest Museum.

Curtis tribute to Myers, from *NAI,* Vol. XV.

Eastwood correspondence to Hodge, in Gidley, *Edward S. Curtis and the North American Indian, Incorporated.*

Description of Indian country in Oklahoma, from the author's visit to Fort Sill and surrounding area, where the Comanche were relocated.

Background on the fall of the Comanche, from *Empire of the Summer Moon,* by S. C. Gwynne, Simon & Schuster, 2010.

Myers letter to Hodge, no date, but received May 28, 1927, Hodge papers, Southwest Museum.

Curtis letter to Hodge, Eastwood getting better, October 8, 1926, Hodge papers, Southwest Museum.

Curtis letter to Hodge, "bum diplomat," May 11, 1927, Hodge papers, Southwest Museum.

Hodge letter to Curtis, "thin-skinned," May 19, 1927, Hodge papers, Southwest Museum.

Curtis letter to Hodge on weak material of the Comanche, December 7, 1927, Hodge papers, Southwest Museum.

Myers letter to Hodge, "I wish I were going," no date, but received on May 28, 1927, Hodge papers, Southwest Museum.

16. THE LONGEST DAYS

All quotations from Curtis log in Alaska on file at UW Library, Special Collections, Curtis papers.

All Beth quotations from her log, Curtis papers.

Population figures on Nome, from census of 1920 and 1930. Personal observations of Nome, from the author's visit to the area.

Eastwood letter to Hodge on dirty Hooper Bay, August 1, 1927, Hodge papers, Southwest Museum.

The rest of the journey, from Curtis log in Alaska, dates as noted in text.

The arrest of Curtis, details from *Seattle Times,* October 10, 1927.

More on Curtis's arrest, from *Seattle Post-Intelligencer,* October 12, 1927.

Warrant and court papers, from *Curtis v. Curtis,* on file at King County courthouse, Seattle.

17. FIGHT TO THE FINISH

"Startling, if humiliating," *Seattle Times,* October 10, 1927.

Clara in court, from *Curtis v. Curtis,* on file at King County courthouse, Seattle.

"shabby, hunched," from *Post-Intelligencer,* October 12, 1927.

$2.5 million figure, from *Seattle Star,* October 12, 1927.

"one of those fanatical persons," *Seattle Star,* October 12, 1927.

Curtis crying like a child, from Meany letter file, undated, appears to be from 1920s, Meany papers.

Document ceding copyright, from Morgan Library archives. There are several documents leading up to it, beginning in 1924. Also later, in a March 1, 1937, letter to a Mrs. Gardner of Seattle, Curtis notes, "The negatives and the copyrights as a whole were transferred to the NAI Inc., and passed completely from my hands," this on file at UW Library, Special Collections.

Curtis letter to Hodge on Christians and Indians, December 7, 1927, Hodge papers, Southwest Museum.

Curtis letter to Hodge, lame hip, January 28, 1928, Hodge papers, Southwest Museum.

Writings on Peyote Society, *NAI,* Vol. XIX.

Quote from Comanche chief Parker on peyote, from Gwynne, *Empire of the Summer Moon.*

Writings on Eskimos, description of pictures, from Gwynne, *Empire of the Summer Moon.*

Curtis letter to Hodge, "my bed," February 20, 1930, Hodge papers, Southwest Museum.

Meany letter to Curtis, January 15, 1932, Meany papers.

Curtis letter to Greene, from Morgan Library archives, April 20, 1932.

18. TWILIGHT

All of Leitch, from correspondence between Leitch and Curtis, SPL.

Letter from Curtis to Meany, down but not out, January 19, 1932, Meany papers.

Death of Clara J. Curtis, from *Seattle Times,* October 22, 1932.

Clara hiding letters from Katherine, as alleged in divorce files, *Curtis v. Curtis,* on file at King County courthouse, Seattle.

Family reunion at Thanksgiving, from Boesen and Graybill, *Edward S. Curtis: Photographer of the North American Indian.*

Last letters from Curtis to Meany, May 12, August 13 and August 18, 1934, Meany papers.

Meany summary of his life achievements, from HistoryLink.org essay 7885.

Sale of *NAI* by Morgan to Lariat, from archival notes in Morgan Library.

Movie *The Plainsman,* from single Curtis mention of it in undated letter, reprinted in Gidley, *Edward S. Curtis and the North American Indian, Incorporated.*

The curious Mrs. Gardner letter, undated, and Curtis's reply to her, March 1, 1937, from UW Library, Special Collections.

Notes on Asahel Curtis, from HistoryLink.org essay 8780.

Myers's death, from Gidley, *Edward S. Curtis and the North American Indian, Incorporated.*

Death of Belle da Costa Greene, burning of personal papers, from Ardizzone, *An Illuminated Life: Belle da Costa Greene's Journey from Prejudice to Privilege.*

Seattle Times obituary of Curtis, October 21, 1952.

New York Times obituary of Curtis, October 20, 1952.

Curtis and his single set of *NAI*, from the author's interview with Lois Flury, who learned of the set from the family and later arranged the sale.

EPILOGUE: REVIVAL

New Mexico account, from Flury interview with the author.

Additional account of how Curtis's plates were sold and resold, from *Popular Photography*, May 1984.

Death of Ella McBride, from HistoryLink.org essay, no number, posted July 21, 2010.

Auction prices, as reported by the houses mentioned in the text.

Biggest price yet for a photo lot, from Artnet.com, October 14, 2005.

University of Oregon sale, from the author's interview with Flury.

Private sale, $1.8 million, as reported on July 11, 2011, by *Fine Books & Collections*, www.finebooksmagazine.com. Price was independently confirmed by the author.

Hopi revival, from the author's visit to Hopi Nation.

Makah, whaling and use of Curtis, from HistoryLink.org, essay 5310.

Modern Coast Salish canoe journey and ritual, from *New York Times*, July 25, 2011.

Discussion of stagings, vetting and poses, from letter to Leitch, and quotes on how Curtis worked, from *New York Times* profile, April 16, 1911.

Momaday quote, from *Sacred Legacy: Edward S. Curtis and the North American Indian*, Simon & Schuster, 2000.

Value of Curtis's work to scholarship of battle, from Philbrick, *The Last Stand: Custer, Sitting Bull, and the Battle of the Little Bighorn.*

Tulalip and Curtis picture in lobby, visited by the author.

Curtis findings on Custer: the ones he did not publish are in the Library of Congress, *The Papers of Edward S. Curtis Relating to Custer's Last Battle*, edited by James Hutchins.

Largest anthropological project ever undertaken, assessment from Curtis scholar Mick Gidley, *Edward S. Curtis and the North American Indian, Incorporated.*

Significance of the film: from *Seattle Post-Intelligencer*, June 9, 2008, containing a good appraisal by film critic William Arnold, and from Holm and Quimby, *Edward S. Curtis in the Land of the War Canoes*.

Census on Indian revival, www.census.gov.

Duwamish, from "The Tribe That Would Not Die," *Seattle Metropolitan Magazine*, March 2009.

PHOTO CREDITS

Frontispiece: Courtesy of Cardozo Fine Art. Princess Angeline: Charles Deering McCormick Library of Special Collections, Northwestern University. Curtis on Rainier: The Mazamas Library of Portland, Oregon. Indians drying bark: The Mazamas Library of Portland, Oregon. *A Piegan Dandy:* Courtesy of Cardozo Fine Art. *Piegan Camp:* Courtesy of Cardozo Fine Art. *Snake Priest:* Courtesy of Cardozo Fine Art. Chief Joseph: Courtesy of Cardozo Fine Art. Theodore Roosevelt: Courtesy of Cardozo Fine Art. Curtis at Sagamore Hill: Library of Congress. *At the Old Well of Acoma:* Courtesy of Cardozo Fine Art. J. P. Morgan: Courtesy of Cardozo Fine Art. *Mosa—Mohave:* Courtesy of Cardozo Fine Art. Belle da Costa Greene: National Portrait Gallery, Smithsonian Institution/Art Resource, NY. *Before the Storm—Apache:* Courtesy of Cardozo Fine Art. *Vanishing Race—Navajo:* Courtesy of Cardozo Fine Art. *Geronimo—Apache:* Courtesy of Cardozo Fine Art. *Cañon de Chelly:* Courtesy of Cardozo Fine Art. *On the Custer Lookout:* Library of Congress. *A Heavy Load—Sioux:* Courtesy of Cardozo Fine Art. Writing cabin: Library of Congress. *Upshaw—Apsaroke:* Courtesy of Cardozo Fine Art. *Bear's Belly—Arikara:* Courtesy of Cardozo Fine Art. *Eagle Catcher—Hidatsa:* Courtesy of Cardozo Fine Art. *The Fisherman—Wisham:* Courtesy of Cardozo Fine Art. *Shore of Shoalwater Bay:* Courtesy of Cardozo Fine Art. Curtis with whale: Courtesy of Cardozo Fine Art. Dancers in canoe: Library of Congress. Wedding party: Library of Congress. *Makah Whaler:* Courtesy of Cardozo Fine Art. Meany with Chief Joseph: University of Washington Special Collections. *Walpi Maidens—Hopi:* Library of Congress. *On a Housetop—Hopi:* Courtesy of Cardozo Fine Art. *A Smoky Day at the Sugar Bowl—Hupa:* Courtesy of Cardozo Fine Art. *Woman and Child:* Courtesy of Cardozo Fine Art. *King Island Village:* Courtesy of Cardozo Fine Art. *Wilbur Peebo—Comanche:* Courtesy of Cardozo Fine Art. Curtis in his eighties: University of Washington Special Collections.

INDEX

Page references in italics refer to photographs.